THE *Pizza* BOOK

THE *Pizza* BOOK

*Everything There Is to Know
About the World's Greatest Pie*

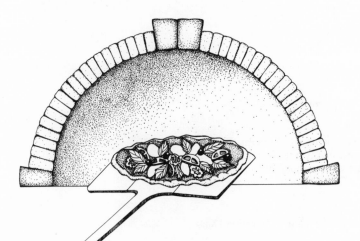

Written and illustrated by
EVELYNE SLOMON

Times BOOKS

Library of Congress Cataloging in Publication Data

Slomon, Evelyne.
  The pizza book.

  Includes index.
  1. Pizza.   I. Title.
TX770.S58   1984   641.8′24   83-45926
ISBN 0-8129-1113-X

Coordinating Editor: Rosalyn T. Badalamenti
Designed by Marjorie Anderson

Manufactured in the United States of America
  85 86 87 88 5 4 3 2

For Bucci

Acknowledgments

My profound gratitude to Amelia Bucci and Paul Camardo and to their families for providing me with their treasured recipes and for inspiring my quest for the perfect pie. I will be forever grateful to Jo Ann McGreevy for her help and encouragement in seeing this book through, and to Irene Sax for opening up doors.

I would like to thank all of the pizza people who let me watch them at work and who answered my many questions. In New York City: to Pete Castellotti, the Baron of Pizza, from John's Pizzeria, for all his help and most especially for allowing me to make pizza in his place; to Larry Goldberg, my trusted pizza confidant from Goldberg's Pizzeria; to Jerry Lombardi for sharing with me his family pizza history; to Carmella Lancieri and her family of Patsy's Pizzeria for more pizza history; and to Vinnie Bondi of La Focacceria for introducing me to authentic Sicilian pizza. In Brooklyn: thanks to Jerry Totonno of Totonno's for continuing an honorable tradition—you're one of a kind. In New Haven: a warm thanks to Salvatore and Flo Consiglio at Sally's Pizzeria for adopting my husband and me into their pizza family; to Ralph Rosselli at Pepe's and Francis Rosselli at The Spot for keeping the legacy of Frank Pepe alive in their pizzerias. In Boston: my heartfelt thanks to Joe Timpone of Santarpio's Pizzeria for all of his hints over the years "to that dame in New York" and for presiding over my desk in the form of a portrait that served as a constant source of inspiration during the writing of this book. In Chicago: to Ike Sewell of Pizzeria Uno and Due for taking the time to recount the story of his famous pizza; to Ed Jacobson of Edwardo's, Rocco Palese of Nancy's and to Charles Smital of the Chicago Pizza and Oven Grinder Factory for talking to me about their unusual versions of Chicago pizza in a pan. In California: to Wolfgang Puck of Spago's in Los Angeles and to Alice Waters and most especially to Joyce Goldstein of the Chez Panisse Cafe in Berkeley for giving me a true picture of California pizza.

A special thank you to Fran Smith at Universal Foods Corporation, for sending me samples of Red Star Quick Rise Yeast to work with before it was available in stores.

My sincere appreciation to the Italian Cultural Institute in New York City for their help in Greek, Latin, and Italian translations. And a very special thanks to my good friend Michael Volonakis for translating and helping me out with Ancient Greek pizza history.

To the Manno family: Antonio, Anne, Martha, and Tony for introducing me to the delights of the Italian-American kitchen.

Thank you to all my official pizza tasters: Phil, Michelle, John, Bard, Kumiko, Chad, Jackie, James, Luca, and Ricky.

To Artie-Lee Kowalski, my ever faithful assistant for all of her help in the pizza workshops—above and beyond the call of duty.

To Bard Martin for his much appreciated photography.

I am indebted to my editor at Times Books, Kathleen Moloney, who now knows nearly as much about pizza as I do, and whose guidance and expertise helped make this book a reality. I would also like to thank Marge Anderson, whose elegant design has made this book truly special; Rosalyn T. Badalamenti, "supreme coordinating editor," for pulling it all together; and Sarah Parsons for all of her ever-cheerful editorial assistance.

Finally and most especially, I would like to thank my husband, Phillip Rivlin, "straight from the heart," for reading through all of those endless drafts and eating all of that pizza and still being as supportive and enthusiastic as ever.

People are always asking how someone like me—who was reared in the tradition of classic French cuisine, who didn't even have a cheeseburger until I was eighteen years old—became so passionately involved with pizza. I'll admit it's a pretty strange turn of events. When I was growing up on Long Island, pizza was something my friends gobbled down after basketball games or sock hops. They adored it, but I could take it or leave it. But then, during my college years, I met Amelia Bucci and Paul Camardo, and life hasn't been quite the same since.

Bucci (as Amelia is known to her friends) and Paul lived in a rambling old Victorian house in Cambridge, Massachusetts, with Tony Manno, Leslie Julian, and other roommates. Life there revolved around the kitchen and it was there that I began my romance with Italian food and that dish called pizza. A self-taught cook of great skill, Bucci makes the most incredible homemade pizza I've ever eaten: thick, crusty pie laden with hearty sausage sauce and tender mozzarella.

In that house, which was full of serious eaters, it was Paul who led the philosophical discussions on who made the best sausage or cheese. He was also adamant about which pizzeria in Boston made the best pie: Santarpio's. "Homemade pizza is in a class by itself. It's delicious, but there's nothing like that pizzeria taste," Paul would say. He was right. My first encounter with truly superlative pizzeria pizza was at Santarpio's, and it was love at first bite. The crust was light, crisp, and thin, and the topping was an extraordinary mingling of tastes and textures. It was a masterpiece.

When Paul took me back into Santarpio's kitchen to meet the master *pizzaiolo*, Joe Timpone, I was fascinated by what I saw. Here Joe turned out pizza after pizza amidst clouds of flour, simmering pots of sauce, tubs of cheese, and a huge revolving oven. "Joe," I said, "your pie is the best I've ever had. What makes it so good?" "It's a secret," he answered with a twinkle in his eye. And from that moment on, I determined to unlock that secret.

When I returned to New York, I was overjoyed to discover that John's Pizzeria makes a pie as good as Joe Timpone's. I soon became a regular, drawn not only by the pizza but also by the lore and the mystique of the pizzeria, with its ancient coal oven and its *pizzaiolo*. Over the years, I have spent many an afternoon talking about and eating pizza with Pete Castellotti, the current owner of John's. Experiencing Santarpio's and John's has inspired me to search out more examples of all types of great pizza.

During the course of my pizza odyssey, I talked to housewives, Italian grandmothers—anyone who would tell me about different varieties of pizza. I traveled all over the United States to sample pies from the best pizzerias. I watched master *pizzaiolos* at their craft, observing their techniques and coaxing bits and pieces of information out of them until I learned their secrets. Then I tested and retested their recipes, and eventually I came up with what I believe are authentic versions of their styles of pizza.

The ritual of pizza-making attracted me from the start. Working with yeast, kneading the dough, watching it rise, and feeling its warmth in my hands provided a pleasure I had never known before. The scents of simmering sauce and baking pizza wafting through the house are only part of the reason that pizza-making became such a popular event in my home. My friends and family love to eat the wonderful pies that come hot out of the oven.

Several years ago when I began teaching courses on classic French and Italian cuisine, I learned that many of my students shared my passion for pizza. Some wanted to recreate old home recipes and others wanted to make pizzeria pizza. Because there was no pizza cookbook I could refer them to, I started the pizza workshop.

It was an instant success. Pizza-making knows no gender or age gap—grandmothers, housewives, construction workers, teenagers, stockbrokers, lawyers, and college students alike came to learn. Many didn't even know how to cook, but they wanted to learn how to make pizza—and they all did.

Teaching those workshops made me appreciate even more the need for a pizza cookbook. Americans eat more pizza than anyone else in the world, yet most are acquainted with little beyond the basic tomato and cheese Neapolitan-style pizza offered in pizzerias. The best way I could think of to tell everyone absolutely everything there is to know about the world's greatest pie was to write the pizza book myself.

—*Evelyne Slomon*

New York City
June 1984

Contents

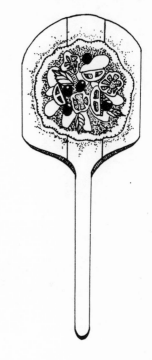

THE *Pizza* BOOK

It has been argued that the Italians did not "invent" pizza. Perhaps this is technically true, but there can be no denying that Italy was most certainly the seedbed out of which the concept would flourish to the fullest. In one form or another, pizza has been a basic part of the Italian diet since the Stone Age, and Italians have devised more ways of interpreting the dish than anyone else.

Italy's culinary heritage is a unique mélange of contributions from other cultures and her own intrinsic, fiercely regional tastes. Pizza, more than any other preparation common to all parts of the country, exemplifies how outside influences were assimilated and absorbed into Italian cuisine.

Italian pizza evolved from the basic concepts initiated by two different cultures: the Etruscans in the north and the Greeks in the south. The older style of the two was brought to northern Italy by the Etruscans, from the Levant area of Asia Minor. This first form of pizza was a crude bread that was baked beneath the stones of the fire. Once cooked, it was seasoned with a variety of different toppings and used instead of plates and utensils to sop up broth or gravies. This notion of a flavored bread as a side dish evolved into what is now known as *focaccia* in Italy. Several hundred years later, when the Greeks colonized the southern part of Italy, the second concept was introduced. The Greeks took the idea of bread as an edible serving dish one step further than the Etruscans. They didn't flavor or top the bread after it cooked: They baked the topping directly on the bread itself, and the topped bread took the place of the main course. This idea paved the way for the pizza as a meal.

In the end, the Romans embraced both the Etruscan and the Greek concepts, and they went on to create an entire repertoire of dishes based on these early prototypes. As a result, all over Italy today there are literally hundreds of styles and variations of pizza, which vary from region to region and town to town. And as far as most people are concerned, pizza was "invented" by the Italians.

1.
THE PIZZA FAMILY TREE

Focaccia

The earliest pizza prototypes originated when Neolithic tribes first gathered wild grains, made them into a crude batter, and cooked them on the hot stones of their campfires. This "bread" was filled and eaten (just like a Mexican tortilla, which also originated in this era). It was not until about 1000 B.C., when the Etruscans arrived in the northern and central parts of Italy from Asia Minor, that there was any improvement or change in this method.

The Etruscans were reputed consumers of a thick gruel known as *puls* or *pulmentum*. This is the same mush that later sustained the Roman army through its many campaigns and that became the basis of several northern Italian staples, including polenta and pasta. The Etruscans baked this mush on stones beneath the ashes of the fire, and the resulting cakes were seasoned with oil and herbs and eaten with broth or meat. The Romans quickly adopted this Etruscan ashcake and called it *focaccia* (from the Latin *panus focus,* meaning fireplace floor bread).

The Romans introduced *focaccia* to all of the lands they conquered; such flatbreads as the *fougasse* or *fouace* of France and even the hearth-cakes of Scotland are related to it. They spread *focaccia* all over Italy as well, making it the oldest and most universal of all styles of pizza.

Greek Pizza

Italians may have made pizza famous, but they certainly did not invent the concept of the dish. Here, the debt is clearly owed to the Greeks.

The Greeks, who occupied the southernmost regions of Italy for over 600 years (from about 730 B.C. to 130 B.C.), were the greatest bakers of ancient times. They had learned their craft from the Egyptians (the first great bakers) so well that they far excelled their teachers. Their methods for refining different flours and their baking technology, which included the use of ovens and special molds for breads, were the most advanced in the ancient world. Greek breads, flavored with seeds, oils, herbs, spices, wine, honey, and eggs, came in all shapes and sizes, and some were even leavened, by means of a primitive sourdough starter method discovered by the Egyptians. The Greeks also instituted the idea of using bread as an edible plate for a meal. Flat, round breads were baked with an assortment of "relishes" (in ancient Greek, a relish meant any-thing spread or baked on bread), such as oils, onions, garlic, herbs, olives, vegetables, and cheese, on top. A rim of crust was left around the bread to serve as a kind of handle.

One of the best accounts of ancient Greek "pizza"—what it was like and how it was eaten—comes down to us in this passage from Plato's *Republic:*

They will provide meal from their barley and flour from their wheat and kneading and cooking these ["... they (the cakes) will also have relishes—salt ... and of olives and cheese; and onions and greens. ..."] they will serve noble cakes and loaves on some arrangement of reeds and clean leaves, and reclined on rustic beds strewn with bryony and myrtyle, they will feast with their children, drinking of their wine there to, garlanded and singing hymns to the gods in pleasant fellowship. ...

The seeds planted in Naples and the surrounding southern Italian regions by the Greeks, however, only served as the impetus for the progression of pizza dishes that was to follow.

Neapolitan Pizza

The Neapolitans, who have historically been impoverished, were also most ingenious at living well, eating well, and making the most out of very little. Neapolitan pizza† made the most of the cheese, herbs, vegetables, fish, and poor meat supply that was available. The one new element that the Neapolitans introduced to pizza in the eighteenth century, and which would forever change the face of this venerable dish, was, of course, the tomato.

It took nearly two centuries for the Italians to build up enough nerve to eat the *pomidoro* (golden apple). The original variety, brought back from the New World in the mid-sixteenth century from Peru and Mexico by way of Spain, was thought to be poisonous and was grown in gardens as an ornamental fruit. But the Neapolitans eventually discovered that this lovely golden fruit (the early tomato varieties were actually

---

*Plato, *The Republic*, Volume I, Books I–V, trans. Paul Shorey (Cambridge, Mass.: Loeb Classical Library, Harvard University Press, 1978), p. 159.

†The earliest Greek ancestor of Neapolitan pizza was called *plakuntos*, which means flat, baked bread. When the Romans adapted this dish, it became known as *placenta* in Latin. In antiquity, *placenta* was a dish of much renown. It was a pie made of the finest flours, a topping of cheese mixed with honey, and a seasoning of bay leaves and oil. *Placenta* was baked on the floor of the hearth alongside the burning wood.

The name pizza comes from a southern corruption of the Latin adjective *picea* (peechia), which described the black tar-like coating underneath the *placenta* as a result of the burning ashes.

yellow) growing abundantly in their gardens tasted as good as it looked. After the first bite of the forbidden fruit, Italy fell head over heels in love with the tomato, and tomato-based varieties of pizza began to make their debut in the Neapolitan repertoire. The tomato swiftly took over as the main component for pizza filling.

But what about cheese? The most famous of all pizza—the tomato and cheese variation—is really a very recent contribution to the genre. In 1889, Raffaele Esposito created a new combination with tomatoes, mozzarella, and basil, to commemorate the colors of the Italian flag, for their pizza-loving Queen Margherita. The monarch was so pleased with this dish that it is still titled in her honor to this day.

But Neapolitan pizza is much, much more than the national dish; it's an institution. Throughout Italy, most pizza is either bought in bakeries or made at home (*casalinga* style). In Naples, though, pizza is rarely made at home; for pizza, one goes to a pizzeria. It is a place where young and old, rich and poor alike come to partake in the ritual of pizza. In the daytime, a pizzeria is where you get a quick and satisfying lunch; at night, it is an inexpensive eating house where family and friends can gather together to eat and drink their fill. Late in the evening, it is a spot where wealthy and fashionable revelers end their night out on the town.

The traditional Neapolitan pizzeria was a no-frills kind of place. Pizza was made in wood-burning ovens, and customers sat at plain marble-topped tables. When the pizza was ready, it was eaten with the hands. The idea was to eat the pie as hot as your mouth could stand it and to wash it down with plenty of sturdy local wine. The art of the *pizzaiolo* was much admired, and each pizzeria had a loyal following.

Modern-day pizzerias, with their neon lights, tiled walls, and cloth-covered tables no longer resemble their nineteenth-century precursors, but they still serve the same function. They are first and foremost a place of the people, where you can get a good but inexpensive meal and enjoy a lively atmosphere. Wherever Neapolitans have migrated, throughout Italy and the rest of the world, they have kept alive the institution of the pizzeria.

The French Connection

French pizza? Yes, it makes perfect sense. Up until the twentieth century, parts of southern France were still under Italian rule. And the food of Provence, with its olive oil, tomatoes, and garlic, owes much more to the Italians than it does to classic French cuisine.

On the surface, French pizza looks very much Italian, but one taste will tell you that the accent is uniquely French. The pizza of Provence is characteristically based on fresh tomatoes, tomato *coulis* (French tomato sauce), highly seasoned cooked onions, anchovies, olives, capers, and pignolis. Aside from garlic, the seasonings include *herbes de Provence* (especially fresh thyme), fennel seeds, walnut oil, and extra-virgin olive oil from the region. The French also do not rely on mozzarella as their only pizza cheese. They are just as likely to use Gruyère, Fontina, Gouda, port salut, chèvre, Roquefort, and Parmesan.

Along the Riviera and the south of France, pizza is popular, and there are several distinct styles. Most of them adhere to the Neapolitan concept of a thin crisp crust, cooked directly over hot stones, with a light topping. They are usually restaurant fare, served in individual *pizzette* portions and almost always baked in a wood-burning stove. *Pissaladière*, the onion-anchovy-olive cousin of Ligurian pizza, and *pizza provençale* are the most common kinds. There are also many quasi-Franco-Italian variations found in little out-of-the-way cafés all over the southern provinces of France. *Pissaladière* comes in three main varieties and has a number of topping possibilities. Most *pissaladière* are cooked in large trays and sold by weight. Depending upon the recipe, *pissaladière* can be thick or thin, delicately flavored or highly seasoned.

Folded Pizza

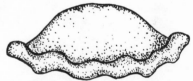

One of the most delightful members of the pizza family comes in the form of a savory turnover, a folded-over pizza that can be filled with any of the more common pizza toppings. Usually called *calzone*, this baked and especially deep-fried turnover is a thoroughly Neapolitan tradition. (The word *calzone* means "pants leg" in Italian. The pizza was so named because it resembled a leg of the baggy trousers worn by Neapolitan men in the eighteenth and nineteenth centuries.) Some *calzoni* are rectangular pieces of dough wrapped around long fillings, such as sausages or pieces of ham and cheese; it is perhaps easier to see the pants-leg shape of the pizza in these examples. In other parts of Italy this kind of pizza is called *mezzaluna* (half-moon), and in the region of Abruzzi it is known as *fiadone*. Still another kind of folded pizza, called *panzerotti*, is generally made with a pastry dough and deep-fried. *Panzerotti* resemble diminutive *calzoni*—they are never larger than 2 to 3 inches, and they're wonderful with drinks. In France, the turnovers are called *chaussons*.

Stuffed Pizza

Pizzas made with fillings of meat, fish, cheese, or green vegetables, on a single crust or encased in a double one, and baked beneath hot stones or in an oven, are the ancestors of all *tortas, tourtes, tarts, quiches, vol au vents,* and *pâtés en croûte.* Wrapping fillings in dough formed the basis of some of history's most popular dishes. Pies of all shapes and sizes, eaten as snacks or meals, were considered food fit for both the commoner and the table of nobility.

According to Apicius, the famous chronicler of ancient Roman cuisine, filled pastries were especially prized and served at the grandest of feasts. But the Roman penchant for excess and the exotic in food seems to have produced the most bizarre combinations—at least to the modern palate. In his *Ars magirica* (*The Art of the Cook*), which is said to be the oldest written cookbook, Apicius gives a recipe for a pie stuffed with cooked sow's teats, fish, chicken, warblers, the bellies of cooked thrushes, "and all sorts of excellent things" chopped together. This mixture was then bound with eggs and oil and seasoned with garum (the sauce-like condiment made of fish innards and lots of salt), wine, and raisin wine, sprinkled with whole black peppercorns and pignolis and baked between two crusts.

While this concoction may not exactly make your mouth water, you can see that the modern stuffed pie, filled with cooked meats, seasonings, and a sauce, is descended from that recipe.

Pitta, sfincuini, pizza rustica, pizza pasqualina, and *torta rustica* are some of the more prominent members of the stuffed pizza branch of the pizza family tree. The dishes are similar only in the fact that they are considered stuffed pies; each has its own history and style. *Pitta* and *sfincuini* are simple, earthy peasant fare. *Pizza rustica* and *pizza pasqualina* resemble a deliciously creamy, savory Italian cheesecake. And *torta rustica,* with its colorful filling, carries the idea of a stuffed pizza to its most impressive height. Most of these recipes are usually reserved for special holidays, but they are so delicious and beautiful to look at that it seems a shame to make them only a few times a year. Any one of these dishes can turn even the most ordinary meal into a festive occasion.

Rolled Pizza

The most unusual looking and obscure members of the entire pizza genre are those filled buns or loaves from Sicily known as *bonata,* The *bonata,* loosely translated from the Sicilian dialect (which differs markedly from town to town and does not translate at all into formal Italian), means "good loaf" or "generous loaf." Generous certainly is an accurate description, as some of the rolled breads are so copiously filled that they constitute an entire meal in themselves.

In this form of pizza, the dough can be rolled around a thick savory filling like a jelly roll. In other cases, they can be wrapped around a thick stuffing much like a *pâté en croûte.* The pies look like long crusty loaves, but when they are sliced, they reveal a beautiful spiral or solid slice of filling enclosed in a crust.

Bonata are better known in the United States as *Stromboli* rolls or pizza rolls. Actually, they are relatively unfamiliar to most Italian-American cooks unless they happen to be of Sicilian extraction, but the rolled pie is such a wonderful concept that I'm sure it will fast become a favorite of all pizza-lovers.

Rolled pizza offers some of the most diverse filling and serving possibilities of all pizza-making. How and when each different pie is served depends upon the kind and the amount of filling that goes into it. Some pies are filled with a small amount of flavoring and are served as snacks or side dishes; other, more amply-stuffed variations are served as main courses. The slice of *bonata* is one of the most appealing ways of serving pizza. The pies can be scaled down so that the slices are the perfect finger food, and they lend themselves particularly well to reheating and freezing. Because most *bonata* are served at room temperature, they eliminate the need to stand over a hot oven and become especially good for parties.

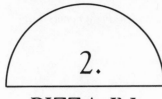

2.

PIZZA IN AMERICA

The first great influx of Italian immigrants to America took place during the latter half of the nineteenth century. Most newly arrived immigrants, too poor to buy bread, made their own by paying the baker a small fee for the use of his oven. In the afternoon, when the bakery wasn't busy, women brought their bread dough to be baked in the coal ovens. Alongside the bread, they baked some extra dough flavored with tomato sauce which had been set aside for that purpose. In the old country it was called pizza. The pizza was always done before the bread and passed out to appease the appetites of hungry children.

As time went on and Italian immigrants became more established, they were able to purchase their own bread, so bakeries started selling large trays of crusty *focaccia*. Consequently, the first pizza sold in America wasn't the classic thin-crusted Neapolitan kind at all but thick Sicilian "bread pie" or baker's *focaccia*.

The Golden Age of Pizza

By the turn of the century, Italians had started up their own bakeries and began selling groceries as well as pizza. The first of these establishments was opened by Gennaro Lombardi, at 53½ Spring Street in New York City, in 1905. This was the first pizzeria in America and the model for subsequent pizzerias throughout the northeast. It wasn't until the early 1930s that Lombardi added tables, chairs, and silverware to his pizzeria, and he also began serving spaghetti. So started the proliferation of pizza and spaghetti parlors that were to become popular with Italians and non-Italians alike. Even so, up until the 1940s pizza and spaghetti were considered to be foreign foods—curiosities to be found in Italian neighborhoods.

In the early 1920s, pizzerias began to proliferate in the northeast. They were family-run institutions, where the secret recipe (every pizzeria has a secret recipe!) was passed down from father to son. The period from the early 1920s to the early 1950s was what I would call the golden age of pizza in America. Before pizza reached large-scale popularity and became doomed to mass production, it was still made just as it always had been in Naples. Pizza came with fresh tomatoes, garlic, with or without mozzarella, with anchovies, or olives, or mushrooms, and sometimes with fresh sausage—that was it. (Meatballs, *pepperoni*, onions, peppers, and other toppings came later to suit the American audience.) Making the dough was a back-breaking chore, and because there was little or no refrigeration, everything had to be fresh and used up each day. The mozzarella was made daily, the tomatoes were fresh or home-canned, and the olive oil was imported from Italy.

In those days the *pizzaiolo*—the pizza cook—was something of a hero. Certainly he was a rare breed. *Pizzaiolos* treated their craft not as a business but as a calling. Their sentiment was best expressed by Signor Gennaro Lombardi himself, when, during a newspaper interview in 1956, he patted his oven and said, "This is what made me a man today."

Postwar Pizza

Most accounts of the history of pizza in America begin during the Second World War when American GIs acquired a taste for it over in Italy and supposedly brought it back to the United States. Pizza skyrocketed to national fame after the Second World War.

Another interesting phenomenon took place in the early forties: the birth of Chicago-style deep-dish pizza. The brainchild of Ike Sewell and Ric Riccardo, this special pizza was developed to suit American tastes and sold at Pizzeria Uno. This regional pizza was just the first of many pizza offshoots based on Italian recipes and reinterpreted through American eyes with American ingredients.

The golden era of pizza in America, a period of little more than thirty years, declined in the early fifties when the character of the traditional pizzeria began to change and the classic pizzeria structure began to crumble. The primary blow seems to have been dealt when the pizzeria as a family enterprise, passed down from one generation to the next, broke up. Second- and third-generation children began to seek out other fields, so in order to keep the business alive, pizzeria owners had to train other newly immigrated minorities. The art of the *pizzaiolo* lost its importance, and pizza-making became a business.

Mass Production

As pizza's general popularity soared, the demands for its swift production became overwhelming. In New York City, the concept of selling pizza by the slice took hold, and soon it became one of the hottest quick lunch items around. Pizzerias began to prebake their pies so that they could always have enough on hand to meet the crush of the crowds. New efficient gas ovens took the place of coal ovens; they could bake many more pies at once, were much less trouble to operate, and were more suitable to high-volume production. Dough machines eased the task of kneading huge masses of dough by hand. And finally, refrigeration eliminated the need for making dough and buying fresh ingredients daily.

Of course, no one of these technological advancements was in itself responsible for the decline of good pizza. Excellent pizza can be achieved with dough machines and gas ovens. No, what killed off authentic pizzas sold through pizzerias was low-quality ingredients. The need for consistency, convenience, and low cost overruled the use of hand-produced or high-quality ingredients, and because labor was at a premium, the less preparation involved in the product, the better. And thus it was that the pizza supply houses emerged. With the suppliers providing the dough, the sauce, and the toppings, all the pizza-makers had to do was to put them together and bake. If all pizzas began to taste the same, it was no wonder: They all came from the same suppliers. Another significant change in the pizzeria came about at this time when the first pizza chains conquered America, making it possible to eat the same mediocre pizza from sea to shining sea.

By the sixties, pizza was mass-produced, but pizza had arrived. It was one of America's most popular foods—up there with hot dogs, hamburgers, and apple pie. In fact, pizza had become so American that we even took credit for inventing it! Frozen pizza was—and is—one of the largest sellers of all convenience foods. As a child, I can remember being treated at neighbors' homes to individual frozen *pizzettes* prepared in the toaster oven; they tasted like salty oregano-tomato-flavored crackers.

Rebirth of Pizza

The health food craze of the 1970s left no pizza unturned. Whole wheat crust, broccoli, walnut, zucchini, carrot, raisin, sprouts, and even tofu went into what I call the guru pizza. America's appetite for the pie could not be controlled; anything from crab meat to pineapple and cherries flambé landed on top of pizza. One would have thought that this was truly the end of great pizza. But no.

In the mid-seventies, American became involved in a gastronomic revolution. Certainly the desire for natural, unprocessed foods was a direct result of the health food fad, but our tastes were moving far beyond mere nutrition. Restaurants featuring Italian, Japanese, Chinese, Mexican, Tex-Mex, and French nouvelle cuisines opened all over the country, and cookbooks and cooking classes enriched our tastes and greatly increased our sophistication. Young American chefs and cooks sought to assimilate foreign influences and combine them with their own culinary heritage. They reexamined local dishes and ingredients and came up with new innovations. And then hard-to-find gourmet ingredients became readily available.

So pizza is definitely not dead. If you need proof, look at the rise of American regional pizza. Different Chicago-style pies have emerged, and New England, Tex-Mex, and California-style pizzas have been developed to add their own delicious variations on the pizza theme. But for those who cling to tradition, a few of those bastions of old pizzeria-style pizza still carry on their craft in New York City, New Haven, and Boston, just as they have for the last fifty years.

The Regional Styles

There are currently three major regional styles of pizza in the United States. Pizza in the East, predominantly known as *New York-style,* is the traditional Neapolitan type with a light, thin crust and a sizzling topping. In many cases it is sold by the slice. Midwesterners wouldn't be caught dead eating that flimsy stuff. Their classic *deep-dish Chicago-style* pizza, a sumptuously thick creation heaped with topping, is not for dainty appetites. It's available only by the pie, and fans customarily wait forty-five minutes while it bakes. Out on the West Coast, this overindulgence seems like an atrocity. There, the trend toward a lighter, more refined version of pizza borrows heavily from the current California Cuisine movement for its inspiration. Individual *pizzettes* with light, chewy crusts and toppings made from combinations of the best imported Italian products and indigenous California ingredients are the hallmarks of this sophisticated pizza. Aside from the major styles, there are several offshoots, especially New England and Tex-Mex styles, and variations are always cropping up. The most significant fact to remember about regional pizza is that no matter where you are, there is fierce loyalty to the local pie. New Yorkers, Chicagoans, and Los Angelenos are all equally convinced that their pizza is the best!

3.

INGREDIENTS

Even in its most complex forms, pizza is still made up of only two main components—a crust and a filling. Why, then, are some pizzas wonderful while others are insipid? What is the secret to great pizza? The answer is simple: *ingredients!* The most important element of pizza-making is knowing the individual characteristics of ingredients and how they will react when they are combined. Technique is also very important, but a truly superlative pie is only as good as the sum of its parts: the flour, oil, cheese, meat, tomatoes, and other toppings. Fortunately, those all-important ingredients are easy to obtain and relatively inexpensive, making pizza one of the most easily affordable pleasures of the table.

With little more than a pair of hands, a bowl, an oven, and your own quality ingredients, you can make pizza that would put the average pizzeria to shame. So don't just skim over this section—*read it.* Ingredients will make or break your pie!

Flour

The most crucial element to the success of pizza crust is the flour you use, so you would do well to acquaint yourself with its peculiarities.

Commercial flour is milled from two major strains of wheat—*Triticum durum* and *Triticum vulgare. Triticum durum* is hard, golden wheat from which semolina is milled to make pasta. It is also used extensively as livestock feed. *Triticum vulgare,* the most widely grown strain of wheat, can vary widely depending upon how and where it was cultivated. The most common cause of variation from flour to flour, however, is the content of a plant protein called *gluten.* And it is the gluten's reaction that gives the dough its character and consistency.

The development of gluten in flour is affected by the addition of liquid, by kneading, and by exposure to heat. The highly absorbent nature of gluten is activated through the introduction of moisture, which forms an entire cell structure of gluten strands in the dough. These gluten strands are built up further when the dough is kneaded, and this promotes strength and elasticity. The amount of gluten present in flour usually determines its ability to raise yeast dough to its highest volume. This is sometimes referred to as a flour's *gluten strength.*

The terms hard and soft in describing flours can be somewhat perplexing, but both are used in pizza-making. Basically, there are two main wheat-producing regions in the United States; one harvests most of our "hard" wheat and the other, our "soft" wheat. Wheat grown in the northern United States near the Canadian border has a short growing season: It starts in the spring and ends with an early harvest in the fall after a short, hot summer. Flour milled from this "spring" wheat is characteristically hard and is prized by bakers for its high-gluten content, which makes it excellent for bread products. The other wheat-producing area, in the Midwest, has a more temperate climate and a longer growing season. Often called "winter" wheat because it is sown in the fall and harvested in the summer, this grain produces a "soft" flour, which is relatively low in gluten content and is highly desirable for pastries, biscuits, quick breads, and sauces.

All-Purpose Flour. This blend of hard and soft flours can vary enormously from region to region. The nationally distributed brands of all-purpose flour, such as Pillsbury and General Mills Gold Medal flour, contain a similar blend of hard and soft flours with a middle range gluten content of about 10 to 11 percent. This makes them strong enough for bread baking and tender enough for most cakes—and just right for pizza.

Most brands of all-purpose flour are bleached, strictly for cosmetic purposes. Bleaching does not affect the way in which flour works, but it does tend to strip it of nutrients. Consequently, most flours are enriched chemically so that vitamins and minerals lost in processing can be replaced.

Pillsbury and General Mills Gold Medal have been used to test many of the recipes in this book with very satisfactory results; they produce tender, rich-tasting pizza crusts and manageable doughs.

Unbleached White Flour. This is an all-purpose flour that is not bleached chemically. Despite its name, this flour is bleached, but it's bleached naturally through aging rather than by processing. Unbleached all-purpose flour also varies markedly from region to region in its blends of hard and soft flours. The brand that I like, Standard Milling Company's Hecker's unbleached flour (called *cerasota* in the midwest), was used to test most of the recipes in this book. To my mind, Hecker's produces the most authentic Italian-style crust because it is very similar to the flour used in Italy. Hecker's has a high percentage of hard flour and a relatively high-gluten content (approximately 13 percent). I have found this blend particularly successful for pizza because it produces hard, crispy crusts and its soft flour content facilitates kneading and cuts down the number of risings needed to roll or stretch the dough out easily.

Bread Flour. The choice of commercial pizzerias, bread flour is milled only from hard, northern spring wheat. Noted for its rising power and strength, this flour creates a dough that can be stretched into the thin circles of pizza. Because of its high-gluten content (approximately 14 percent), bread flour (sometimes called "high-gluten flour") requires more liquid than other flours, more kneading, and two risings in order to ensure manageability. This dough demands respect: It must be allowed to rest and to double in bulk twice before shaping or it will shrink back on you as you try to roll or stretch it out. Pillsbury distributes an excellent bread flour to most supermarkets in 5- to 10-pound bags; it is the same commercial flour that many pizzerias use—only they buy it in 50- to 100-pound sacks!

Note: The increased amount of kneading and rising times develop the fine crumb structure of this crust, which is characterized by a thin, crisp exterior and a chewy interior. This dough will *rise*, so if a very thin crust is your aim, assemble the pizza as quickly as possible and bake it right away.

Whole Wheat Flour. Stone-ground whole wheat flour is more healthful than its high-speed, steel-rolled whole wheat counterpart. Steel rollers mill the wheat kernel into a finer flour, but in the process, some of the nutrients of the whole grain are destroyed. The time-honored method of grinding wheat between two huge stone disks maintains the integrity of the grain and retains its natural goodness, giving baked products a more substantial texture and a rich nutty taste. This dense flour absorbs more liquid than white flour and forms a slightly sticky dough; it is also less elastic and consequently a bit harder to roll out because it has the tendency to tear. Whole wheat flour produces a chewy pizza crust with a satisfying flavor.

Semolina Flour. Often called pasta flour, semolina is made from hard durum wheat. Pizza dough made from this flour requires additional water, takes longer to rise, and is tricky to roll out. Despite the extra bother, the end justifies the means—a hard, crispy, buttery tasting crust is your reward.

Yellow Cornmeal. Cornmeal mixed with water makes polenta, and baked polenta serves as the basis for several types of pizzas from northern and central Italy and for *pizza minestre*. In general, though, the cornmeal used in pizza is sprinkled on oiled pizza pans before the dough is pressed into the pan to prevent sticking and to add extra crunch to the crust.

Avoid over-processed finely ground yellow cornmeal. Use stone-ground coarse yellow cornmeal which has superior flavor and texture.

Baker's Yeast

Yeast, a living fungus that feeds off of carbohydrates and grows to several hundred thousand times its original volume, is indispensable to the leavening of pizza dough. Baker's yeast comes in two forms: compressed cake and granulated active dry yeast. Brewer's yeast, which has no leavening power, is an excellent source of protein and is often added to baked goods as a nutritional supplement.

Compressed Yeast. Compressed baker's yeast has a very short shelf life. Usually packaged in waxed paper, which does not offer adequate protection from temperature fluctuations or exposure to moisture, compressed yeast is sometimes rendered ineffective before it reaches your grocer's shelf. Because it is almost impossible to ascertain the freshness of compressed yeast at the supermarket, I suggest you purchase it in bulk from a health food store or a bakery. I buy 1-pound cakes of baker's yeast, either Red Star or Budweiser, a commercial brand distributed by Anheuser-Busch. Compressed yeast should be light tan or gray in color, should feel firm to the touch, and should have a pleasant, yeasty smell. A dark outer crust or an acrid sour smell are indications of deterioration. You can freeze unused portions of cake yeast for as long as 2 months. Just seal the yeast first in plastic wrap and then in aluminum foil. Even if you're not freezing the yeast, keep it well sealed in plastic wrap to prevent it from drying out and store it in the refrigerator. It should keep for about a month. Because of its unstable nature, compressed yeast should always be *proofed* to determine if it is still active before using it in recipes (see page 45 for proofing details). Compressed yeast does not activate in liquids cooler than 90 degrees and will perish in temperatures greater than 115 degrees. Despite its unpredictable nature, cake yeast does lend a subtle delicious yeasty flavor to bread or pizza crust that is extremely satisfying.

Granulated Yeast. Granulated active dry and compressed yeast are interchangeable in recipes (1 2-ounce cake equals 3 ¼-ounce packages), but I prefer the convenience and predictability of dry yeast. Dry yeast comes in individually sealed packages printed with an expiration date, so there's no need to proof it. If it's stored in a cool dry place, it has a shelf life of about a year. Dry yeast dissolves instantly, and it can withstand temperatures of up to 130 degrees when it is mixed with a small amount of flour. The higher liquid heat tolerance of dry yeast is a particular boon, because it hastens the rising action of the dough and allows the cook a greater margin of error in judging temperature. I have used Fleischmann's and Red Star active dry yeast with equal success. Both brands are free of preservatives and are available at supermarkets. Dry yeast can be purchased in bulk at your local health food store at quite a savings (1 level tablespoon of dry yeast equals 1 package). However, the newest kind of dry yeast now available is a super-active strain which actually raises the dough in half the time. Red Star's is called Quick Rise and Fleischmann's is called RapidRise. Again, both brands are highly recommended. Sold in ¼-ounce packages or 4-ounce jars, this yeast is interchangeable with traditional dry yeast. If you store granulated yeast in the refrigerator in a clean dry, airtight container, it should remain good for about a year. When in doubt, proof dry yeast just as you proof cake yeast.

Oils and Shortening

Oils play a major role in pizza-making. Vegetable or corn oil is rubbed into baking pans or screens to prevent pizza from sticking during baking. Drizzled directly on top of pizza, fruity green olive oil enhances the flavor of the topping and prevents it from drying out. Brushing it on stuffed and rolled pizza helps to promote a golden crust. Golden olive oil used in pizza dough improves flavor, acts as a tenderizer, and makes the dough more manageable. Furthermore, the addition of olive oil to the dough produces a crust with a very hard exterior and a crumbly, rough-crumbed interior—not unlike a coarse Italian bread. I find these crusts especially suitable for deep-dish pizzas with juicy fillings because they can absorb sauce without getting soggy.

Unopened bottles of olive oil will keep well for over a year, but once they have been opened, the less refined oils will go rancid faster than the processed ones. If the temperature in your kitchen tends to rise above 80 degrees, store the oils in the refrigerator. Don't worry if they cloud; they will clarify after a few minutes at room temperature. Under refrigeration, oils can keep almost indefinitely.

Extra-Virgin Olive Oil. These oils are the most expensive, because they are still made almost entirely by hand. The olives are hand picked, graded of the highest quality, and pressed manually. These painstaking methods produce a very limited quantity of intensely flavored, dark green oil. Use these delicately flavored oils on top of pizza, in the dough, or as a marinade for toppings, but not for sautéeing or for preparing pans. Italian extra-virgin olive oils that I recommend are Badia a Coltibuono, Colavita (the two most expensive, at around $20 a bottle), and Olivieri and Mancianti, which are a bit less expensive but also excellent.

Virgin Olive Oil. Made from the first pressing of lesser grade olives (through a high-yield hydraulic press), virgin olive oil is less costly than extra-virgin—and less distinct. The heat of the steel press destroys much of the delicate flavor and character of the oil. Virgin olive oils are light green in color with a slightly fruity taste, and like their extra-virgin relatives, they have a low burning point. Use them in the same ways as you use extra-virgin oils.

Pure Olive Oil. Pure olive oil is made from the second or even the third pressing of olive pulp. Mechanically pressed, these golden oils are of good quality but lack the fruity intensity of the virgin oils. The additional refinement of these oils makes them more heat resistant (and thus suitable for sautéing), as well as flavoring when a light olive flavor is desired. Some of the most common Italian brands available in America are Amastra, Olio Sasso, Bertolli, and Berio.

Note: The best olive oils come from Italy and France. In general, French extra-virgin olive oils tend to be lighter in color and taste than their Italian counterparts, but are on the whole excellent. Excellent French extra-virgin olive oils include James Plagnio, Hilaire Fabre, and Artaud Frères.

Walnut Oil. I have found walnut oil a very exciting alternative to olive oil both in pizza crusts and on toppings where a nutty, rich flavor is desired (such as Herbed Goat Cheese and Walnut Oil-Dressed Bitter Greens Pizza). Walnut oil, like virgin olive oil, has a low burning point, so it should not be used for sautéing. It also spoils easily, so it should be refrigerated when your kitchen's temperature reaches 80 degrees.

Vegetable Oil. These light, flavorless oils have a high burning point and are used mostly in the cooking of pizza rather than as one of its flavoring agents. Use them to grease the bowl in which the dough is to rise and to oil the pizza pan or screen to prevent the pizza from sticking. Any corn oil or safflower oil will do for greasing bowls and pizza pans.

Lard. A pure animal shortening that is obtained through the melting down of pork or beef fat until all of the impurities are rendered out, natural lard can be refrigerated for months. Lard imparts a rich flavor and a distinctive flaky texture to pizza dough when used in place of olive oil. Pure lard can be purchased from a butcher or a specialty pork store. Solid vegetable shortening and processed lard should *never* be used, since they tend to give the dough a disagreeable, greasy taste. If natural lard is not available, substitute bacon fat or oil.

Tomatoes

The fate of the fresh tomato in the United States has been sad to watch. A "real" tomato is rare to our supermarkets, even when tomatoes are "in season." But when the supplies from the farmer's market or friend's gardens keep me in fresh tomatoes up to my neck, my pizza-making activities reach a fever pitch. Nothing tastes quite like a fresh vine-ripened tomato crushed on a piece of golden, crispy crust and infused with the heady scents of freshly picked herbs—but that is only a seasonal treat. At other times of the year oil-packed sun-dried tomatoes or canned tomatoes are usually much better than those insipid, greenish-pink impostors found in supermarkets.

Fresh Tomatoes. The Italian plum or egg tomatoes you can buy at the supermarket or greengrocer were bred for cooking purposes. They have sweet, firm flesh, few seeds, low moisture content, and low acidity. In the summertime, though, there are many types of local tomatoes that can be used for pizza.

Prepare fresh tomatoes for pizza in the following manner. Select firm ripe tomatoes; over softness indicates deterioration. Cut the tomato across its circumference; hold it cut side down and gently squeeze out the seeds and excess liquid. The tomatoes may then be sliced or chopped for use in and on pizza. Some tomatoes have thick skins, and you may want to peel them before you seed them. To do so, simply immerse the tomato in boiling water to cover for 30 seconds. Then put the tomato in cold water to cover. The skin will peel off easily with your fingers or with a paring knife. Then, proceed with the seeding instructions. Fresh tomatoes will continue to give off liquid while they cook on top of a pie, so be sure to rid them of their excess moisture and seeds before using them. Otherwise your pizza will be soggy.

Sun-Dried Tomatoes. One sun-dried tomato has the concentrated taste of a hundred fresh ones. As an avowed tomato lover, I don't make this claim lightly. My first taste of a sun-dried tomato on a bleak winter day was like a ray of summer sun! Like other dried foods, dried tomatoes contain all of the concentrated flavors that the drying process has locked in and intensified. Virtually all sun-dried tomatoes are imported from southern Italy, where they are a familiar and colorful sight. Many Italians pluck the tomatoes from their own home gardens and hang them out along the walls of their houses to dry under the Mediterranean sun. Thrifty Italian housewives took advantage of this natural method of preservation long before the advent of canning. Reconstituting the tomatoes was simply a matter of picking a few tomatoes from the wall and plunking them down into hearty sauces, soups, stews, and the like. Another popular preparation for dried tomatoes calls for keeping them in olive oil and herbs. Tomatoes prepared in this way are excellent tossed in salads, for antipasto, on pasta, or on pizza. Sun-dried tomatoes are still somewhat of a rarity in the United States, but as the demand slowly increases, so too will the supply. Sun-dried tomatoes can be had from California. They are usually sold dry in bulk and tend to be much tougher than the Italian ones because of their thick skins. Here are some tips on how to select and use the ones most commonly available now.

Sun-dried tomatoes are sold in bunches, resembling red prunes that have been strung together, or they are packed in jars with olive oil and seasonings. The jars are what are most commonly available in the United States. The price of sun-dried tomatoes varies greatly—anywhere from $4 to $18 per pint. As with extra-virgin olive oils, price is reflective of quality ingredients and superior taste. Unfortunately, unlike olive oils, there is no grading system on which you can base your decision. It has been my experience that the more intensely red the tomatoes, the better the quality and taste. Taste is, of course, the final measure; there are so many different styles, and each flavors the tomatoes with a different mixture of herbs, garlic, oil, and sometimes vinegar. Keep trying until you find the one you like.

There is one brand that stands out far above the rest—Pumate Sanremo from Liguria, Italy. These are the most succulent, tender, and flavorful of all the sun-dried tomatoes I have tried. The makers of Pumate Sanremo have raised the lowly dried tomato from its peasant origins to the level of *haute cuisine.* Pumate are bright red in color, made from only the finest quality tomatoes, and packed in extra-virgin olive oil that has been seasoned with herbs. They are the costliest of all sun-dried tomatoes, but they are well worth it. Each 10-ounce jar contains 20 to 25 whole tomatoes—enough to make 4 or 5 large pizzas. The oil takes on a lovely reddish hue and is imbued with the flavor of the tomatoes and herbs that have steeped in it. Use the oil in pizza or tossed with pasta with some sweet butter as a sauce. It is also absolutely delicious on its own, soaked up on a piece of crusty bread.

To use dried tomatoes on pizza, simply tear them into bite-sized pieces and proceed with the recipe instructions. Once the jar is opened, store the unused portion in the refrigerator. Keep all leftover tomatoes submerged beneath a thin layer of oil, adding more olive oil if necessary. Tomatoes stored in this way will keep for months.

Sun-dried tomatoes are available in Italian markets, *salumerias*, specialty food stores, and through mail order. Pumate Sanremo are imported into this country solely by Dean and Deluca in New York, which distributes the tomatoes through mail order and specialty food stores.

Canned Tomatoes. All canned tomatoes are not created equal, and just because the label says *imported* doesn't mean you're getting more taste for the extra cost. The only imported tomatoes that I feel warrant your searching for are those Italian brands that indicate somewhere on the label that they are *Genuine San Marzano Tomatoes*—not San Marzano "quality" or San Marzano "type." San Marzano tomatoes are the original Italian plum tomatoes, bred for cooking purposes. The climate and soil of San Marzano produce the most full-bodied, sweetest, and least acidic tomatoes available in cans. Some brands with Italian names are deceptive, for if you squint at the fine print on the label, you will often find that these tomatoes come from Spain, Israel, Argentina, or even California. Don't be fooled. Stick to domestic whole Italian-style tomatoes packed in purée if you can't find genuine San Marzano tomatoes.

Canned whole tomatoes, generally packed in their own juice, are the tomatoes you'll most often use on pizza. To prepare them, crush them roughly with a fork or with your hands. (It's much better to use your hands.) Some recipes will call for draining the tomatoes in a sieve first to rid them of their excess liquid. Crush the drained tomatoes in exactly the same way, reserving the juice for soups or pasta sauces.

Tomato Purée, Concentrated Crushed Tomatoes, and Tomato Paste. These are all different concentrations of puréed tomatoes. Tomato purée is just what the name implies, but a good deal of salt has been added during the processing. I much prefer buying whole tomatoes and crushing them myself. Tomato purée makes a flat-tasting, over-salty pizza sauce and should be avoided.

Concentrated crushed tomatoes are puréed tomatoes that have been slowly cooked down to a rather thick purée. This is a very popular base for tomato sauce and is, I believe, frequently responsible for making them heavy, acidic, and undigestible.

Tomato paste is a further concentration of concentrated crushed tomatoes that has been cooked down past the thick purée stage to an extremely thick sweet paste. Use tomato paste to give sauces depth and flavor, but never use it alone. Too much paste can also cause sauces to be oversweet and difficult to digest. Most pizzerias use canned tomato or pizza sauces. Because the sauces are usually preseasoned, oversalted, oversweetened, and extended with fillers they are an insult to good taste.

Always start from scratch. If you don't have time to cook a sauce, simply crush drained canned tomatoes directly onto a prepared crust, add a liberal sprinkling of herbs, garlic, and seasonings, and you can create an "instant" sauce that is absolutely delicious.

Cheese

What kind of cheese is best on pizza? Really any cheese that melts well. We tend to think of mozzarella as synonymous with pizza, but it was not actually used on pizza until the second half of the nineteenth century in Naples. There were many different alternative cheeses for pizza before mozzarella, and there are innovations being discovered every day. Any mellow cheese that has a good melting capacity can be a candidate for pizza. Experiment with different kinds of cheeses but keep in mind that domestic variations of imported cheeses have neither the fine taste nor the melting properties of the originals. Here is a list of the most traditional cheeses used in pizza-making, along with some of the latest trends.

Mozzarella. America produces more mozzarella than any other nation in the world. The demand for this cheese is in direct relation to the rise in popularity of pizza in this country. Unfortunately, mozzarella has changed so much over the years that it is barely recognizable as the ethnic food it once was. The continued "improvement" of mozzarella has had little to do with quality of taste; rather, it has been one of convenience. Mozzarella is now judged on such merits as "mouth feel" (the industrial term for texture), meltability, grinding, slicing, or shredding

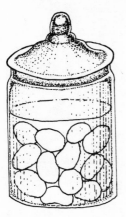

ease, and shelf life—everything but flavor. The subject of mozzarella is a constant source of debate among pizza-makers, commercial or not. For the sake of clarity, I will confine our discussion of "pizza" cheese, as mozzarella has come to be known, to three main categories: fresh, low-moisture, and non-dairy imitation analogs (mozzarella substitutes).

Buffalo Milk Mozzarella.   Authentic mozzarella made from buffalo milk is in a class by itself; its slightly tangy, delicate flavor is unique, and its creamy texture defies grating. Buffalo milk mozzarella is extremely perishable and rare even in Italy, where most mozzarella is now made from cow's milk. Nevertheless, more and more specialty food stores and cheese stores in cities all over the United States are beginning to sell this delightful cheese.

Genuine buffalo milk mozzarella is made in the form of small white balls (about the size of a jumbo egg) or is smoked, and is always stored in brine. Be sure to use the cheese within 2 or 3 days of its purchase. Otherwise it will dry out and spoil unless you get some brine to store it in. (The brine will preserve it for 5 to 7 days longer.) To use it on pizza, dry off the cheese with a paper towel and crush it with your hands directly onto the pie. The high butterfat content of buffalo milk causes the cheese to burn at high temperatures; to avoid this, add the cheese during the last 5 minutes of baking time. No other mozzarella compares with the luscious texture and distinct flavor of this Italian original; it is well worth its higher cost for the occasional extra-special pizza.

Fresh Cow's Milk Mozzarella.   Fresh mozzarella is still made throughout the United States in the time-honored Italian tradition. It is an art that has survived through Italian-American families, who continue to make it from scratch daily. Not long ago, the sight of white balls of cheese floating in brine was familiar only in Italian *salumerias* (pork butcher shops) and stores specializing in *latticini* (milk products), which were rarely found outside old Italian neighborhoods. But as the demand for this quality cheese seems to be on the rise, it is becoming more and more accessible at fine cheese stores and specialty markets.

Cow's milk mozzarella is slightly rubbery in texture and somewhat blander in taste than its buffalo milk relative, but despite its differences in character, it melts into long, tender strings on pizza and is absolutely delicious.

Preservative-free, fresh mozzarella comes in three types: regular, nonsalted, and smoked. The nonsalted type is the most perishable, lasting only a day or two at the most; the salted kind lasts up to a week if it is tightly wrapped in plastic wrap or—better still—if it is kept in a container with some of its brine. Smoked mozzarella keeps the longest—about 2 weeks if tightly sealed in plastic. All of these types of mozzarella can be frozen for several months, but they won't melt quite so well and they may be a little tough when defrosted and cooked. Because of its limited production, fresh mozzarella tends to vary slightly from family recipe to recipe. Some will be more or less moist or more or less salty than others. In general, these cheeses bubble and brown in oven temperatures of 500 degrees when they are baked for more than 15 minutes. I get excellent results by slicing the cheese into ¼-inch-thick slices or cutting it into 1-inch cubes. This allows the cheese to melt without getting tough and rubbery. I don't advise grating mozzarella for use on top of pizza, as this causes the cheese to release too much water and to become dried out and over-browned. Because buffalo milk mozzarella is rare and expensive, I prefer to use cow's milk for almost all of my pizzas, and I strongly recommend it.

Processed Mozzarella. Sold in supermarkets from coast to coast in familiar ½-pound, 1-pound, and 2-pound packages, processed mozzarella is by far the most readily accessible type of mozzarella. This kind of cheese is made with either whole milk or skim milk in a manner similar to that of fresh mozzarella, only on a much larger scale. There is very little difference in taste and texture between whole milk and skim milk mozzarella in their uncooked state; when cooked, though, whole milk mozzarella tends to brown more rapidly, and skim milk doesn't melt as well. Both kinds taste far more of salt than of cheese. Most of these cheeses are natural, but some do contain additives and preservatives. A quick glance at the label will tell you what you are buying. The best processed mozzarella has no preservatives, but it should keep well for up to 2 weeks if sealed in plastic wrap and for several months when frozen. Processed mozzarella does not have the delicate flavor and texture of fresh, but when it is paired with a fragrant tomato sauce or other toppings, it still makes a very good pizza.

Low-Moisture Mozzarella. Born and bred for pizza, this ultra-refined version of mozzarella is the number one choice of professional pizzamakers. Low-moisture mozzarella contains roughly 45 to 50 percent moisture, as compared with fresh mozzarella, which can contain 60 percent moisture. Less moisture makes the cheese harder and dryer, which in turn makes it easier to grind, shred, or slice. There are two types of low-moisture mozzarellas: full-cream and part-skim mozzarella cheese. Full cream is the more expensive because it contains the largest percentage of butterfat. It also has the best flavor and best melting qualities. Part-skim mozzarella can be purchased in several different grades, at a substantially lower cost—depending on the butterfat content. Many pizza-makers blend the two together in an effort to economize.

On the whole, low-moisture mozzarella is the model pizza cheese. It is consistent, it handles beautifully, and it melts into great strings. Unfortunately, though, its flavor has very little in common with the flavor of authentic mozzarella.

Nondairy Analogs. The most recent development in pizza cheese is the introduction of a totally nondairy imitation mozzarella "analog," made entirely from vegetable fat. The use of mozzarella analogs is widespread in the frozen pizza industry and, to a growing extent, in pizzerias. I mention it here not to recommend its use but to warn you about it. Analog cheese substitutes have been called the wave of the future; if so, I don't want any part of it.

Scamorza. Originally from the Italian province of Abruzzi, where cheese plays a major role in almost all of the dishes, this egg- or pear-shaped cheese is part of the mozzarella family, and it can be substituted for mozzarella in nearly any recipe. Dried on the outside, with a soft, creamy interior, scamorza is widely used in pizza both as a substitute for mozzarella and on its own. Some varieties are smoked, and others are spiced with black pepper. The slightly pungent taste of this unusual cheese is brought out in cooking; uncooked, it remains an extremely pleasant and mild cheese. Imported scamorza is rare. Your best bet is to purchase it from a good *salumeria* or, better yet, from an Italian food store. If the owners are from the south of Italy and make their own fresh mozzarella, they are bound to make scamorza as well. Scamorza keeps well when sealed tightly in plastic wrap and refrigerated. It travels well, too, and is available through mail order.

Caciocavallo. A semi-hard cheese with a smooth skin that ranges in color from pale yellow to brown, caciocavallo traditionally comes in the shape of an elongated, lopsided figure eight. The outside color of the skin determines its age and use. Paler outside skin indicates a young cheese with a soft interior (good for cooking or eating as is), while a darker outside skin is a sign of age; with age comes hardening, which makes the cheese more suitable for grating. The pungent flavor of caciocavallo becomes more pronounced as it ages. Caciocavallo imported from Italy comes in large rounds and is sold by the wedge. The larger cheeses are dry and excellent for grating. Use caciocavallo along with mozzarella on pizza or in fillings for the rolled and stuffed variations. Caciocavallo is available in most fine cheese stores or through mail order.

Provolone. Imported Italian Provolone, with its full, sharp flavor and excellent melting capacity, is clearly superior to domestic Provolone, which tastes dry and dull and does not melt properly. Imported Provolone is easily found in most supermarkets or cheese stores. Use Provolone mixed with other cheeses on pizza or in fillings for added flavor.

Ricotta. Whole or skim milk ricotta is a creamy curd cheese that resembles cottage cheese—except that it is much finer in texture and flavor. The fat content of ricotta seems to have little effect on cooking qualities; therefore, whole and part-skim ricotta are interchangeable. Ricotta is used primarily as a filling in the stuffed variations of pizza, such as *calzoni* and *sfincuini*. Cottage cheese is not an adequate substitute for ricotta, because cottage cheese is too salty and it gives off too much moisture while cooking.

Ricotta Salata or Dura. This imported Italian cheese is dry, and somewhat more akin to a sharp, salty goat cheese (chèvre) than to its creamy, mild American counterpart. It is used in stuffings for filled pizzas like *pitta*, *calzoni*, and *sfincuini*. A mild feta or dry goat cheese can be substituted if Italian ricotta salata is unavailable.

Fontina. True Italian Fontina is a mild, creamy cheese that melts beautifully and is superb on pizza. Swedish and Danish Fontinas, though less creamy than the Italian, are very good substitutes, and so are imported Dutch cheeses such as Gouda and Edam.

Pecorino Romano. A sharp grating cheese, Romano is a favored ingredient in the cuisine of Romans and among the Genovese in Italy, especially in sauces like *pesto*. For optimum flavor, Romano should be kept tightly wrapped in plastic in the refrigerator and grated only as it is needed. Try including a generous sprinkling of Romano along with mozzarella for a more intense cheese taste on pizza. Buy only fresh Romano, not the bottled or canned variety.

Parmesan. The most popular grating cheese of northern Italy, Parmesan is characteristically a sweet, nutty-tasting semi-dry cheese. It should be moist and warm yellow in color if it has been stored properly; if it has not, the cheese develops an off-white color and a slightly pungent flavor. Look for the words *Parmigiano-Reggiano* on the rind of the cheese. This will assure you that the cheese is first rate. Stay away from bottled or canned pregrated Parmesan. It's often made from lesser quality cheeses and cut with things other than cheese to prevent spoilage. Store Parmesan by wrapping it tightly in plastic wrap and refrigerating it. Grate only as much as you need.

Goat Cheese. Goat cheese is not a traditional Italian ingredient for pizza, but its tangy flavor seems to have a natural affiliation to pizza. There are a number of imported French or Italian goat cheeses now available; they range from dry to creamy in texture and from mildly pungent to extremely sharp in taste. Some are shot through with black pepper or rolled in the aromatic herbs of Provence. There are also excellent domestic goat cheeses made in California and New York State that are beginning to make their way to local markets. Goat cheese does not melt into strings as mozzarella does, and its cooked texture is not much different from its raw state. It remains creamy on top of pizza and, of course, in fillings. The goat cheeses I recommend are Montrachet (without the black ash coating), Boucheron, Saint Maure, Valencay, and Saint Saviol.

Cheddar. White Vermont, New York State, and Canadian Cheddar cheeses are popular toppings for pizza in New England. The intense flavor of the sharp cheeses makes them an obvious choice for pizza. Processed Cheddar melts better than natural, but the taste of the natural is much better. If you are not from the Northeast, Cheddar cheese on pizza may seem a bit strange. Just think of it as a giant grilled cheese sandwich—only better!

Monterey Jack. This West Coast favorite, a mild-tasting, all-natural, white Cheddar-like cheese with excellent melting capacity, is a major ingredient in Tex-Mex cooking. Witness the rise of two southwestern regional specialties—taco pizza and chile pizza—that are untraditional but great.

Anchovies

Look for the imported ones in cans packed in oil or sold in bulk and packed in salt. Be sure to rinse off anchovies that have been packed in salt before using them in any of the recipes. There are no substitutes for anchovies. If you don't like them, leave them out!

Capers

The little berries gathered from caper bushes growing along the Mediterranean are still hand-picked and still expensive. Available in two sizes—large and nonpareil—capers usually come packed in brine or vinegar. The larger, less expensive ones are just fine for pizza-making. A little goes a long way, so use capers sparingly on pizza to give it that fresh taste of the Mediterranean.

Olives

The best are the black, wrinkled, oil-cured ones of Italy and the fat, juicy, black, purple, and green ones from Morocco or Greece. My favorites, the tastiest olives of all, come from the south of France. These tiny purple Niçoise olives, marinated in olive oil and the herbs of Provence, are expensive, but they're well worth the money. As a rule, olives on pizza where they can be seen are not pitted. But if you can't see them, do pit them. To pit an olive, just squeeze the olive until the pit comes out between your fingers. If the olive is dried out, you may have to cut it with a small paring knife to get the pit out. Olives keep for several months in a jar or other airtight container and will stay especially moist and plump if you include a bit of their brine along with them. Olives packed in salted water are not suitable for pizza. Their bland, salty flavor adds nothing to the pie.

Peppers

Peppers, sweet or hot, make a welcome addition to pizza. Crisp green peppers provide crunch, and mellow roasted or sautéed red peppers lend a subtle, smoky taste. Hot peppers can add a bit of zing or a fiery kick to a pizza, depending on how much you use.

Sweet Peppers. Green peppers and red peppers are actually the same plant; as a green pepper matures, it turns from green to red and develops a soft, succulent, sweet fleshy taste. Green or red bell peppers are the most commonly available, but it's worth trying to find those long skinny green, yellow, and red peppers sometimes referred to as "Italian frying peppers" or simply "frying peppers." Don't confuse them with hot peppers which are thinner and darker green or red with thick skins. To make peppers more digestible, skin them or sauté them until they just begin to soften before using them on pizza. To remove the skin from peppers, put them about 3 inches below the flames of a broiler and turn them with tongs every few minutes until the skin is black and blistered. Put the peppers in a bowl and cover it with plastic wrap for about 10 minutes. This will cause the peppers to steam and will make it easier to peel away the charred skins with a paring knife.

Hot Peppers. Every September, I begin my hot pepper ritual by selecting tiny dark green, thick-skinned specimens, threading them with kitchen twine, and hanging them to dry and to blaze ruby red in my kitchen. The fall harvest of hot peppers provides me with their fire throughout the winter. Chili powder or hot red pepper flakes are pale substitutes for the real thing, as the powder and flakes have little or no flavor of their own. You can control the degree of fire by how much of the pepper you expose in cooking. Leaving it whole will impart a mildly hot bite. If you bruise the whole pepper by crushing it, it becomes hotter still, and crushing the whole pepper releases all of its volatile oils. *A word of caution:* Whenever you handle hot peppers, don't rub your face or eyes with your hands, and always wash your hands well with soap and warm water when you are finished. Pepper oils get trapped in the pores of your skin and will burn the soft, sensitive tissue of your face and eyes on contact. (I wear rubber gloves when I handle hot peppers.)

Hot peppers packed in vinegar can be purchased and can be stored in the refrigerator for months.

Mushrooms

Fresh mushrooms should have smooth, unblemished skin and should be creamy white in color. Purchase mushrooms loose by the pound from large baskets, because those that are prepackaged in wrapped containers are treated with sodium bisulfate to retard spoilage. Treated mushrooms tend to retain moisture and give off much more liquid during cooking than natural ones do. This accounts for their mushy texture and lack of flavor. Even natural mushrooms can be ruined by overwashing. Mushrooms in general are highly absorbent and should never be rinsed under water, because they will absorb too much water and will no longer have any taste of their own. The best method is to wet a paper towel, squeeze out the excess water, and wipe the mushrooms clean. Before they are used on pizza, mushrooms should be sautéed in a small amount of oil for about 5 minutes, or until they give off all of their liquid. Canned mushrooms are unacceptable for pizza; their rubbery texture and bland flavor will add nothing to your pie.

Meats

Traditionally, meats such as sweet or hot sausages, salami, *prosciutto*, *pepperoni*, *pancetta*, and ham were mainly used for flavoring purposes on pizza and not as primary ingredients. A little of any of these meats goes a long way, so it's not necessary to use any of them in large quantities to get a totally satisfying taste.

Fresh Sausage. Good Italian sausage is very hard to find outside of Italian specialty stores or fine butcher shops. Try to find a reputable merchant, preferably one who makes his own sausage. Most "Italian-style" sausage sold in supermarkets is of poor quality and can legally contain fillers, preservatives, and a large percentage of fat. All sausage must contain 30 percent fat for it to have any flavor, but the rest should be made of good-quality pork and such fresh seasonings as fennel, black pepper, hot pepper, parsley, garlic, and cheese. The most common varieties of Italian sausage are *sweet* and *hot*. Sweet sausages are made with black pepper, garlic, and fennel seeds or sometimes with cinnamon; hot sausages can contain any of the aforementioned plus bits of red pepper and paprika, which is what gives them their reddish color. Fresh sausage will keep for about a week in the refrigerator and for several months in the freezer. Used in the crust as a flavoring, in sauces, or as a topping, good sausage can mean the difference between a great pizza and a mediocre one.

Dried Sausage. Dried sausage is merely fresh sausage that has been allowed to dry out under controlled temperature conditions. Most places that sell good-quality fresh sausage usually sell good dry sausage as well. Dried sausage comes in the same variations as fresh—sweet and hot—and it resembles a thin salami. Dried sausage is interchangeable with *pepperoni* and salami in most recipes. Use it sliced on top of pizza and in fillings for the rolled and stuffed variations.

Pepperoni. Without a doubt America's favorite pizza topping is *pepperoni*, followed by Italian sausage, mushrooms, and green peppers. (*Pepperoni* is uniquely an American pizza phenomenon—there is no such thing as *pepperoni* pizza in Italy.) *Pepperoni* is similar to dried sausage except that it is made with a mixture of beef and pork and is smoked. The combination of meats, seasonings, and the smoking process give *pepperoni* its particular taste. *Pepperoni* can be kept refrigerated for months; use it on top of pizza and in pizza fillings. To avoid burning *pepperoni*, layer it under the sauce; it will stay moist while the pizza bakes.

Salami. Genoa salami, Sicilian salami, and *soprassatta* are all excellent for pizza. Imported salami is not necessarily better than some of the quality handmade ones available at Italian specialty food stores. Look for a large percentage of meat in the salami. If there is a large portion of light-colored or white fat in the mixture, it is an indication of lesser-quality salami. Salami is interchangeable with dry sausage in recipes.

Prosciutto. *Prosciutto* is ham that has been salted and then air-cured. Usually *prosciutto* is sliced paper-thin and eaten with melon or fruit as an appetizer, but for pizza it is used in chunks. The best cut for this purpose is the "*prosciutto* heel," which is the bone at the end of the piece of ham. This piece can no longer be sliced into neat slices and is usually sold at a savings to those who know enough to ask for it. *Prosciutto* heel is found only in Italian food stores. If you can't find *prosciutto* heel, buy a chunk of *prosciutto* in most delis or even in some supermarkets. The best brands of *prosciutto* in the United States are made by Citterio and John Volpi Company. *Prosciutto* can be frozen for months and keeps well for several weeks in the refrigerator when properly wrapped in plastic (if mold forms on the outside, it can be scraped away). Use *prosciutto* in pizza dough, *focacce*, and pizza fillings.

Pancetta. Almost exactly like unsmoked bacon, *pancetta* is salted and flavored with black pepper and is used extensively in pizza fillings. Slab bacon may be substituted for *pancetta*, but it must first be blanched in boiling water for 10 minutes. *Pancetta* in one piece can be purchased at good Italian delis, pork stores, or *salumerias*.

Ham and Canadian Bacon. Ham is often found in traditional Italian pizza, but Canadian bacon seems to be gaining in popularity as a topping in the midwestern and southwestern parts of the United States. It is delicious on breakfast pizzas. Both ham and Canadian bacon can be found in most supermarkets and require no precooking.

Herbs are used throughout pizza-making—in the dough, the sauce, the toppings, even the cheese. Unfortunately, herbs are often stale before you bring them home, and stale herbs do absolutely nothing for pizza. Here are some tips on how to get the most out of your herbs.

First of all, herbs and spices don't last forever. That old bottle of oregano or basil you've had tucked away for ages is useless, so throw it out. (I make it a practice to renew my herbs every fall, preferably with ones I've dried myself.) Try to find a merchant who sells high-quality dried herbs. All too often herbs sold in large bags or bins may look quaint in the store display, but they may have been sitting around in a warehouse for the last 2 years. Quality dried herbs are still greenish, not gray or brown, and have a strong aroma. Try to buy herbs in small amounts and replace them with fresh stock a few times a year. Don't be fooled by "bargain" bulk, prepackaged bags. Bargain herbs usually have bargain flavor. Ground herbs are always inferior to the whole leaf forms, because they have a somewhat acrid aftertaste. Whenever possible, use fresh herbs rather than dried; their delicate flavor is quite refreshing on pizza. Dried or fresh herbs are interchangeable in most recipes: The rule of thumb is to use twice as much fresh as dried.

Garlic. Garlic is good for you. Its medicinal properties were appreciated by the ancients, who used it in their cooking to ward off disease. Of course, the little bulb has an extremely strong flavor, and too much of it may cause those who indulge to ward off more than just disease! Seriously though, garlic is one of the essential *essences* of pizza, flavoring sauces, fillings, and toppings. Only fresh garlic is acceptable on pizza. Never adulterate your creation with garlic powder, garlic salt, or garlic flakes; they are difficult to digest, they have an unpleasant aftertaste, and they are more expensive than the real thing.

Look for large, rounded, well-developed cloves on a smooth, unblemished head. Purple-colored outside skins denote the most flavor, but the more common pure white heads will do just fine. Separate and peel the cloves as you need them. To facilitate peeling, smack them with the flat side of a knife to loosen the skin. The power of garlic is directly related to the amount of surface area revealed; thus, finely minced garlic is more potent than garlic that has been sliced. Garlic lightly crushed with a knife and finely chopped is even stronger than minced. But the most potent essence of all is extracted with a garlic press, which releases all of the oils. This last strength is reserved for making garlic oil, which you can brush on pizza crust to flavor it and give it a lovely golden brown color.

If the lingering odor of garlic on your hands bothers you, rinse your hands with cold water and rub them liberally with table salt. The salt acts as an extractor and removes the garlic oil from the pores of your skin. Be sure to use *cold* water—hot water opens the pores up and traps the garlic oil in! This old trick comes courtesy of Julia Child's *Mastering the Art of French Cooking.*

Oregano. How fitting that the herb most frequently associated with pizza was once considered a symbol of peace and happiness by the Romans. Oregano is actually a potent variety of wild marjoram. The best and most fragrant of all oregano comes from Greece and is sold in large bunches in most Greek or Italian markets. Unlike the oregano in the shake-top jars that most pizzerias use—which is only a ghost of the fresh herb—Greek oregano is extremely flavorful and should be used with restraint.

marjoram

Marjoram. Sweet marjoram is similar to oregano in flavor, but it is much sweeter and infinitely more delicate. I prefer to use fresh or dried marjoram rather than oregano on pizza because it blends with rather than dominates the other flavors in the pie. Marjoram is very easy to grow, and it makes a beautiful potted plant for a sunny windowsill all year 'round.

Basil. Nothing quite duplicates the lovely fragrance and intense flavor of fresh basil. Once the herb is dried, however, it loses a lot of its flavor. One way to guarantee a steady supply of fresh basil to flavor pizza, sauces, soups, or stews throughout the year is to freeze it in small portions. In the summer, when big, healthy bunches of fresh basil are plentiful, I freeze small packages of basil. I stack five leaves, roll them up tightly, and wrap them in foil, and put the packets in a plastic bag. The little basil packages keep in a sealed plastic bag in the freezer for up to a year. Freezing affects the color and texture of basil (so you can't use it raw), but it retains its refreshing taste. To use the basil, simply unwrap one package (one should be adequate for one pizza) and throw the frozen basil leaves into the sauce. To cook on pizza, let the leaves defrost for about 15 minutes, or until they are soft enough to handle, and use them on top of the pie as you would fresh basil.

To use fresh basil, snip the leaves with scissors or tear them with your hands. Basil bruises easily (and becomes bitter), so handle it gently. Always select basil that is bright green and fresh looking; limp, wrinkled leaves with black spots are sure indications that it is past its prime.

Fresh basil on pizza is thoroughly Italian. Genuine Neapolitan pizza is made only rarely with oregano. The natural affinity of basil and tomatoes on pizza has long been recognized as one of the classic combinations in Italian cuisine.

Rosemary. An herb steeped in tradition, rosemary has long been considered the symbol of friendship, loyalty, and remembrance. Its highly aromatic, pungent flavor has the tendency to dominate a dish, so it should be used with caution. Rosemary has small thin leaves like tiny pine needles and looks rather like a small shrub. Fresh rosemary has the best flavor—it is far more fragrant than dried—but dried is adequate for most recipes. Don't use preground rosemary, as it has a strong and bitter flavor, but do grind down whole rosemary or pulverize it in a blender just before using it. Fresh rosemary is available at most good-quality greengrocers the year 'round. If you can't find any fresh rosemary at your local markets, try growing a pot of this hardy perennial on your own—a windowsill with a southern or western exposure will do just fine. Rosemary has enjoyed a long association with pizza. From the time when *focacce* were embellished with only oil and herbs, it has remained a key flavoring in toppings and in the dough itself.

Sage. An often underrated herb because of its widespread misuse, sage has come to be known for its use in poultry seasoning. The slender gray-green leaves of sage carry with them a distinctively warm and slightly pungent flavor that compliments pork and fish as well as poultry and all manner of stuffings. Sage was particularly favored by the Romans, who used it very often in stews or as a wrapping for bits of meat and sausages to be grilled.

sage

Avoid ground sage at all costs. Buy sage in the whole leaf state and pulverize it as you need it. Sage is an excellent accent for toppings that include sausage, bacon, mild cheeses, or eggplant, but it does not go well with tomatoes.

Thyme. There are literally dozens of species of cultivated thyme, but the one considered to be the best for culinary purposes is called French thyme. Other varieties of thyme are grown for ornamental purposes and are not suitable for cooking. French thyme is grown all over the world, but the most fragrant still comes from Provence in the south of France. Whether in the fresh or dried state, good French thyme is characterized by its strong smell. Thyme is an extremely strong herb, so exercise caution when using it. Southern Italians are particularly fond of thyme and use it in a number of dishes, but no other country along the Mediterranean uses thyme quite so lavishly as the French do. Thyme is the major seasoning in *pissaladière*—France's answer to pizza.

Herbes de Provence. Herbs growing wild along the roads and in the fields of the countryside in the back hills of the French Riviera fill the air with their fragrance. The effect is intoxicating. It's no wonder that the cuisine of Provence is so lively with its profusion of herbs. Small pouches or bundles of mixed fresh or dried herbs are sold in all of the marketplaces of Provence. No two mixtures are alike, as they are hand-picked from wild and cultivated herbs and vary from place to place. *Herbes de Provence* usually contain any combination of wild thyme, oregano, marjoram, sage, rosemary, wild fennel seeds, and sometimes lavender. They are available in this country at specialty food stores and through mail order. Use these unusual herb mixtures on any French pizza variations and as an all-around pizza flavor enhancer.

Parsley. Curly leaf parsley and flat leaf parsley (sometimes called Italian parsley) are the two most common varieties of parsley in this country. The flat leaf kind has a stronger flavor and is better for cooking; curly parsley is less robust and more useful as a garnish. Fresh parsley, abundant the year 'round, is perhaps the easiest of all herbs to buy fresh, so there's no reason to bother with dried parsley flakes; they don't taste like parsley anyway.

Onions. Sweet red Bermuda onions or yellow Spanish onions or the egg-shaped red Italian onions, *cippole,* are best for pizza. Sautéing the onions first for a few minutes in a bit of olive oil brings out their sweetness and makes them easier to digest than using them raw.

Chives and Scallions. These members of the onion family are not traditional on pizza, but they are nevertheless extremely tasty additions. Chives resemble long thin green blades of grass, and their delicate onion flavor is especially suited to more delicate pizza toppings and fillings. Always use fresh or frozen chives. Dried or freeze-dried chives have little or no taste.

Similar in flavor but much stronger are scallions, which are sometimes also known as spring or green onions. Scallions have a small white

parsley

bulb with long, slender green leaves and can be used from top to bottom in fillings and on toppings when a light onion flavor is desired.

Fennel Seeds. Fennel seeds and anise seeds are very similar in flavor. Both are reminiscent of licorice, but fennel is slightly sweeter and more aromatic than anise. Fennel is used to flavor Italian pork sausages, to cure black olives, in sauces, and as a distinctive seasoning on pizza.

Salt. One of my biggest gripes about commercially produced pizza is its high concentration of salt. The crust, the low-moisture mozzarella, canned tomato sauces, the garlic salt, the *pepperoni* and sausages all contain too much salt. You will find that homemade pizza will be much less salty and far more delicate than anything you've ever had in a pizzeria, even though fresh cheese, fresh sausages, and other ingredients contain plenty of salt. Ignore the salt shaker when you're making pizza. Try freshly ground black pepper instead. For those of you on low-sodium diets, take heart—you can now enjoy this forbidden pleasure. Omit the salt in the dough and use fresh tomatoes, fresh herbs, and unsalted fresh mozzarella.

Pepper. The incomparable taste of freshly ground black pepper is a must in pizza-making. Whether it is very coarsely ground in pizza dough or used to add just the right hint of spice to a topping, pepper is an important pizza seasoning. Preground black pepper has little or no taste in comparison. Buy yourself a pepper mill and add a bit of spice to your life.

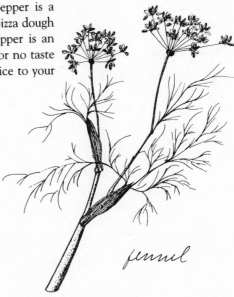

fennel

4.

EQUIPMENT

Perhaps the greatest misconception proliferated about pizza-making is that it requires lots of special equipment. Nothing could be further from the truth. Your home oven, a bowl, a pan, and a good pair of hands are all that you really need to make pizza. Of course, some ovens work better than others, different pans give different effects, and a good pair of hands might be assisted by a machine such as a food processor or an electric mixer. If you do decide to stock up on equipment, you'll be happy to find out that there is very little in the way of equipment for pizza-making that is expensive. You can outfit yourself to the hilt with pizza pans, stones, oil cans, peels, and cutting wheels, and spend less than the price of a single copper saucepan.

But before you buy anything, read this section carefully and purchase only what you think you really need. Learn to use it well before going on to experiment with other kinds of pans and pizza.

The Pizza Oven

Traditionally, pizza was baked in wood-fired or coal-fired brick ovens, which not only supplied intensely dry heat (700 to 800 degrees) but also imparted a distinct flavor and texture to the crust as well. Unfortunately, few pizzerias still use these ovens, because operating them is such an arduous task: The daily routine of shoveling hard wood or coal onto one side of the oven deck, stoking it up until it is red hot and waiting as long as 5 hours until it was fired up is, to say the least, labor-intensive. Furthermore, it takes someone with great skill to use a brick oven. Each oven's interior has its own hot spots, and the *pizzaiolo* must know the oven well enough to be able to judge the pie by eye and to know where to move it next. This may not seem overly difficult when a single pizza is being baked at a time, but when upward of 10 pies are cooking at once, anyone less than a master of the oven will probably charcoal-broil the whole lot!

Today, even in Italy, most coal- or wood-burning ovens have been replaced by gas-fired ones. Gas is much more dependable and accurate, and it is easier to fire up; with but a flick of a switch, it can be ready to use in about an hour. But gas does not infuse the crust with that wonderfully toasty, charcoal flavor that is characteristic of brick-oven pizza.

However, despite my fondness for brick-oven pizza, most of the greatest pizza I've ever had has come out of a gas-fired oven—my own.

The only quality of a pizza oven that cannot be duplicated at home is the brick-oven taste. Aside from that, as long as your oven gets very hot (500 to 550 degrees), you're in business. To get the most heat out of your oven, line its floor with unglazed quarry tiles, leaving an inch border all around for air. I have measured up to a 50-degree temperature difference from the lowest position of the oven rack to the floor of the oven itself. The floor is the hottest part of your oven, and that's the best place to bake thin-crusted Neapolitan-style pizza.

Most ovens lined with quarry tiles or fitted with pizza stones take 1 hour to reach a maximum temperature of 500 to 550 degrees. However, not all pizza is baked at such high temperatures. Deep-dish pan pizza or rolled and stuffed pies rarely require temperatures of over 450 degrees.

Beware of oven thermostats, as they can vary as much as 75 degrees over or under the temperature indicated. You can check your oven's accuracy with a good-quality oven thermometer. Place the thermometer exactly where you would a pizza, heat up the oven, and compare readings. This will ensure even results and properly cooked pizza.

Quarry Tiles

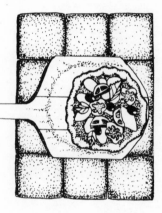

The least expensive and easiest way to convert your oven to a pizza oven is to use unglazed quarry tiles as your pizza deck. Unglazed quarry tiles are made of hard red clay that is very similar to the kind used in brick ovens. They act in the same way, too, by providing intense hot and dry heat.

Buy unglazed quarry tiles at a ceramic tile supplier. You will need only a few. To determine what size you need, measure your oven floor, leaving an inch border of clear space all around (so the hot air can circulate). Have the tiles cut to size. This allows you more room to maneuver and to make larger-size pies.

There are pizza tiles available from mail order or cookware stores at three or four times the price of quarry tiles. They work just as well, but they can't be cut to size. They simply are not worth the extra cost.

Do not buy sealed or glazed tiles for pizza-making. The idea is to take advantage of the clay's porous, absorptive qualities, and once the stone is sealed, this is no longer possible. Pay attention to the thickness of the tiles; thicker stones take much longer to heat up and tiles that are too thin can break easily. Most tiles or stones are just under ½ inch thick and should take about 1 hour to reach a temperature of 500 degrees.

Note: If you have an electric oven that has a heating element on its floor, lay the tiles on an oven rack and set the rack at its lowest position.

Baking Stones

There are a number of pizza stones on the market to choose from. I find the round pizza stones extremely limiting (the pizza can only be round and only as large as the stone) and difficult to use (it's not easy to aim the pizza off of the peel so that it fits exactly over that circle of stone), but the rectangular ones are adequate. The Old Stone Oven Corporation makes a 14- by 16-inch rectangular pizza baking stone that is made of sturdy, thick, heatproof ceramic and can accommodate a full-size rectangular pizza. Despite the fact that it's expensive (about $22), I strongly recommend it.

Pans

Pizza pans made of black steel, which is noted for its ability to retain heat, are clearly the choice over aluminum, because their superior browning capabilities produce a very crispy pizza crust. Pans should be thick enough not to warp when exposed to intense heat.

To care for black pans, lightly grease them with flavorless vegetable oil each time before baking. Don't ever cut pizza in the pan, or you'll scratch the finish and the next pizza you bake in that pan will stick. Don't be alarmed if the pans develop discolorations in the finish after baking. The spots are caused by the acid of the tomatoes; the stains do not affect the pans' performance in any way.

Brick Oven Black Steel Bakeware pans coated with Carbonite are made by Speko Products, Inc., and are available in most cookware stores. They resist staining and have a relatively nonstick surface.

Aluminum pans needn't be seasoned, and they do not develop a patina finish like black pans. They tend to need a heavier application of oil before baking a pie than black pans do because their surface reflects heat rather than absorbing it. I do not cut pizza in these pans either, because scratching the surface of any baking pan—whether the finish is removed or not—causes sticking and diminishes the pan's performance and cleaning ease.

Tray Pans. These round or square black steel or aluminum pans are excellent for thin- or medium-crusted pies. Their low rim (about ½ inch) facilitates the removal of hot pizza, so that it merely slides off the pan. Rimless pans and baking sheets are not necessarily called pizza pans, because they are really considered all-purpose pans and can be used for a number of other baking tasks. The exact dimensions of these pans vary slightly from manufacturer to manufacturer. In general, the round pans come in 10-, 12-, and 15-inch diameters, and square pans come in 12- and 14-inch sizes. The rectangle is usually 12 by 16 inches.

Jelly Roll Pans. Jelly roll pans are excellent all-around pizza pans as they can accommodate a large thin- or thick-crusted pie. Their short sides (1 inch) are tall enough to support a thick pizza and low enough for easy removal of the pie with a spatula. The standard size for most jelly roll pans is 12 by 16 inches, and they are available in both black steel and aluminum. Try to have one of each. Black steel is better for Neapolitan- or Sicilian-style pies, but aluminum keeps rolled and stuffed pizzas, which require longer cooking times, from burning on the bottom.

Deep-Dish Pans. Black steel is a must for deep-dish pies, because pizza cooked in aluminum with high sides tends to steam rather than bake—especially when it is smothered with gooey sauce and cheese. Deep dish pans have 1½- to 2-inch sides, which should be more than adequate to hold any Sicilian- or Chicago-style deep-dish pizza. These pans are available in diameters of 6-, 10-, and 14- to 15-inch rounds or in 12- and 14-inch squares.

Pizza Screen. The best method for cooking Neapolitan-style pizza is to bake it directly on the deck of the oven or on a pizza stone. But there is always the problem of getting the pizza onto the stone or deck in one piece. This feat takes a fair amount of practice, but with a pizza screen, you'll never have to worry about pizza burning on the back wall of your oven. What's more, you can become a master at the direct stone-baking method from the first time you use one.

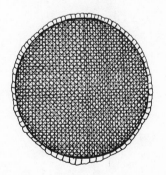

This miracle of modern pizza-making is nothing more than a heavy wire mesh edged with wire tape. It supports the pizza while letting the dough make direct contact with the heated oven deck or pizza stone. These inexpensive screens come in 8-, 10-, 12-, 14-, 16-, 18-, and 24-inch diameters. (The limit of most residential ovens is 18 inches. Don't forget to measure the inside of your oven before shopping.)

Food Processor

Having this mighty machine is like having an extra pair of hands in the kitchen. It makes pizza dough in 30 seconds, and it can slice, chop, and grate ingredients for toppings. Some of the larger models can make up to two recipes for pizza dough at once. However, not all food processors are heavy duty enough to handle pizza dough. Make sure you read the manufacturer's directions for your machine before proceeding with any of these recipes or you may find pizza dough to be the demise of your processor. I have two food processors, a Robot Coupe and a Cuisinart, both of which I used to test batch upon batch of pizza dough. I recommend them both.

Electric Mixer

Only heavy duty stationary electric mixers are strong enough to knead pizza dough. Most hand mixers would overheat under the strain. My old standby, the ever sturdy Kitchen-Aid mixer, kneads enough dough for 2 full-size pizzas in about 5 minutes. If you have another type of stationary mixer, be sure to read the manufacturer's directions before attempting to knead pizza dough with it.

Pizza Peel

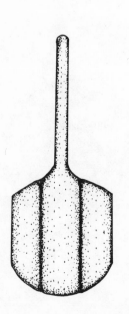

The peel is used to move thin Neapolitan-style pizza into and out of the oven. A rimless cookie sheet or a thin piece of wood could serve this function, but they certainly aren't as authentic. The pizza peel, symbol of the *pizzaiolo*, is for seriously hooked pizza fanatics. It is not the kind of tool you can merely tuck away in a drawer: For one thing, it's too big! Display it proudly and be prepared to rise to the challenge when your friends ask if you can really use that thing!

Select a peel only slightly larger than the pizza you intend to make. Be sure the peel can fit in your oven and that the handle isn't too long for your kitchen. Most pizza peels are made of wood, and wooden ones are best. There are also heavy-use commercial types of peels, which have a metal palette and a wooden handle.

Most of the utensils needed for pizza-making, with the exception of a
cutting wheel, a cutting tray, and an olive oil can, should already be part
of the average kitchen. If they aren't yet part of yours, now is the time to
acquire some of the little but extremely useful tools you've just not gotten
around to buying.

Cutting Wheel. To slice through a pizza with ease, select a cutting
wheel that is strong and sharp. Professional cutting wheels have sturdy
handles, blade guards, and blades that are 3 to 4 inches in diameter. I
have sliced through thousands of pies with my trusty Dexter pizza wheel,
which is all metal and features a replaceable blade. Considered by many
to be the best cutting wheel, the Dexter costs about three times as much
as some of the other professional wooden-handled cutting wheels, but it's
a small price to pay for a superior knife. And you don't have to buy a
whole new wheel each time the blade gets dull.

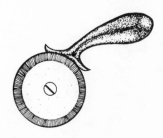

Bread Knife. A large, serrated bread knife is a good alternative to the
pizza wheel for cutting pizza. It is indispensable for cutting very thick
pizza, especially the rolled or filled kinds.

Cutting Tray. This large, round aluminum tray looks like a rimless
pizza pan, but it's much too lightweight to cook in. Transfer the hot pizza
from its pan onto one of these trays before cutting it up into serving
pieces. A large cutting board works equally well and may actually look
better—even if it is less authentic.

Spatula. Every cook should have a good heavy duty spatula to use as a
third hand when lifting foods, especially a whole pizza from pan to plate.
An 8-inch professional spatula will serve you well.

Dough Scraper. A small flexible stainless steel strip with a sturdy
wooden handle is perfect for scraping up sticky dough from work surfaces.
The scraper helps complete the task of kneading pizza dough quickly and
efficiently without leaving half of it to dry up on the work surface. Dough
scrapers make fine pastry cutters and are excellent too for portioning out
raw dough.

Olive Oil Can. A lovely object to behold, and useful, too, the Italian
oil can will allow you to drizzle the merest stream of olive oil onto your
pizza. The graceful traditional form comes in either tin or stainless steel.
A sleek, modern version is available only in stainless steel.

Cheese Grater.   The sturdy, four-sided stainless steel graters with a handle clean easily and give greater stability than the flat kind.

Bowls.   Stoneware, glass, or stainless steel bowls are all fine to use for the dough to rise in. But the plastic wrap that seals in moisture and heat during the rising time seems to stick better on stoneware or glass than it does on stainless steel.

Bio-Therm Thermometer.   If you have trouble guessing what "lukewarm" or "not too hot" means in terms of proofing temperatures, you will always be right with a Bio-Therm thermometer. This accurate little gadget can test all kinds of temperatures from 0 to 220 degrees. Whether you need to know the internal temperature of a roast or the correct temperature of butter for puff pastry, this thermometer will make an extremely useful addition to your *batterie de cuisine.*

Work Surface.   The traditional work surface of professional pizzamakers is marble, but any smooth, clean material will work just as well. Formica, wood counters, or rubber chopping boards are fine for kneading and rolling out pizza dough.

Additional Utensils.   You'll need a heavy duty wooden spoon for mixing dough, a set of measuring spoons, dry and liquid measuring cups, a mortar and pestle, a pepper mill, a sieve, a rolling pin (I prefer an Italian-style straight pin without handles or ball bearings, because it gives me more control while rolling out the dough), and plastic wrap for sealing the bowl during the dough's rising time.

The best pizza you'll ever eat can be made in your home oven. The techniques are simple, the variations are endless, and the results are immediate. These tried and true methods were developed in my pizza workshops for students who had little or no previous experience with making pizza. We've discussed ingredients and equipment, and before you read about dough and try your hand at the 30-Minute Pizza or some more ambitious recipe, read this section about the basic techniques.

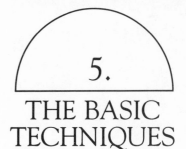

5.
THE BASIC TECHNIQUES

Proofing Yeast

Despite the advances of modern active dry yeast—especially the use of the expiration date—there will still be some occasions when you may need to proof yeast before using it in a recipe. Proofing is the process by which yeast's effectiveness is determined. The whole procedure takes only about 15 minutes, and it can avert a potential disaster.

1. Measure out 1 cup of warm tap water (110 to 115 degrees) into a small bowl. (The amount of warm water will vary from recipe to recipe. This amount corresponds to Basic Pizza Dough, page 56.)

2. Crumble 1 cake of compressed yeast or sprinkle 1 ¼-ounce package of active dry yeast over the water.

3. Add a pinch of sugar. (This does not flavor the dough. Yeast feeds off sugar and it will not foam up without it.)

4. Stir gently with a fork to dissolve. The mixture should be a light, creamy color. If the water remains clear and the yeast clumps at the bottom of the bowl without dissolving, this is an indication that the water temperature was wrong. It was either too hot (thereby killing the yeast) or too cold to activate it. Temperature miscalculations are difficult to compensate for. Once the yeast has been killed as a result of overheating, it cannot be resuscitated, and warming the mixture up because it was too cold to activate it is risky. The best solution is to start over again with some more water and yeast. (A Bio-Therm thermometer saves time and takes the guesswork out of this procedure.)

5. Let the dissolved yeast sit in a warm, draft-free place for 15 minutes. At the end of that time, a thin layer of whitish foam should appear on the surface of the mixture. The foam indicates that the yeast is active.

Kneading

Kneading is the rhythmic push, twist, and fold action that develops the gluten in flour while slowly incorporating it into the dough. When kneading the dough by hand, always add the flour in small amounts, as it will be absorbed into the dough at its own rate. The amount of flour used in the dough will vary according to the kind of flour used and under which weather conditions it was made. (A humid day will require more flour; on a dry day, less will be required.)

If you add too much flour too quickly, the dough will become dry, crumbly, and difficult to knead; it may even tear in spots. This can easily be corrected by removing all excess flour from the work surface and adding a few drops of water at a time to the dough while continuing the kneading process. As soon as the dough is soft and all of the dry lines of raw flour have disappeared, it has reached the proper consistency. (Don't add too much water too quickly or the dough will get sticky.) Pizza dough should be smooth and elastic, not sticky. Once the dough no longer sticks to your hands, do not overwork it; knead it only until it feels springy to the touch. Too much kneading will overdevelop the gluten in the dough and render it tough and unmanageable.

Rising

During the rising time, yeast gives off carbon dioxide and raises the millions of tiny gluten cell structures within the dough, which is why it doubles in volume. Risings promote good flavor and crumb texture in the crust and ease in handling when stretching or rolling out the dough.

Once the dough has been properly kneaded, it is then placed in an oiled bowl and sealed tightly with plastic wrap. Oiling the bowl facilitates the dough's rising by allowing it to slide up the sides of the bowl rather than sticking to them. Sealing the bowl with plastic wrap helps keep the dough moist and makes it rise faster by trapping in the excess heat from the carbon dioxide given off by the yeast. The best place for the dough to rise is in a warm, draft-free place, such as a pilot-lit gas oven. If your oven does not have a pilot light, turn it up to 200 degrees for 10 minutes and turn it *off before* you insert the dough, or it will begin to bake! After about 30 to 45 minutes (or 15 to 20 minutes if you are using one of the fast-rising dry yeasts), the dough should have doubled.

Once the dough has doubled in bulk, do not let it continue to rise without first punching it down or it may over-rise and collapse. Pizza dough is generally able to undergo 4 complete risings before the yeast will begin to use up its leavening power and the dough will no longer rise. Refrigerating the dough is the best solution to prolonging the risings if it is not to be used within 2 hours as the yeast's activity is slowed down by the cold. Give refrigerated dough 30 minutes to reach room temperature before using it. However, after 4 prolonged risings in the refrigerator (about 36 hours) the yeast will become ineffective and the dough will go flat.

Shaping

There is more than one way to shape a pizza. Some methods are more suitable to certain crust types than others and you'll learn that you don't have to flip a pizza a mile high in order to turn one out like a pro. Here are a few ways to start you off.

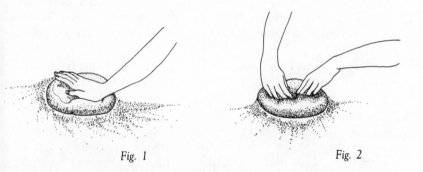

Fig. 1   *Fig. 2*   *Fig. 3*

Method I. The most direct way of shaping pizza is to flatten the dough with your hands into the general shape of the pan *(Figs. 1–3)*. This method is most suitable for medium- and thick-crusted pies.

Press the dough directly into a prepared pizza pan with your fingertips or the heel of your hand, working from the center out, until a natural rim is formed. The dough should be evenly distributed over the bottom of the pan. (Do not use this method on pizza screens because the dough will be pushed down into the mesh.)

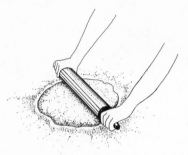

Fig. 4

Method II. Rolling the dough out with a pin is a good all-around technique for shaping most pizza (*Fig. 4*), but it is vital to the thin, even crusts of rolled and stuffed pizza and for such difficult-to-stretch doughs as whole wheat, semolina, and some of the flavored crusts.

1. Lightly dust the dough and work surface with flour.

2. Press the dough out to the desired shape and roll it out to 1 inch larger than the pan size. Pick up the dough often and turn it over while rolling. This stretches the dough and prevents it from sticking to the work surface. If it should stick at any time, dust it and the work surface with some flour.

3. Fit the dough into a prepared pan or onto a pizza screen or use it for rolled or stuffed pizza.

Method III. The classic Neapolitan stretching method makes the thinnest pizza in the world and is the preferred technique of most master pizza-makers. Once the dough has doubled in bulk, punch it down, knead it for 1 or 2 minutes, and let it rest, covered with a dish towel, for 15 to 20 minutes before stretching it out.

1. Shape the dough into a flat circle of about 1 inch thick.

2. Dust both sides of the dough and the work surface lightly with flour. (Frequent dustings of flour throughout this entire procedure are very important. Without them the dough will be too wet and soft to stretch.)

3. Starting from the center, slap the dough with your hand, pressing down firmly and quickly. Continue in a circular direction; working evenly from the inside out. Don't press the outer edge of the circle. That's how the pizza's puffed rim is formed.

4. When the inside portion of the dough is ½ inch thick, or the dough is two thirds the desired diameter, begin stretching it. Lift the dough off of the work surface and drape the edge over your open fists. Hold your hands together (*Fig. 5*), and then move them apart about 12

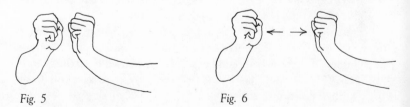

Fig. 5   Fig. 6

inches—stretching the dough over them as you do *(Fig. 6)*. Move the right hand to where the left one was under the dough and, starting once again with both hands together, stretch the dough over your fists. Continue this procedure a few more times until the dough is the right size. As the circle becomes larger and thinner, let the stretched part drape onto the work surface or you may tear it *(Fig. 7)*. Always stretch the dough close to the thicker outer edge as the center becomes thinner. If you poke a hole in the dough, just pinch it closed. Be careful not to stretch the dough less than ⅛ of an inch thick in the center or the filling may leak.

5. Carefully fit the dough onto a prepared pan or screen or on a floured pizza peel.

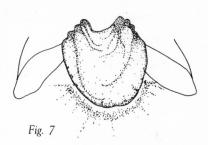

Fig. 7

Method IV. The ultimate show in pizza-making is the act of flipping a disk of dough high over your head into a perfect pizza. You may be surprised to learn that most professionals shun flipping; they regard it more as a form of entertainment than as a mark of excellence. But if it's showmanship you want, or if you've always had the desire to know the secret of flipping, here it is.

The prerequisites to flipping a pie are coordination, a high ceiling, perfectly conditioned dough, and lots of practice. Dough that is too dry or too wet will not stretch, nor will dough that is too warm (you'll end up poking a hole into it) or dough that is too cold (it tears). The dough should feel soft and cool but not cold enough to be stiff. Try conditioning the dough by refrigerating it: Once the dough has doubled in bulk, punch it down, knead it for a few minutes, and refrigerate it for about 15 minutes before attempting this method.

1. Shape the dough into a flat circle about 1 inch thick.

2. Dust the dough on both sides and the work surface lightly with flour. (Frequent dustings of flour throughout this entire procedure are essential.)

3. Starting from the center, work the dough with your fingertips, pressing down firmly and quickly. Continue in a circular direction, working from the inside out. Don't press the outer edge of the dough circle; leave the rim intact.

4. When the inside portion of the dough is ½ inch thick, begin stretching it. Lift the dough off the work surface and drape the edge over your open fists. Holding your hands together, move them apart about 12 inches—stretching the dough over them as you do. Move the right hand to where the left one was under the dough and starting once again with

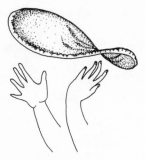

Fig. 8

both hands together, stretch the dough over your fists (*Figs. 5–6*). Continue this procedure a few more times until the dough is two thirds the desired diameter. Now you are ready to flip.

5. Posture is important, so stand up straight. Place your feet about 12 inches apart, with your weight evenly distributed.

6. Center your fists under the dough and raise your arms to chest height. Relax your shoulders. Don't tighten up.

7. Open your hands slightly. Begin the motion by bringing the right hand toward you about 12 inches apart from the left, now quickly switch hand positions, flicking your wrists as you bring your left hand toward you and your right hand away. (It is important that this motion be completed in one smooth, quick action. Practice it without the dough to get the feel of it.) This action starts the pizza spinning like a top, and the final flicking of the wrists sends it aloft (*Fig. 8*). Don't attempt to fling the dough more than a foot or two until you get better at it—height comes with practice.

8. Catch the dough as it lands on your fists.

9. Repeat. Avoid flipping the pizza more than twice. If you did not get it thin enough, complete the final stretching over your fists.

Assembling

Eating pizza by the slice can be a messy undertaking if the pie has not been properly assembled. A single bite can send the whole mass of hot dripping cheese and sauce off the dough and onto your lap. How can you avoid "pizza slide"? It's all in the construction of the pie. Here, then, are some of the finer points of "slide-proof" pizza construction (see *Fig. 9* for a pizza cross section):

1. Leave an inch rim of dough around the pie. It will act as both a handle and a natural barrier to prevent the filling from leaking out.

2. The center of the pie should always be under-filled. The toppings will naturally gravitate there during baking and tend to make the pie over-soft.

3. Lay the cheese down first. This lines the dough and prevents it from getting soggy. Also, the cheese melts through the topping, not over it, and this holds everything together on top of the pie.

4. *Pepperoni* or other dried sausage and raw garlic, which have the tendency to burn on top of the pie, go on next.

5. Layer the sauce over next and then any other toppings, such as sausage, mushrooms, and the like.

Keep in mind that deep-dish pies are strictly knife and fork food and, therefore, are not subject to pizza slide. Because deep-dish pies take longer to cook, add the cheese during the final 5 to 10 minutes of baking time.

Fig. 9

Seasonings

The seasonings given for the recipes in this book are to my own taste. You may find that a bit more of this or a little less of that is more to your liking. Keep in mind, though, that seasoning pizza is a bit like applying perfume—the right amount dabbed in the correct places sends out a subtle and enticing scent, but too much perfume is cloying. A perfectly good pizza can be ruined by a heavy hand with the seasonings. Herbs and the like are meant to accentuate the main ingredients not to overpower them. Learning to season pizza properly is the final subjective touch you will add to your pizza creation—that special something that will make it your very own.

Baking

Thin-crusted pizza can be baked directly on the oven deck, on a pizza screen, or in a pan. Medium- or thick-crusted pies must be baked in a pan that supports them. The easiest way to bake thin pizza is to fit it into a pan, but the most authentic method—which gives the best results—involves the use of the pizza peel. Learning to construct an ultra-thin pizza directly on a peel and to slide it off—in one piece—in the oven is the sign of an accomplished pizza-maker; it takes practice. But using a pizza screen under the dough will give you a similar great *bake* on the crust and prevent messy spills in your oven.

The Direct Stone Method. This is the classic technique for achieving ultra-thin, crisp, Neapolitan-style pizza. An oven outfitted with quarry tiles or a pizza stone (see Chapter 4 on Equipment for how to set up a home pizza oven) must be preheated to 500 degrees for 1 hour in order to be hot enough. Pizza cooked directly on hot stones takes the least time (5 to 10 minutes) of all methods to bake.

Try this method out on smaller-sized pies at first, as they are much easier to handle. If they should stick to the peel, you can still salvage them by using a large spatula to push them off onto a prepared pizza pan if necessary. A large pie, on the other hand, is not very easy to slide off the peel intact if it should stick.

1. Preheat the oven to 500 degrees for 1 hour.

2. Flour the pizza peel, carefully lay the stretched dough over it, and assemble the pizza as quickly as possible. Don't leave the filled pie on the peel for long, as it tends to form moisture beneath the dough and causes the pie to stick. Don't pile too many toppings on the pie or you'll never get it off the peel.

3. Give the peel a jerk to make sure the pie isn't sticking (*Fig. 10*).

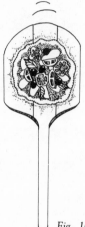

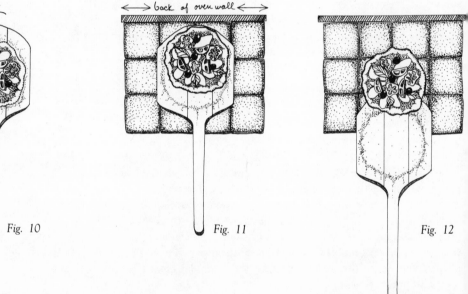

Fig. 10

Fig. 11

Fig. 12

4. Slide the peel all the way into the oven. Holding it right over the pizza stone or oven deck, give it a short forward jerk (*Fig. 11*), to start the pie sliding, and quickly pull the peel straight back in one sweep. The pie should come to rest on the oven deck or pizza stone (*Fig. 12*).

5. To remove the pie from the oven, lift one edge with a spatula and slide the peel beneath it. Transfer the pizza to a cutting tray to serve.

Pizza Screen Method. To avoid guesswork and messy burnt pizza in your oven, use a commercial pizza screen. It will make you a pro from your first pie. Pizza cooked on a screen takes a bit longer to bake (10 to 15 minutes), but it is very nearly every bit as crispy as pie made without one.

1. With your hand or a pastry brush lightly oil a pizza screen with vegetable oil, place it on a pizza peel, and fit the dough on the prepared screen.

2. Assemble the pizza.

3. Continue with step 3 of the preceding baking method.

4. When the pie is cooked, remove it from the screen by loosening it with a spatula and sliding it off the screen before serving.

Pan Baking. Pizza pans must be lightly oiled with vegetable oil and dusted with coarsely ground yellow cornmeal before using or the pie will stick during baking. Pans can be used alone or in conjunction with pizza stones. If you are using the two together, take care not to let the pizza burn, as it will cook faster. To check on the pie's progress, slip a spatula under a portion of the pizza to lift it just enough to reveal the color underneath, which should be golden brown when done. Pizza cooked in pans takes the longest time to cook (15 to 45 minutes) because the heat must penetrate the metal pan first. Use a spatula to loosen the pizza and help slide it off the pan before cutting.

Cutting and Serving

For a thin pie, use the cutting wheel. Start from the center of the pie and cut outward into the thicker edges of the crust. For thick pies, wait about 5 minutes or so before cutting. Like lasagne, deep-dish pizza benefits from sitting a bit before serving. A serrated bread knife is the most appropriate tool for cutting into a deep-dish pizza, and a spatula will make serving those thick gooey slices that much easier and neater.

Yields

What is a normal serving of pizza? Well, it depends—upon the appetites and what the toppings and crust thicknesses are. Generally speaking, the thinner crusted, lighter pizzas serve fewer people than the deep-dish or

Sicilian styles do. Some toppings are richer than others; and that makes a difference. The number of suggested servings in the "yield" notation of each recipe is based on sensible portions. After all, I can't be responsible if your homemade pizza is so delicious that you end up eating an entire pie by yourself!

Each recipe will specify the number of servings, but most of the doughs using 3 to 3½ cups of flour will result in these yields: One 18-inch round ultra-thin crust serves 3 to 4 as a main course or 8 as an appetizer; one 12- by 17-inch medium or thick crust serves 4 as a main course or 8 as an appetizer; one 15- to 16-inch round thin crust serves 3 to 4 as a main course or 8 as an appetizer; one 15- to 16-inch round thick crust serves 4 as a main course; four 10-inch round thin crust, individual dinner size; six 8- to 6-inch round thin crust, individual first course or luncheon size; ten to twelve 4-inch round thin crust *pizzettes*, appetizer size or finger food.

Reheating, Partial Cooking, and Freezing

Leftover pizza can be reheated by loosely wrapping it in aluminum foil and heating it in a preheated 400-degree oven for about 15 minutes or more, depending upon the thickness. Open the foil during the final 5 minutes to let the cheese brown.

Most pizza can be very successfully precooked to freeze and/or reheat at a later time. To precook pizza, omit the cheese (if the recipe calls for any) and bake the pie for only half the time required in the recipe. The dough should have risen and begun to color when the pie is removed from the oven to cool. To finish the pie, preheat the oven to 400 degrees and reheat the pie for about 15 minutes or so. Add the cheese during the final 5 minutes of baking time.

To freeze pizza, wait until the pie has cooled down completely before wrapping it up tightly in foil and placing it in the freezer. Once you've had your own homemade frozen pizza, there'll be no going back to the dismal quality and taste of commercially frozen brands.

To reheat your fresh frozen pizza, preheat the oven to 400 degrees and simply put the alumunim package, straight from the freezer, on a pan and pop it into the oven. Open the foil on top for the last 10 minutes of baking time. Thin-crusted pies take about 30 minutes to reheat, medium crusts take 45 minutes, and thick crusts can take up to an hour.

Freezing Raw Dough. Raw pizza dough can be frozen for up to 4 months. The dough should be frozen directly after the kneading is completed. Instead of letting it rise in a bowl, shape the dough into a flat disk and freeze it in a zip-lock plastic freezer bag.

Dough that has doubled once or twice can also be frozen. Punch it down and proceed with the general freezing instructions. Label the plastic bag with the number of risings that the dough has already undergone. Labeling is important. Without it you'll have no way of knowing how many risings the defrosted dough can go through before it can't rise any longer.

Frozen dough can be slowly defrosted in the refrigerator over a 24-hour period and then brought to a workable temperature in a warm, draft-free place for about an hour or so. Or frozen dough removed directly from the freezer can be defrosted in about 2 hours or less by setting it in a warm (80-degree) place. Waiting for frozen dough to double is not necessary. It can be used as soon as it warms up enough to stretch or roll out into a pizza.

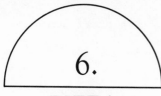

6.

PIZZA DOUGHS

If there was ever an ideal formula for pizza dough, this might very well be it. This simple recipe—flour, water, yeast, and salt—is so versatile that it can be used to make nearly all of the pizzas in this book. The results are so varied that you might think a different dough was used for each pie.

How can one dough be used time and time again without tasting the same? The answer lies not in the ingredients but in how they are put together. Different rising times, ways of shaping the dough, and baking methods all affect the texture of the final crusts, and, of course, the various toppings and fillings contribute to its flavor.

The beauty of pizza-making lies in its inventiveness. If you master the Basic Pizza Dough you'll not only have the means of making most of the pies in this book, you'll be able to take your pizza where no pizza has gone before—to the creation of your own "perfect pie"!

Basic Pizza Dough

Yield: See page 53.

1 **cup warm tap water (110 to 115 degrees)**
1 **package active dry yeast**
3 **to 3½ cups all-purpose white flour**
½ **teaspoon salt**

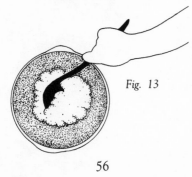

Fig. 13

1. Pour the water into a medium-sized mixing bowl and sprinkle in the yeast. Stir gently with a fork until the yeast has dissolved and the liquid turns light beige in color.

2. Add 1 cup of the flour and the salt. Mix thoroughly with a wooden spoon. Add a second cup of flour and mix well. After the second cup of flour has been mixed in, the dough should start coming away from the sides of the bowl and should begin to form a soft, sticky mass (*Fig. 13*). It is now ready to be kneaded

3. Measure out the third cup of flour. Sprinkle some over the work surface and flour your hands generously. Remove all of the dough from the bowl and begin to work the mass by kneading the additional flour in a bit at a time.

4. To knead the dough, use the heel of your hand (or both hands, if you wish) to push the dough across the floured work surface in one sweep (*Figs. 14–15*). Clench the dough in your fist and twist and fold it over (*Fig. 16*). Use the dough scraper to help gather the wet dough that sticks to the work surface into a ball while kneading (*Fig. 17*). Repeat this action over and over again, adding only as much flour as it takes to keep

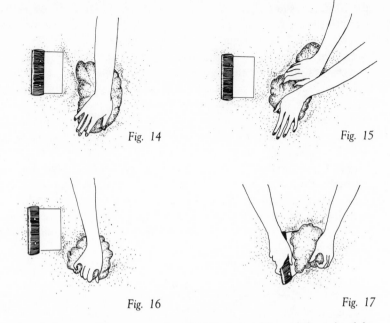

Fig. 14

Fig. 15

Fig. 16

Fig. 17

the dough from sticking to your hands. Work quickly and don't be delicate. Slap and push the dough around to develop its gluten and to facilitate its rolling out. (Kneading pizza dough is a great way to relieve pent-up aggression!)

5. When the dough no longer feels sticky, push the heel of your hand down into it and hold it there for 10 seconds. This will test its readiness; if your hand comes up clean, the dough is done. If it sticks, a bit more kneading will be necessary. Once the dough is no longer sticky, do not overwork it by adding more flour. Continue kneading only until the dough is smooth and elastic (it should spring back when pressed) and no lines of raw white flour show. The whole process should take 5 to 10 minutes. Now it's time to let the dough rise.

6. Lightly oil a 2-quart bowl with vegetable oil. Roll the ball of dough around in the bowl to coat it with a thin film of oil. Tightly seal the bowl with plastic wrap to trap in the moisture and heat from the yeast's carbon dioxide gases. This will help the dough rise faster.

7. Place the bowl in a warm, draft-free place, preferably in a gas oven with a pilot light. For electric ovens, set the thermostat at 200 degrees for 10 minutes and then turn the oven off; this should provide enough warmth to raise the dough. *Be sure the oven is off* before you put the dough inside, or it will begin to cook! Let the dough rise for 30 to 45 minutes.

8. Once the dough has doubled in bulk, punch it down by pushing your fist into it. All of the gases will quickly escape, and the dough will collapse. Remove the dough from the bowl and knead it again for about 1 minute.

9. The dough is now ready to be patted or rolled into pizza, or to undergo additional rising. (All doughs made with bread, high-gluten, or semolina flour really need a second rising time, anywhere from 15 minutes to 1 hour, to develop their gluten potential. Added rising times and further kneading produce a more refined, even crumb structure in pizza crust and create lighter-textured *foccace.*)

10. To raise dough a second time, add a bit more oil to the bowl and repeat the procedure indicated for the first rising. The dough is now ready to be shaped.

Pan Rising.   For a slightly thicker crust, let the dough rise again in the pan for 10 to 20 minutes before baking.

Refrigerated Rising.   If you wish to have pizza the next day or evening, prepare the dough through step 6 and refrigerate it overnight. The next morning it will have doubled; punch it down, knead it for about 1 minute, and return it to the bowl. Let the dough rise again until you are ready to use it that night. Take the dough out of the refrigerator 30 minutes before you want to stretch it out, or it will be stiff and difficult to handle.

Food Processor Method

WORKING WITH A food processor is so fast that it will take you longer to gather the ingredients together than it will take to make the dough. Save time by getting organized before starting the recipe. Premeasure the flour and salt and have the yeast ready. And be sure to read the section on food processors in the Equipment chapter before you begin.

1. Fit the work bowl of your processor with either a steel blade or a special dough blade if your processor has one.

2. Pour in the hot tap water (up to 115 degrees) and sprinkle in the yeast. Turn the machine on and off once or twice to dissolve the yeast.

3. Add 3 cups of flour and the salt to the work bowl and process continuously until the dough forms a ball. (Often, with a steel blade, the dough won't go into a ball but will form a layer under or over the blade. This is fine.)

4. Test the dough by squeezing a portion in your hand. If it sticks, add a dusting of flour and process until it is no longer sticky. Dough that is too dry has the tendency to crumble. If it's dry, add water a tablespoon at a time until the right consistency is reached. (Bread flour, high-gluten, or semolina flours can require up to 4 tablespoons of additional water.)

5. Remove the dough from the processor. Knead it briefly into a ball and proceed with the Basic Pizza Dough recipe from step 6.

Flavored Doughs

thyme

DIFFERENT FLAVORINGS CAN be kneaded into basic pizza dough for some delicious variations. Prepare the dough as usual, letting it double in bulk; punch it down and knead in the flavoring of your choice until it is well distributed. Refrigerate the dough for 15 to 20 minutes before stretching or rolling it out or let it go through another rising before shaping it.

Note: Sometimes flavored doughs become sticky after the additional ingredients have been kneaded in. If this happens, simply knead in a small amount of flour until the dough is smooth and no longer sticks.

Prosciutto or Sausage Dough

4 ounces *prosciutto*, cut into ¼-inch dice, *or* 4 ounces fresh sausage meat, removed from the casings and crumbled

Cheese Dough

¼ cup freshly grated Provolone, caciocavallo, Parmesan, or Romano cheese

Onion Dough

1 small sweet onion, peeled, minced, and cooked until translucent in 1 teaspoon olive oil, *or* ¼ cup finely chopped white part of scallions

Herb Dough

1 teaspoon dried thyme, crumbled dried sage, or dried rosemary, *or* 1 to 2 tablespoons fresh marjoram, fresh mint, fresh oregano, fresh sage, fresh thyme, fresh rosemary, fresh parsley leaves, fresh chives, or fresh basil (separately or in combination of 2 herbs)

Sicilian-Style Dough

Yield: 1 15- to 16-inch round thick-style crust.

THE ADDITION OF olive oil in this dough creates a marked difference in the flavor and texture of the finished crust. It has a more cake-like, more tender interior and a harder, thicker outer crust, which is particularly well-suited to deep-dish, heavily sauced or filled pizza. It also rolls out extremely well and is excellent for some of the rolled and stuffed variations of pizza which call for thin, strong crusts.

¾ **cup warm tap water (110 to 115 degrees)**
1 **package active dry yeast**
3 **to 3½ cups flour**
¼ **cup olive oil**
½ **teaspoon salt**

1. Pour the water into a medium-sized mixing bowl and sprinkle in the yeast. Stir gently with a fork until the yeast has dissolved and the liquid turns light beige in color.

2. Add 1 cup of the flour, the olive oil, and the salt. Mix thoroughly with a wooden spoon. Add a second cup of flour to the bowl and mix well. After the second cup of flour has been mixed in, the dough should start coming away from the sides of the bowl and should begin to form a soft, sticky mass.

3. Continue with step 3 of the Basic Pizza Dough recipe on page 56.

Note: For an extra thick crust, let the dough rise in the pan for 20 to 30 minutes before filling.

Food Processor Variation

Follow the same procedure as indicated in the Food Processor Method (page 58), adding the oil in with the water.

Sicilian-Style Variation for Large-Size Pizza and Chicago-Style Stuffed Pies

Yield: 1 12- by 17-inch large Sicilian-style thick crust, *or* 1 15-inch round stuffed Chicago-style pizza.

Follow the directions for Sicilian-style dough (page 60), using these proportions.

Note: If you use a food processor, remember that this recipe can be made only in the larger-sized food processors.

1½ **cups warm tap water (110 to 115 degrees)**
1 **package active dry yeast**
4½ **to 5 cups flour**
½ **cup olive oil**
1 **teaspoon salt**

Whole Wheat Dough I

Yield: See page 53.

PIZZA DOUGH MADE from 100 percent whole wheat flour tends to feel somewhat stickier and softer than white flour dough. Sometimes it requires a few additional tablespoons of water to give it the right consistency. Whole wheat dough does not stretch as white flour dough does, and at times it tears while being rolled out with a pin. Don't worry. Just pinch the hole together and keep on rolling.

Whole wheat dough's naturally nut-like flavor is better paired with spicier pizza fillings; it tends to overpower the more delicate ones.

1. Pour the water into a medium-sized mixing bowl and sprinkle in the yeast. Stir gently with a fork until the yeast has dissolved and the liquid turns light beige in color.

2. Add 1 cup of the flour, the olive oil, and salt and stir with a wooden spoon. Add a second cup of flour and mix again. After the second cup of flour has been mixed in, the dough should be soft and should start to come away from the sides of the bowl. Add more water by the tablespoonful if the dough appears to be too crumbly and dry.

3. Continue with step 3 of the Basic Pizza Dough recipe on page 56.

1 **cup warm tap water (110 to 115 degrees)**
1 **package active dry yeast**
3 **to 3½ cups stone-ground whole wheat flour**
½ **cup olive oil**
½ **teaspoon salt**

Whole Wheat Dough II

Yield: See page 53.

WHOLE WHEAT DOUGH can be made lighter in taste and texture by adding a small proportion of white flour to the recipe. The interior of this dough is almost cake-like, and the crust is less crisp than Whole Wheat Dough I. But the dough is much easier to handle and rolls out extremely well.

1 cup warm tap water (110 to 115 degrees)
1 package active dry yeast
1 cup all-purpose white flour
½ cup olive oil
½ teaspoon salt
2 to 2½ cups stone-ground whole wheat flour

Follow the instructions for Whole Wheat Dough I, but substitute the cup of white flour for the first cup of whole wheat flour in the recipe.

Black Pepper-Lard Dough

Yield: See page 53.

THIS RECIPE DESCENDS from one of the oldest known kinds of pizza crust. The Romans, who were very fond of black pepper, used a similar but richer dough, which included eggs and honey.

Naturally rendered pork lard is essential to this crust. If you can't get any, use the same amount of olive oil in the recipe. Black pepper-lard dough is an excellent all-purpose pizza dough. It is good, thick and doughy, under a zesty sauce, or rolled out thin for *calzoni* and rolled or stuffed pizza.

1. Pour the water into a medium-sized mixing bowl and sprinkle in the yeast. Stir gently with a fork until the yeast has dissolved and the liquid turns light beige in color.

2. Add 1 cup of the flour, the salt, pepper, and lard and mix thoroughly with a wooden spoon. Add a second cup of flour and mix again. After the second cup of flour has been mixed in, the dough should be soft and sticky and should start to come away from the sides of the bowl.

3. Continue with step 3 of the Basic Pizza Dough recipe (page 56).

1 **cup warm tap water (110 to 115 degrees)**
1 **package active dry yeast**
3 **to 3½ cups flour**
½ **teaspoon salt**
½ **teaspoon coarsely ground black pepper**
2 **heaping tablespoons naturally rendered pork lard (approximately 2 ounces)**

Semolina Dough

Yield: See page 53.

SEMOLINA FLOUR IS usually associated with pasta, but it also produces the most crispy and flavorful pizza crust. Dough made from this hard durum wheat flour is especially suitable for moist fillings. It makes excellent *calzone* and double-crust pizza because it resists getting soggy.

Semolina dough is much less elastic than basic pizza dough made with white flour, so it must be rolled out rather than stretched. The dough should feel moist but not too sticky, and it may require a few extra tablespoons of water to attain the right consistency. If it sticks while it is being rolled out, dust the dough lightly with a small amount of flour. (If the dough tears, that means it is too dry. Just gather it up into a ball and add a small amount or water, knead the dough until it is softer, and give it a 15-minute rest before continuing.)

1 **cup warm tap water (110 to 115 degrees)**
1 **package active dry yeast**
1 **cup all-purpose white flour**
¼ **cup olive oil**
½ **teaspoon salt**
2 **to 2½ cups semolina flour**

1. Pour the water into a medium-sized mixing bowl and sprinkle in the yeast. Stir gently with a fork until the yeast has dissolved and the liquid turns light beige in color.

2. Add the all-purpose flour, olive oil, and salt and stir with a wooden spoon. Add 1 cup of the semolina flour and mix. After the cup of semolina flour has been mixed in, the dough should be soft and should start to come away from the sides of the bowl. Add more water by the tablespoonful if the dough appears to be too crumbly and dry.

3. Continue with step 3 of the Basic Pizza Dough recipe (page 56).

Polenta Pizza Crust

Yield: 1 14- to 15-inch deep-dish pizza.

BAKED POLENTA MAKES an especially toothsome pizza crust. The brief precooking makes a crisp outer crust and preserves the soft, chewy, almost pudding-like interior. The rich corn and cheese flavor of this crust goes particularly well with thick meat sauces, Italian-style greens, or Chicago-style pizza fillings.

1 **cup water plus 2 cups milk,** *or* **3 cups milk**
½ **teaspoon salt**
1 **cup coarsely ground yellow cornmeal**
4 **tablespoons melted butter or olive oil, plus additional oil for greasing the baking pan**

1. Preheat the oven to 400 degrees.

2. Lightly coat a pizza pan with vegetable oil. Sprinkle it lightly with coarsely ground yellow cornmeal.

3. Bring the water, milk, and salt to a boil in a medium-sized saucepan.

4. Pour the 1 cup of cornmeal into the saucepan in a steady stream, stirring constantly with a wooden spoon.

5. Cook, stirring, until the polenta pulls away from the sides of the pan (2 to 3 minutes).

6. Remove from the heat and stir out the lumps with a fork. Add 2 tablespoons of melted butter or oil and let the polenta cool for a few moments before mixing in the egg and cheese.

7. Rub your hands with olive oil (to prevent sticking) and press the polenta into the prepared pizza pan. Make sure it comes up the sides of the pan about 1½ to 2 inches.

8. Brush the dough with the remaining 2 tablespoons of melted butter or olive oil and bake for 30 minutes. (This pre-baking ensures a crunchy crust.)

9. The pie can be prepared ahead to this point. To finish it off, add just about any deep-dish or Chicago-style filling and bake at 400 degrees for 20 to 30 minutes longer.

1 **whole extra large egg, beaten**
¼ **cup freshly grated Parmesan cheese, optional**

Flaky Pizza Dough

Yield: 1 12- by 17-inch pizza.

WITH THIS ELEGANT CRUST beneath it, pizza could hardly be called humble pie. This synthesis of two traditional doughs creates a new and utterly delicious variation of pizza crust that stands apart from all the rest. It combines the savory flavor of Italian pepper-lard crust with the incredible lightness and flakiness of French puff pastry.

Flaky Pizza Dough is the most complex of all pizza crusts, but it is well worth the effort. The real working time for this dough is actually very little and it can be spread out over two days if necessary. The techniques involved are drawn from those of classic puff pastry but are simple enough for even the beginning cook to succeed. It is a "forgiving" dough: If the lard melts or leaks or if it tears a bit, the crust will still come out.

The secret of this recipe lies in the way lard can be worked into a basic pizza dough to form hundreds of tiny layers of flaky crust. The dough undergoes two swift workouts, with the use of double turns (a quick method for achieving the many layers of classic puff pastry in nearly half the time) before it is rolled out into its final form. Refrigerating the dough between steps helps to maintain the fragile layers of lard and relaxes the gluten in the flour to make rolling easier. If the dough appears soft or if it leaks a bit, don't worry. Just dust the dough with flour and keep on going!

1 **recipe Basic Pizza Dough (see page 56), refrigerator risen for at least 2 hours. (This can be made the day before and allowed to rise overnight in the refrigerator.) Additional flour for dusting Coarsely ground black pepper to taste**
8 **ounces cold, naturally rendered pork lard**

1. Press the dough out into a rough rectangle with your fingers and roll it out into a 16- by 22-inch rectangle (*Fig. 18A*). Sprinkle the work surface and the dough often while rolling and remember to pick up the dough often to prevent it from sticking.

2. Spread the lard evenly over the dough leaving a 1½-inch border all around the dough.

3. Sprinkle the surface of the lard liberally with coarsely ground black pepper.

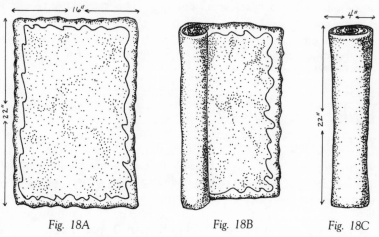

Fig. 18A   Fig. 18B   Fig. 18C

4. Roll the dough into a jelly roll, starting from one of the shorter sides (*Fig. 18B*). Press the dough gently into a 4- by 22-inch rectangle and even out the ends (*Fig. 18C*).

5. Fold the top edge of the dough over to the center of the rectangle and repeat with the bottom of the dough so that the ends meet at the center. Fold the top end over the bottom, as if you were closing a book or a pad of paper (*Fig. 19A*). For side view see *Fig. 19B*.

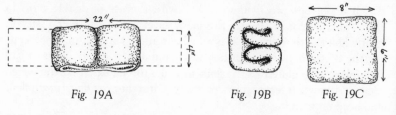

Fig. 19A   Fig. 19B   Fig. 19C

6. Press this dough package lightly into a fat 6- by 8-inch rectangle and dust it liberally with flour (*Fig. 19C*). Don't worry if some lard escapes.

7. Seal the dough in plastic wrap and let it rest in the freezer for 30 to 45 minutes.

8. Roll out the chilled dough into a 12- by 16-inch rectangle, dusting with flour to keep it from sticking. [It will be soft and the lard will leak a bit, but that's okay. (*Fig. 20A*).]

9. Fold the 12-inch sides of the dough to the center and fold one side over the other. You should now have a 6- by 12-inch rectangle (*Fig. 20B*).

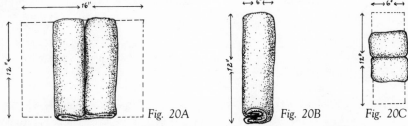

Fig. 20A   Fig. 20B   Fig. 20C

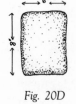

Fig. 20D

10. Press the rectangle down lightly with a rolling pin and give it another double turn (*Fig. 20C*). Press the package of dough into another 6- by 8-inch fat rectangle and return it to the freezer for another 30 to 45 minutes (*Fig. 20D*).

11. Roll the dough into an even 16- by 12-inch sheet, dusting it with flour to keep it from sticking and fit it into an oiled pizza pan that has been sprinkled with cornmeal. Refrigerate the dough for at least 30 minutes or up to 3 to 4 hours before baking

12. Preheat the oven to 450 degrees.

13. Bake the dough blind (without a filling) for 20 to 25 minutes so that it will rise.

14. Top the crust with the filling of your choice. (Robust, non-liquid fillings—any of the French *pissaladière*, goat cheese, greens with cheese, or sun-dried tomato combinations, for example—are especially good on this crust.) Return to the oven for 15 to 20 minutes longer. Serve hot or at room temperature.

To Freeze. Freeze the dough in the baking pan after step 11. Once the dough is frozen solid, remove it from the pan and wrap it tightly in aluminum foil.

To Reheat. Preheat the oven to 400 degrees. Remove the dough from the foil and place it on an oiled baking sheet. Bake it frozen for about 25 to 30 minutes, or until it is lightly colored and puffed. Raise the oven temperature to 450 degrees. Remove the dough and add the topping. Bake for an additional 15 to 20 minutes.

Note: Try not to roll the edges of the dough too much because this will prevent it from rising as much as it should.

Provençale Olive Oil Pastry Dough

Yield: 1 12-inch tart, *or* 4 8-inch main-course *chaussons*, *or* 6 6-inch appetizer or luncheon *chaussons*.

I'VE USED THIS Provençale tart crust recipe for years. It's one of the easiest doughs to handle, because you don't have to worry about the butter melting.

2 **cups flour**
¼ **teaspoon salt**
1 **extra large egg**
½ **cup green fruity olive oil**
4 **tablespoons water**

1. Combine the flour and salt in a medium-sized mixing bowl.
2. Beat the egg, olive oil, and 3 tablespoons of the water together in another small bowl.
3. Stir the wet ingredients into the dry with a wooden spoon and mix until the dough begins to hold together. Add the last tablespoon of water if the dough seems a bit too dry.
4. Gather the dough into a ball and knead it on a clean unfloured surface until it is no longer sticky and feels smooth to the touch.
5. Put the dough into an oiled bowl, cover the bowl tightly with plastic wrap, and let it stand at room temperature for about 45 minutes before rolling it out.

Roman Pepper Pastry Crust

Yield: 1 12-inch tart shell, *or* 4 8-inch main-course *calzoni* or *chaussons*, *or* 6 6-inch appetizer-size *calzoni* or *chaussons*, *or* approximately 30 3-inch *panzerotti*.

THIS IS AN EXCELLENT tart or *panzerotti* dough. The lard makes it flaky, extremely flavorful, and easy to roll out. It is interchangeable with Provençale Olive Oil Pastry Dough for *chaussons*.

1. Mix the flour, salt, and pepper together in a medium-sized bowl.

2. Mix the egg and 2 tablespoons of the water together in a small bowl.

3. Add the lard to the dry ingredients and rub the flour between the palms of your hands until it is evenly distributed.

4. Stir in the egg-water mixture and work the dough with your hands until it is smooth. Add the remaining water 1 tablespoon at a time if the dough appears too dry.

5. Put the dough into an oiled bowl, cover the bowl tightly with plastic wrap, and let it stand at room temperature for about 30 minutes before rolling it out.

Processor Method

1. Put the flour, salt, pepper, and lard into the bowl of a food processor fitted with a metal blade. Process for 30 seconds.

2. Add the egg and mix with 2 on–off pulses.

3. With the machine running, add the additional water 1 tablespoon at a time until a ball forms.

4. Check to see if the dough is sticky. If it is, add a dusting of flour.

5. Put the dough into an oiled bowl, cover the bowl tightly with plastic wrap, and let it stand at room temperature for 15 to 30 minutes before rolling it out.

2 **cups flour**
¼ **teaspoon salt**
½ **teaspoon coarsely
   ground black pepper**
1 **extra large egg, beaten**
4 **tablespoons water
   (approximately)**
½ **cup packed down natu-
   rally rendered pork lard**

Rich Egg Pizza Dough   (Brioche)

Yield: 1 thick-crusted 12- by 17-inch pizza, *or* 1 full *torta rustica*.

FOR AN ELEGANT change of pace, this rich *brioche*-like dough makes a thick, utterly delicious pizza crust. French Provençale pizza or *pissaladière* fillings are exceptionally good on it. Its most spectacular presentation, though, comes in the form of *torta rustica* (page 200) with its majestic crown of dough leaves and multilayered colorful filling.

This dough is characteristically soft. Work it only until it no longer sticks to your fingers. For an extra golden, shiny finish, brush a thin coating of egg white glaze (1 egg white beaten with a tablespoon of water) over the top of the dough.

4 tablespoons sweet butter, cut into 4 pieces
2 tablespoons sugar
¼ cup instant nonfat dry milk powder
¾ cup water
1 package active dry yeast
4½ to 5 cups all-purpose white flour (not bread flour)
1 teaspoon salt
3 extra large eggs, beaten

1. Put the butter, sugar, dry milk powder, and water in a small saucepan. Stir briefly to dissolve the solids and heat the mixture over medium heat until bubbles begin to appear around the sides of the pan. Remove from the heat and pour the mixture into a large mixing bowl.

2. When the liquid mixture no longer feels too hot to the touch (no more than 130 degrees), sprinkle the yeast over it and stir with a fork until the yeast dissolves.

3. Stir in 2 cups of the flour, the salt, and eggs with a wooden spoon.

4. Add about a cup of flour ½ cup at a time, stirring until the dough forms a soft, sticky mass and comes away from the sides of the bowl.

5. Dust your hands and the work surface liberally with some of the remaining flour. Remove the dough from the bowl and knead in the remaining flour a bit at a time, until the dough is smooth and elastic and no longer sticks to your hands. Don't try to push all of the flour into the dough. You may not need it all.

6. Roll the dough around in an oiled bowl, cover the bowl tightly with plastic wrap, and let it rise in a warm, draft-free place until it has doubled in bulk (about 1 hour).

7. Punch the dough down, knead it briefly, and return it to the bowl. Recover with plastic wrap and let it double again before using. (This dough *must* go through 2 risings.)

8. After the dough has doubled in bulk a second time, it is ready to be rolled or pressed into shape.

Note: For thicker crusts, let the dough rise in a prepared pizza pan for 30 minutes before baking. This dough should not be baked at temperatures above 400 degrees or it will burn.

Processor Method

Use *only* a processor with at least an 8-cup capacity.

1. Add the warm liquid ingredients to the bowl of the food processor and dissolve the yeast with an on–off pulse.

2. Add 2 cups of the flour, the salt, and beaten eggs to the bowl and process until just mixed. Add 2 more cups of flour and process until a smooth dough forms.

3. Remove the dough from the processor and finish kneading the remaining flour into the dough until it is no longer sticky.

4. Continue with step 6 of the recipe.

The final major component of pizza that we must explore is the sauce. Don't go through all of the trouble of obtaining fresh mozzarella, herbs, sausage, and a delicious crust and then add a canned tomato sauce to your creation. That would be an insult to your pie! Besides, making an excellent tomato sauce is easy.

A well-seasoned tomato sauce opens up another dimension to pizza by adding a certain complexity and depth of flavor to the dish. Pizza sauce does not require lengthy cooking. A tasty sauce can be made in as short a time as 15 minutes, and within an hour, it reaches its peak. When a sauce is cooked longer than an hour, it loses its freshness and becomes heavy.

The choice of tomato sauce versus plain tomatoes makes a critical difference to the sensitive palate of the pizza connoisseur. When all of the ingredients cook together on top of a pie from a raw state, one is presented with a certain separateness of tastes. The flavors have just begun to merge on the pie, and each bite is a symphony of ingredients that still manage to maintain their distinct integrity. The vegetables are crisp, in contrast with the softness of the cheese and tomatoes. On the other hand, cooked sauces and toppings create a different sensation. When onions are sautéed to a golden translucency, this brings out their natural sugars and renders them intensely sweet, mellow, and more digestible than when they are raw. In pizza with cooked sauce and cooked onions, the flavors are melded together. And finally, when the onions are first melted down and then cooked in the sauce itself, they become integral to the sauce and lend it their natural sweetness and add overall body.

Steps to the Perfect Sauce

1. Because the acid in tomatoes reacts with unlined aluminum and causes the sauce to taste bitter, you should always use a non-aluminum pan to make tomato sauce.

2. Never use fresh tomatoes for pizza sauce. Fresh tomatoes should not be cooked before they go on top of pizza, but rather, they should be put directly on top of the pie to preserve their light delicate taste.

3. Always maintain the sauce at a gentle simmer; high heat will cause it to burn and go bitter.

4. Try not to be heavy handed with tomato paste, for it tends to make a sauce heavy.

7

PIZZA SAUCES

5. A properly made tomato sauce does not require sugar. If you prefer a slightly sweeter sauce, add a finely chopped carrot and/or a finely chopped onion to sweeten it naturally.

Basic Pizza Sauce

Yield: Approximately 4 cups, or enough for 3 large pies.

1 **2-pound, 3-ounce can whole tomatoes packed in tomato purée or juice**
2 **fresh basil leaves, or 1 teaspoon dried basil, dried oregano, or dried marjoram**
1 **garlic clove, peeled, crushed, and minced**
2 **tablespoons tomato paste, optional**
Freshly ground black pepper to taste
Pinch of salt, optional (canned tomatoes have plenty of their own salt)

1. Pour the contents of the tomato can into a 2-quart, heavy non-aluminum saucepan and coarsely crush the tomatoes with a fork or your hands.

2. Add the herbs, garlic, tomato paste, pepper, and salt.

3. Bring to a bubble over medium heat, stirring to mix the seasonings.

4. As soon as the sauce begins to bubble, turn the heat to low and maintain the sauce at a gentle simmer.

5. Cook, uncovered, stirring from time to time, for a minimum of 15 minutes and a maximum of 1 hour.

Storage: The sauce will keep for about a week in an airtight container in the refrigerator. It can also be frozen for up to 4 months.

Note: Leftover pizza sauce makes a zesty pasta sauce and is delicious on *focaccia*.

Variation

Onion. In the same saucepan, sauté 1 small, finely chopped sweet onion in 2 tablespoons of olive oil until the onion is just translucent. Then proceed with the recipe.

Meat Flavor. In the same saucepan, sauté the meat of 2 Italian sweet or hot sausages, which have been removed from their casings and roughly crumbled, in 1 tablespoon of olive oil. Cook the sausage meat for 1 to 2 minutes over medium heat until it is no longer pink. Then proceed with the recipe.

Joe Timpone's Pizza Sauce

Yield: Approximately 3 cups of sauce.

Purée the tomatoes and juice and pour the purée into a nonaluminum saucepan. Add the remaining ingredients and stir to mix well. Bring to a boil over medium heat, turn the heat to very low, and simmer the sauce, uncovered, for 30 minutes, stirring occasionally.

1 **28-ounce can Italian-style tomatoes packed in their own juice**
3 **ounces tomato paste**
1 **teaspoon salt**
Freshly ground black pepper to taste

Salsa for Pizza

Yield: Approximately 2 cups of sauce.

THIS LOW-CALORIE SAUCE is also excellent on meats and fish.

Mix all of the ingredients in a large jar or plastic container. Then cover tightly and shake until all the ingredients are well combined. Let the sauce stand at room temperature for about 1 hour before using. Drain the excess liquid from the sauce before using it on pizza.

Note: The more chili peppers, the hotter the sauce.

The *Salsa* will keep in a tightly covered container in the refrigerator for about 5 days. It can also be frozen for at least 3 months.

½ **pound fresh tomatoes, seeded, drained, and finely chopped**
2 **to 4 fresh hot chili peppers, finely chopped**
1 **medium-sized sweet onion, peeled and finely chopped**
2 **garlic cloves, peeled, lightly crushed, and minced**
½ **teaspoon ground cumin**
Salt to taste
1 **tablespoon finely chopped fresh cilantro (Chinese parsley) leaves, optional**

Tomato Coulis

Yield: Approximately 3 cups of sauce.

THIS SAUCE IS excellent hot or cold and can be used as a pasta sauce or over chicken, seafood, or veal. It also makes an original cold or warm soup base.

1 tablespoon extra-virgin olive oil
1 small sweet onion, peeled and finely chopped
1 28-ounce can whole tomatoes, basil leaf removed
1 garlic clove, peeled and lightly crushed
2 tablespoons finely minced fresh parsley leaves
½ teaspoon ground cumin
Salt and freshly ground black pepper to taste

1. Heat the oil in a nonaluminum saucepan and sauté the onion over medium heat until it is just lightly golden.

2. Purée the tomatoes through a food mill or sieve and add them to the saucepan along with the garlic, parsley, cumin, and salt and pepper. Bring to a boil over medium heat. Lower the heat and simmer the sauce, uncovered, for 45 to 60 minutes.

Gravy

Yield: Approximately 3 cups of sauce.

THIS SAUCE CAN be used for pasta.

2 tablespoons olive oil
1 medium-sized sweet onion, peeled and minced
1 28-ounce can whole tomatoes
1 2-ounce can anchovies, drained

1. Heat the olive oil in a 2-quart nonaluminum saucepan. Add the onion and sauté over medium heat until the onion is golden.

2. Purée the tomatoes through a food mill or sieve and add them to the saucepan along with the remaining ingredients. Bring to a boil, lower the heat, and simmer, uncovered, for 1 hour. Remove the bay leaf before using or storing the sauce.

Note: This sauce can be refrigerated in a tightly covered container for up to 1 week. It can also be frozen for up to 4 months.

1 small bay leaf
1 tablespoon finely chopped fresh parsley leaves
   Pinch of dried thyme
   Freshly ground black pepper to taste

Sicilian Ragu

Yield: Approximately 3 cups of sauce.

1. Heat 2 tablespoons of the oil in a 3-quart nonaluminum saucepan. Add the onion, celery, and carrot and sauté over low heat until the vegetables just begin to color. Use a slotted spoon to remove the vegetables to a plate. Set aside until needed.

2. Add the remaining tablespoon of oil to the pan and sauté the ground pork until it is lightly browned. Pour off and discard any excess fat from the pan and return the vegetables to the pan.

3. Purée the tomatoes and add them to the saucepan along with the mint, parsley, and salt and pepper. Bring to a boil, lower the heat, and simmer, uncovered, stirring occasionally, for 1½ hours.

Note: The sauce may be refrigerated in a tightly covered container for up to 1 week. It can also be frozen for up to 4 months.

3 tablespoons olive oil
1 small sweet onion, peeled and minced
1 celery stalk, minced
1 small carrot, scraped and minced
½ pound ground pork, or ½ pound plain Italian sweet sausage meat (seasoned with black pepper but not fennel), removed from the casings and crumbled
1 28-ounce can whole tomatoes
2 to 3 sprigs fresh mint, or ¼ teaspoon dried thyme
2 tablespoons minced fresh parsley leaves
   Salt and freshly ground black pepper to taste

Eggplant-Sausage Sauce

Yield: Approximately 4 cups of sauce.

IN THIS RECIPE, the eggplant is cooked in a rich meaty sauce, and the result is a hearty, stew-like consistency. This substantial filling requires a deep-dish crust.

3 tablespoons olive oil
1 pound unpeeled eggplant, trimmed and cut into 1-inch cubes
1 pound hot or sweet Italian sausage meat, removed from the casings and crumbled
1 garlic clove, peeled and crushed
½ a 28-ounce can whole tomatoes with liquid, roughly chopped
½ teaspoon dried marjoram or dried oregano Salt and freshly ground black pepper to taste

1. Heat the olive oil in a medium-sized nonaluminum saucepan. Add the eggplant cubes and sauté them over medium heat for about 5 to 7 minutes. Use a slotted spoon to remove the eggplant cubes to a plate. Set them aside until needed.

2. Add the sausage meat to the saucepan and sauté until it is no longer pink. Add the crushed garlic and cook for 1 minute. Add the tomatoes, marjoram, and black pepper and mix well. Simmer for 5 minutes.

3. Return the eggplant to the pan and cook the sauce, uncovered, over low heat for 30 minutes, stirring occasionally.

Note: The sauce can be made in advance and stored in an airtight container in the refrigerator or frozen.

Variation

For a totally vegetarian sauce, omit the sausage and substitute 1 pound of trimmed and washed zucchini, cut into 1-inch pieces. Sauté the zucchini in 2 tablespoons of olive oil for just 2 minutes. Then proceed with the recipe as given.

Bucci's Sausage Sauce

Yield: Approximately 4 cups of sauce.

1 tablespoon olive oil
1 pound Italian sweet sausage meat, removed from the casings and crumbled

1. Heat the oil in a medium-sized nonaluminum saucepan. Add the sausage meat and cook over medium heat, stirring constantly, until the meat is no longer pink. Add the crushed garlic and cook for 1 minute longer.

2. Crush the tomatoes roughly and add them with the purée or juice to the saucepan. Stir in the pepper and oregano and bring to a boil. Lower the heat and simmer, uncovered, for 1 hour.

Variation

Use 1 pound of Italian hot sausage instead of the sweet sausage and omit the herbs.

Note: The success of this sauce and the pizza it is used on is totally dependent on the quality of the sausage you use. The better the sausage, the better the pie.

1 garlic clove, peeled and crushed
1 28-ounce can whole tomatoes packed in purée or juice
Freshly ground black pepper to taste
½ teaspoon dried oregano, or 1 or 2 fresh basil leaves

Jane Butel's Pecos River Bowl of Red

Yield: Approximately 8 cups.

HERE IS A recipe from Jane Butel's *Chili Madness* (Workman Press, New York, 1980), which I have adapted for pizza. This is a straightforward classic, medium-hot Texas-style chili, and it's superb on pizza.

1. Melt the lard in a large heavy pan over medium heat. Add the onion and cook until it is translucent.

2. Combine the meat with the garlic, ground chilis, and cumin and add the mixture to the pan with the onions. Cook, stirring to break up any lumps, until the meat is evenly browned. Stir in the water and salt and bring to a boil. Lower the heat and simmer, uncovered, for 2½ to 3 hours, stirring occasionally, until the meat is very tender and the flavors are well blended. If the chili dries out, add a bit more water to keep it moist, but not too wet; if it is too wet, it will make the pizza soggy.

Note: This chili can be frozen for up to 3 months.

2 tablespoons lard, sweet butter, or bacon drippings
1 large sweet onion, coarsely chopped
3 pounds lean beef, coarsely ground
3 medium-sized garlic cloves, minced
4 tablespoons ground hot chili powder
4 tablespoons ground mild chili powder
2 teaspoons ground cumin
1½ cups water
1½ teaspoons salt

Sun-Dried Tomato Pesto

Yield: Approximately 1½ cups of sauce.

1 garlic clove, peeled
¼ pound drained oil-
   packed sun-dried
   tomatoes
¼ cup pignolis
½ cup extra-virgin olive
   oil

Put the garlic in a blender or food processor and blend until it is finely chopped. Add the tomatoes and pignolis and blend until a paste is formed. With the machine running, gradually add the oil in a thin stream. Blend until a smooth sauce forms.

Béchamel Sauce

Yield: Approximately 1¾ cups of sauce.

1½ cups milk
3 tablespoons sweet
   butter
2½ tablespoons all-purpose
   white flour
   Pinch of salt
   Pinch of white pepper
   Pinch of freshly grated
   nutmeg, optional

1. Pour the milk into a small saucepan and heat it over low heat until small bubbles appear along the sides of the pan. Remove the pan from the heat immediately or the milk will boil over. Set aside until needed.

2. Melt the butter in a heavy 1-quart nonaluminum saucepan. Whisk in the flour all at once and cook over moderate heat for 1 minute, whisking constantly. Do not let the mixture take on color or it will turn bitter. Remove the pan from the heat and begin whisking in the hot milk, ¼ cup at a time, stirring constantly to prevent lumps from forming. Continue whisking until all of the milk has been incorporated.

3. Season the sauce with salt, pepper, and nutmeg. Bring the sauce to a boil over medium heat, whisking constantly until the sauce is very thick. Use immediately or set aside until needed.

Note: This sauce may be refrigerated in a tightly covered container for at least 1 week. It can also be frozen. If the sauce seems a bit too thick when you want to reheat it, add a small amount of milk or water, stirring until you have the proper consistency—like slightly whipped cream.

Pissaladière Onion Base

Yield: Approximately 3 cups of sauce.

Heat the olive oil in a large frying pan. Add all the ingredients and stir to mix well. Cook, uncovered, over medium heat for 45 minutes, stirring occasionally to prevent the mixture from scorching. The onions are done when they have melted down to almost the consistency of a purée and all of their excess moisture has evaporated (see Note). Remove the bay leaf before using or storing the sauce. The sauce may be prepared in advance and frozen or reheated.

Note: Traditionally, the liquid exuded by the onions while they are cooking is used to make the dough. During the first 15 minutes the onions are cooking, draw off the liquid with a spoon and transfer it to a measuring cup. If there isn't enough liquid for the dough recipe, add water to make the amount needed. Heat the liquid gently until it is just warm and dissolve the yeast in it. Be careful not to heat the liquid too much or it will kill the yeast. If you can't determine the temperature of the liquid by touch, use a thermometer. The onion liquid imparts a wonderful taste to the dough and this makes the extra attention well worth the effort.

¼ cup olive oil
3 pounds large sweet yellow or red onions, peeled and thinly sliced
4 garlic cloves, peeled and crushed
1 tablespoon dried French thyme leaves, or 2 tablespoons fresh thyme leaves
1 bay leaf
½ teaspoon coarsely ground black pepper

Italian Greens

Yield: 1½ to 2 cups.

ITALIANS MASTERED THE art of stir-frying and braising their greens centuries before anyone in the western world had any notion of the technique. The process is simple, quick, and very useful for a variety of Italian dishes.

When using the greens on pizza, broccoli rabe, sometimes called Chinese broccoli, provides a delightfully sharp taste in contrast with the mellow flavor of mozzarella. If you find broccoli rabe too bitter, substitute regular broccoli or any other green. Experiment with cheese, too: Try Bel Paese or scamorza with the greens. I am particularly fond of smoked mozzarella with greens.

To turn these greens preparations into a light pasta sauce, simply add a bit more olive oil and ½ cup or so of the pasta cooking water to the greens. (The pasta water contains starch from the cooked pasta and adds more body to the greens.) Toss the sauce with the pasta and some grated cheese.

4 tablespoons olive oil
2 pounds spinach, Swiss chard (green leaves only), dandelion, arugola, escarole, chicory, beet tops, watercress, or any wild greens, washed, dried, and coarsely shredded
2 garlic cloves, peeled and minced
Salt and freshly ground black pepper to taste

1. Heat the oil in a large frying pan. Add the greens and cover the frying pan. Cook over medium heat, stirring every 30 seconds to prevent the greens from scorching. The greens will wilt in a few minutes.
2. Add the garlic and salt and pepper and cook, uncovered, for 2 minutes longer. Drain well before using on pizza.
Note: If you use frozen spinach, defrost it first and squeeze out as much excess liquid as possible. Then follow the cooking directions for the fresh greens.

THE SECOND GROUP of greens have thicker stems and require additional cooking with some added liquid.

1 pound broccoli, broccoli rabe, or Swiss chard (white stalks only)
4 tablespoons olive oil
2 garlic cloves, peeled and minced
Salt and freshly ground black pepper to taste

1. Wash the greens in several changes of cool water. Discard any woody or tough stems and chop the greens into small pieces.
2. Heat the oil in a large frying pan. Add the greens and sauté over high heat for 1 minute. Add the garlic and salt and pepper and stir over high heat for 2 to 3 minutes longer, or until the vegetables turn bright green.
3. Add the water, cover the pan, and cook until the greens are tender, 2 to 5 minutes, depending on the type of green used. Drain well before using on pizza.

Variations

To use the greens as a pasta sauce, add 2 tablespoons of olive oil and ½ cup pasta cooking water for every pound of cooked greens. Toss the pasta and greens with ½ cup of freshly grated Parmesan cheese.

To make a soup, see the recipe for *pizza minestre* on page 90.

Ratatouille

Yield: Approximately 4 cups of sauce.

THIS SAUCE IS also good on pasta and as a crêpe filling or served cold as an appetizer.

1. Heat the oil in a heavy 3-quart saucepan. Add the eggplant and sauté for 5 minutes, stirring occasionally. Add the zucchini, onion, and green pepper and sauté for 5 minutes longer, or until the onion is limp.

2. Add the remaining ingredients and bring to a boil over medium heat. Lower the heat and simmer, uncovered, for 35 minutes, or until the eggplant is very tender.

Note: *Ratatouille* can be made in advance and stored, tightly covered, in the refrigerator. It can be frozen and reheats very well.

¼ cup olive oil
1 1-pound eggplant, cut into 1-inch cubes
2 medium-sized zucchini, washed, trimmed, and cut into thick slices
1 large sweet onion, peeled and roughly chopped
1 large sweet green pepper, roughly chopped
1 cup drained whole canned tomatoes, coarsely chopped
2 garlic cloves, peeled and minced
1 bay leaf
1 teaspoon dried French thyme
Salt and freshly ground black pepper to taste

Tapenade

Yield: Approximately ⅔ cup of sauce.

TAPENADE, THE MARRIAGE of anchovies and olives, is one of the staples of the cuisine of Provence in France, and it has produced a number of delightful offspring. With the addition of a bit more oil, *tapenade* becomes a pasta sauce, a dip for raw vegetables, and a dressing for warm cauliflower or potato salad. In its more solid form, it is an unusual and refreshing spread and a stuffing for vegetables—not to mention its possibilities on pizza.

½ cup oil-cured black
olives (about 30),
pitted
1 garlic clove, crushed in
a garlic press
1½ tablespoons drained
capers
1 2-ounce can anchovies,
drained
4 tablespoons olive oil
Juice of 1 lemon

Combine all the ingredients in a blender or food processor and blend until a smooth sauce is formed.

Pesto

Yield: Approximately ¾ cup of sauce.

BASIL IS NOT the only main ingredient from which *Pesto* can be made. The word "pesto" in Italian means to pound or bruise, and it refers to the technique, not the ingredients in the recipe. Nuts and olive oil that have been pounded to a paste are the traditional thickeners of the sauce, but almost any other herb or flavoring can be added or substituted. Try experimenting with other *Pesto* bases, such as anchovies, *Tapenade*, pickled hot peppers, or roasted pimientos—use your imagination!

1 cup very tightly packed
fresh basil, fresh mint,
or Italian parsley
leaves, or any combina-
tion to make 1 cup
¼ cup olive oil
¼ cup freshly grated
Pecorino Romano or
locatelli cheese

Put the herbs, oil, and cheese in a blender or food processor and purée until a smooth sauce is formed.

Note: The *Pesto* will keep for weeks under a ¼-inch layer of olive oil in a tightly covered container in the refrigerator.

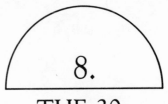

8.

THE 30-MINUTE PIZZA

Now that you've read all of that tantalizing information on how to make the greatest pizza in the world, your desire for pizza must be so strong that you can almost smell it baking. If this is so, you are suffering from a basic need common to all pizza-lovers—the need for instant gratification. Because I know what it's like to experience those uncontrollable pangs, I devised this recipe.

After a great deal of experimenting, I have found that the new fast-rising dry yeasts can be used in water temperatures of up to 130 degrees when mixed in with some flour. The higher temperature pushes the already ultra-fast rising yeast to begin its action immediately, thereby eliminating the rising time of the dough. What's more, it produces a dough that is instantly stretchable. With these two breakthroughs in the pizza-making process, I discovered that after just 30 minutes of preparation and cooking, I could sit down to the best "instant" pizza I'd ever eaten. Granted, the crust was not quite as light as that of fully risen dough, but it was nonetheless crispy, chewy, and totally satisfying. Best of all, a fresh, naturally delicious pizza can be had in less time than it takes to order one out, to reheat a frozen pie, or to make pizza from a mix. With this time-saving method, pizza joins the ranks as one of the quickest, easiest, cheapest, and most nutritionally complete hot dishes you can prepare in half an hour.

The "instant" concept of the 30-minute pizza is a challenge to your spontaneity and creativity. The variations that can be drawn from fresh, frozen, or canned provisions and the possibilities that leftovers can provide are limitless. Try to keep a stock of pizza supplies on hand to work from when that irresistible urge for pizza strikes. Here are a few suggestions:

Instant Pizza Makings

Cans: Anchovies, sardines, clams, tuna, whole tomatoes, artichoke hearts.

In the Refrigerator: Red Star Quick Rise or Fleischmann's RapidRise dry yeast (it keeps for months), *pepperoni*, dried sausage, salami, sausages, bacon, ham, cooked or uncooked chopped or diced meat, olives, hot peppers, capers, sun-dried tomatoes, and any kind of cheese that melts.

In the Freezer: Mozzarella can be coarsely sliced while it is still frozen; frozen sausages can be boiled in water to cover for 5 minutes, which softens them up enough to slice on top of pizza. *Pesto*, frozen in zip-lock bags, can be defrosted in 3 minutes if it is immersed in simmering water.

Produce: Fresh or dried herbs, garlic, scallions, onions, tiny zucchini, and ripe tomatoes.

Leftovers: Tomato sauce or other pasta sauces, steamed or sautéed vegetables, *Ratatouille,* or Chili.

Flour: Keep flour in a clear container so that you'll know when it gets down below the danger level of less than 3 cups.

10 Easy Steps to the 30-Minute Pizza

On your mark . . .

1. Preheat the oven to 500 degrees.

2. Lightly coat a pizza pan or screen with vegetable oil, or a pizza peel with flour (depending on the baking method you choose). Sprinkle the pan lightly with coarsely ground yellow cornmeal.

3. Lay out all of the remaining equipment: medium-sized mixing bowl; 1 cup dry measure; 1 cup liquid measure; measuring spoons; dough scraper; and rolling pin (optional).

Get set . . .

4. Gather all of the ingredients for the dough:

1 package fast-rising dry yeast

3 cups all-purpose white flour (Bread or high-gluten flour is not right for this recipe.)

1 cup hot tap water (120 to 130 degrees)

½ teaspoon salt

5. Line up all of the topping components:

½ pound mozzarella or other melting cheese, thinly sliced or cut into 1-inch cubes

1 cup tomato sauce (or other kind of sauce), or 1½ pounds fresh tomatoes, seeded, drained, and roughly chopped

2 garlic cloves, peeled and minced, optional

½ teaspoon dried oregano, or 5 to 6 fresh basil leaves, shredded, or 1 tablespoon chopped fresh herbs, such as parsley leaves, thyme, or marjoram

Freshly ground black pepper to taste

2 tablespoons olive oil

Use one or more of the following additional toppings:
½ pound Italian sausage, removed from the casings and crumbled or sliced

¼ pound *pepperoni* or dried sausage or salami, thinly sliced
1 small sweet green pepper, seeded and thinly sliced
1 small sweet onion, peeled and thinly sliced
1 2-ounce can anchovies, drained
12 to 15 olives

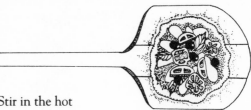

Go!

6. Mixing: 5 minutes.

Mix the yeast with 1 cup of the flour in a mixing bowl. Stir in the hot tap water and blend until no raw flour shows. Stir in a second cup of flour and the salt and mix quickly until the dough comes away from the sides of the bowl. The dough is ready for kneading.

7. Kneading: 5 minutes

Dust the work surface and your hands with some of the third cup of flour and turn the dough out of the bowl. Knead in the remaining flour a bit at a time, using the dough scraper to help prevent sticking. Don't treat the dough gently—push and pull at it vigorously. Knead only until the dough is no longer sticky. It should be smooth and elastic and should spring back slightly when pressed.

8. Assembling: 5 minutes.

Press the dough out into an 8-inch circle with your fingertips and then roll or stretch it out into a 15- or 18-inch pizza shell. Fit the shell onto a prepared pan or screen or on a floured pizza peel.

Assemble the toppings and finish with a drizzling of olive oil.

9. Bake: 15 minutes.

Bake until the crust is golden and the topping is bubbly. (For a well-done crust cook 5 minutes longer.) While the pie is baking, toss a salad, set the table, uncork a bottle of wine, and light the candles.

10. Serve

Voila! The 30-minute pizza meal! Cut the pizza into wedges and enjoy.

Yield: Serves 4 as a main course or 6 to 8 as an appetizer.

Note: Pies cooked directly on the oven deck or on pizza screens cook faster than those cooked in pans.

You can use conventional dry yeast for this recipe, but if you do, the crust won't begin to rise so quickly and it won't stretch so well. For that reason, it must be rolled out with a pin, and the texture of the crust will be heavier.

30-Minute Processor Variation

THE PROCESSOR MAKES this recipe virtually instant, because it eliminates nearly 10 minutes of the mixing and kneading time in the Master Recipe.

1. Follow steps 1 and 2 of the Master Recipe, using this list of equipment instead: food processor fitted with a steel blade or a plastic dough blade; 1 cup dry measure; 1 cup liquid measure; measuring spoons.

2. Continue with steps 4 and 5 of the Master Recipe

3. Blend the yeast and 1 cup of the flour in the bowl of the processor, using 1 on–off pulse. With the machine running, pour in the hot water. Stop processing and add the salt and remaining 2 cups of flour. Process with on–off pulses until the dough begins to hold together. Then let the machine run continuously until a ball of dough forms. (The whole procedure should take a little more than 1 minute.)

4. Proceed with steps 8 through 10 of the Master Recipe.

Pizza bread, or *focaccia,* baked under the fire and flavored with oils and aromatic toppings, is the ancient forerunner of most pizza as we know it today, yet its character has not changed much since it first became popular. Admittedly, most *focacce* (the plural form) are more refined now, because they are made with leavened doughs and baked in ovens, but the concept of the dish is still thoroughly northern Italian.

Northern Italians think of *focaccia* as snack food, a flavored bread that can be eaten still warm from the oven as is, or split and filled like a sandwich, or eaten as an accompaniment to soup, meat, or stews. Unlike southern Italian-style pizza, *focaccia* is not a meal in itself. Northerners never pile ingredients on top of their *focaccia:* They believe it should be enjoyed in its pure state, as a chewy, pleasantly flavored bread with small bursts of flavor throughout the dough or on top. Virtually all recipes for *focaccia,* even those from the South, are loyal to this style.

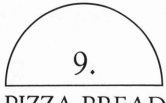

9.
PIZZA BREAD

Focaccia Dough Master Recipe

Yield: Most *focacce* are served as a side dish and are the equivalent of approximately 1 1½-pound loaf of bread.

THERE IS NOTHING difficult about making *focaccia.* After all, it is nothing more than pizza dough with ingredients added to the dough or sprinkled on top, and, in its most primitive state, it didn't even require an oven. In the traditional sense, *focacce* make great snacks and are wonderful with soups or stews, but beyond gravy sopping, their potential has yet to be developed. Some *focacce* are baked in whimsical shapes that would certainly add a festive touch to a brunch or a buffet table, and their delightful flavorings make them perfect companions to a variety of cheeses or dips. Herb *focacce* make exceptional stuffings for poultry and the like, and they also make superb bread crumbs. *Focacce* can be split, filled, and cut into wedges for spectacular sandwich presentations at a party or a picnic. And finally, some of these breads make fantastic pizza crusts—not traditional, but still delicious.

Basic pizza dough makes a very traditional *focaccia,* bready and chewy. Sicilian-style dough, because of the extra olive oil, makes a thicker, harder crust and a more tender interior. Both are equally good.

1. Follow all the directions of the Basic Pizza Dough (page 56).

2. Put the dough in an oiled bowl and seal it with plastic wrap. Follow the directions for rising times given in the Master Recipe. Some of these recipes will require a second and even a third rising. Once the dough has doubled in bulk, punch it down, knead it briefly, and return it to the oiled bowl. Repeat this procedure for the second rising. The second rising is not strictly necessary, but it makes for a breadier, thicker, better texture. If time is of the essence, eliminate the second rising in the bowl and shape the dough directly in the pan. If you do so, let it rise in the pan for 20 to 30 minutes before baking.

3. *Focacce* range from crisp cracker-like flatbreads of about ½ inch thickness to the thicker, breadier variations that rise to about 2 inches. Any of the following recipes may be made thick or thin, but if they are better suited to a particular thickness, I will indicate it. For most of the recipes, if the dough is pushed out into a 14- to 15-inch circle, a thin, crisp *focaccia* will result. If you decrease the circle to 10 to 12 inches, the *focaccia* will be thicker and more like bread. Rolling out *focacce* with a pin is not necessary. Simply press them out into an oiled pan with your fingertips, leaving the indentations in the dough. The small hollows hold in bits of topping or olive oil.

4. Black pans are not necessary to attain a proper crust texture with *focacce*. Prepare any pan as you would for pizza, with a thin coating of vegetable oil and a dusting of coarsely ground yellow cornmeal. The recommended pan size is a 15-inch round or a 16-inch square.

5. The oven temperature ranges from 400 to 450 degrees, and the cooking times are longer than for Neapolitan pizza, from 20 to 25 minutes. The lower temperature and longer cooking time allow the *focaccia* to develop a golden crust and a chewy interior without burning.

Baker's Focaccia

Yield: Serves 6 to 8 as a side dish.

FOCACCIA IN ITS most pristine form contains only oil and coarse salt. In Italy, bakeries usually sell it by the piece. Baker's *focaccia*, as it is sometimes called, may also contain some slivers of garlic or thin slices of onion. Italians enjoy it as a satisfying snack straight from the oven with no further embellishments.

For a lovely buffet presentation or as a great picnic item, I like to make round *focacce* that I split and fill with savory combinations and then cut into sandwich wedges. Try this garlicky flat bread spread with just some sweet butter.

1. Preheat the oven to 400 degrees.

2. Lightly coat a 15-inch round or 12-inch square baking pan with oil and sprinkle it lightly with coarsely ground yellow cornmeal.

3. Press the dough out into a 10- to 12-inch circle directly in the baking pan. Let the dough rise in the pan for 30 minutes.

4. Brush the dough with the olive oil and press the garlic slivers into the dough with your fingertips. Sprinkle with a little of coarse salt.

5. Bake for 35 minutes, or until just golden.

Variations

For a thinner, crisper, more cracker-like crust, press the dough out into a 15-inch round pan and bake for only 20 minutes. Don't let it burn.

Substitute ½ cup of thinly sliced onions for the garlic.

1 **recipe Basic Pizza or Sicilian-style Dough (see pages 57–60), ready to use**

2 **to 3 garlic cloves, peeled and finely slivered**

1 **tablespoon olive oil Coarse salt to taste (preferably Kosher salt)**

Filled Focaccia

Only the thicker variation of *focacce* can be split like a large bun. Here is a suggested combination, in order of the layers: On the bottom half of a split *focaccia* arrange well-dried arugola leaves, thinly sliced imported Italian salami, slices of Fontina or Bel Paese cheese, thin slices of ripe tomatoes or drained oil-packed sun-dried tomatoes, a generous sprinkling of drained capers, and thinly sliced Bermuda onions. Spread the top of the *focaccia* liberally with sweet butter. Cut into 6 to 8 wedges.

Piadina (Savory Griddle Cakes)

Yield: 6 *piadina*.

PIADINA, A DIRECT descendant of Neolithic pizza, is a regional specialty of Emilia-Romagna. In the mountainous part of this region, peasants still cook these primitive breads on a heated terra-cotta slab called a *testo*. At one time, *piadina* was the most renowned form of bread in the area, but now it has become rustic fair and is served up mostly to tourists.

Making *piadina* is exactly like making wheat flour tortillas. The dough is nearly the same, except that *piadina* contain a small amount of baking soda, which renders them a bit lighter than a tortilla.

Piadina can be served with a selection of fillings, such as sausage, salami, *prosciutto*, cheese, or sautéed vegetables. The *piadina* is wrapped around the filling and popped into your mouth. This kind of pizza is perfect for informal occasions.

4 cups flour
1 teaspoon salt
½ teaspoon baking soda
⅓ cup melted pure pork lard or olive oil
⅓ cup milk
½ to ⅓ cup water

1. Mix the flour, salt, and baking soda together in a bowl. Add the melted lard, milk, and just enough water to form a dough.

2. Remove the dough from the bowl and knead it for 5 to 8 minutes, adding a small amount of flour if the dough becomes too sticky.

3. Divide the dough into 6 uniform pieces. Roll out each piece to a ¹/₁₆-inch thickness. Use light dustings of flour to prevent sticking.

4. Heat a cast-iron skillet or a frying pan as you would for making pancakes. When a drop of water sizzles across the surface, the pan is sufficiently heated to cook the *piadina*.

5. Let the *piadina* cook for 1 minute at a time on either side. Turn them over often to prevent scorching. When small brown spots form on one side (after 4 to 5 minutes), they are done.

6. Keep them warm and serve with an assortment of fillings.

Elvira Camardo's Pizza Minestre

Yield: Serves 4 as a main course or 6 as an appetizer.

ONE OF THE simplest yet most satisfying pizza combinations ever is this recipe for *pizza minestre*, a modern-day version of the hearthcakes baked on stones and eaten with broths made from wild greens.

In the Camardo family, *minestre* (soup) usually starts out with greens of some kind—cooked in oil, with garlic and, perhaps, some hot red pepper—and is built upon with some added chicken or beef broth, or puréed tomatoes and possibly some bits of onion or carrot. It simmers quickly and fills the house with a hearty aroma. The *minestre* is served piping hot over thick, crusty wedges of a rough cake made of cornmeal mush flavored with garlic and chunks of sausage throughout.

1. Preheat the oven to 450 degrees.
2. In a large bowl, combine the cornmeal, flour, salt, pepper, garlic, and sausage meat.
3. Pour in just enough water to form a smooth paste.
4. Grease a 10-inch cast-iron skillet or other ovenproof frying pan with half of the lard or oil.
5. Spread the dough into the prepared frying pan and top with the remaining lard or oil.
6. Bake for 45 to 60 minutes, or until the dough pulls away from the sides of the pan and is lightly browned.
7. Remove from oven and let rest for 5 minutes before unmolding. Use a spatula to ease the pizza from the pan. It can be eaten hot or cold or reheated.

Variations

Substitute ½ cup of sautéed chopped onions *or* freshly grated Parmesan cheese for the sausage meat in the pizza.

2 cups coarsely ground yellow cornmeal
1 cup flour
½ teaspoon salt
Freshly ground black pepper to taste
1 garlic clove, peeled and minced
½ cup Italian sweet or hot sausage meat, crumbled
2 cups boiling water
2 tablespoons lard or olive oil
1 recipe *Minestre* (recipe follows)

Minestre Base

Yield: 4 to 6 servings.

1. Put one recipe of sautéed greens of your choice (see page 79) in a large saucepan.
2. Add 6 cups of chicken or beef broth or 1 28-ounce can of tomatoes, puréed, plus 1 cup of broth.
3. Bring the greens and liquid to a boil. Simmer for 20 minutes over low heat. To serve, put a wedge of pizza in the bottom of each bowl and pour some *minestre* over it.

Panetto di Ramerino (Rosemary *Focaccia*)

Yield: Serves 6 to 8 as a side dish.

THE ROBUST FLAVOR of this rosemary *focaccia* goes well with assertive dishes and is particularly good for soaking up pan juices from roasts. Sometimes it is worth making this recipe just to use it as a base for stuffing poultry, since it imparts a lovely fragrance to the overall dish. *Panetto di ramerino* also makes an interesting pizza dough.

Rosemary is a very potent herb, so use it sparingly. Fresh rosemary is always preferable to dried, in this recipe and in general.

1 recipe Basic Pizza or Sicilian-style Dough (see pages 56–60), ready to use

2 teaspoons fresh rosemary, finely chopped, or 1 teaspoon dried rosemary leaves, coarsely crushed

2 tablespoons olive oil
Coarse salt to taste

1. Preheat the oven to 400 degrees.

2. Lightly coat a 15-inch pizza pan with vegetable oil and sprinkle it lightly with coarsely ground yellow cornmeal.

3. Punch the dough down and knead in the rosemary until it is well distributed.

4. Press the dough out into a 12-inch circle in the baking pan and let it rise for 20 minutes.

5. Brush the dough with olive oil and sprinkle it with coarse salt.

6. Bake for about 30 minutes, or until the crust is just golden.

Pane con Salvia (Sage Bread)

Yield: Serves 6 to 8 as a side dish.

ONE OF THE most popular of the herb *focacce* is made with sage. The long, gray-green leaves of fresh sage impart a wonderful aroma and a delicate taste to this *focaccia*. Be sure to use fresh or dried sage, though, powdered sage is overpowering. In this recipe, the sage is added to the flour before the dough is made. Introducing the sage early on in the recipe, rather than kneading it in after the first rising, distributes the flavor more fully throughout the *focaccia*.

1. When the dough has doubled in bulk, punch it down and knead it briefly. Return it to the oiled bowl and reseal with plastic wrap. Let it rise a second time.

2. Preheat the oven to 400 degrees.

3. Lightly coat a 15-inch round pizza pan with vegetable oil and sprinkle it lightly with coarsely ground yellow cornmeal.

4. Once the dough has doubled again, press it into a 12-inch circle; then fit it into the prepared pan. Let the dough rise for 30 minutes.

5. Brush the dough with olive oil and bake for 30 minutes, or until the crust is golden.

Variations

For a garnish, arrange fresh sage leaves in the shape of a fan on top of the dough before it rises in the pan.

Herb Focaccia. Use only half the amount of sage indicated in the recipe and mix 1 teaspoon of dried thyme with the first cup of flour.

Marjoram Focaccia. Substitute the same amount of marjoram for sage. Mix with the first cup of flour.

Fresh Herb Focaccia. Use ¼ cup of the following, finely chopped, alone or in combination: parsley, mint, scallions, or chives. *Do not mix them in with the first cup of flour*, because their high moisture content will cause them to release their juices and make the dough green. Knead the fresh herbs in by hand after the first rising.

Note: These herb-scented breads make a perfect foil for a cheese tray, or as an accompaniment to soups. The leftovers make the best croutons ever.

¼ **cup tightly packed fresh sage leaves, or 2 tablespoons dried whole leaves, pulverized in a food processor, in a blender, or with a mortar and pestle, and blended into 1 cup of flour**

1 **recipe Basic Pizza or Sicilian-style Dough (see pages 56–60) made with this sage flour and ready to use**

1 **tablespoon olive oil**

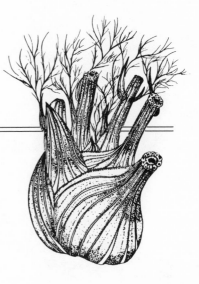

Focaccia di Finocchio (Fennel Bread)

Yield: Serves 6 to 8 as a side dish.

FENNEL HAS LONG been held in high esteem by Mediterranean peoples for its delicate flavor and medicinal qualities. Italians, who call it *finocchio*, are particularly fond of the herb. They use the entire plant: Its green feathery leaves are used in salads and marinades, and its seeds flavor soups, stews, and pastries. But it is the white bulbous "heart" of the plant that is most prized.

Although frequently confused, anise and fennel are not the same herb. They belong to the same family, and both have long been recognized as digestive aids, but only the seeds of the anise plant are used in cooking. The Romans ended their rich meals with a kind of sweet spiced *focaccia*, which was heavily scented with fennel or anise seeds. (Pieces of crisp, raw fennel are still a traditional finale for a large Italian meal.) The ancient version resembled a giant cookie and was made with eggs, black pepper, nuts, wine, and honey. This modern recipe is not sweet or spicy, but it still makes a delicious flatbread.

1 **recipe Basic Pizza or Sicilian-style Dough (see pages 56–60), ready to use**
1 **tablespoon olive oil**
2 **garlic cloves, peeled and minced**
4 **teaspoons fennel seeds**

1. Preheat the oven to 400 degrees.

2. Lightly coat a 15-inch round or square baking pan with oil and sprinkle it lightly with coarsely ground yellow cornmeal.

3. With your fingertips press the dough into a 10- to 12-inch circle in the pan.

4. Brush the dough with olive oil and press the garlic pieces and then the fennel seeds into the dough with your fingers.

5. Let the dough rise in the pan for about 20 minutes.

6. Bake for 10 to 30 minutes, or until the crust is just golden.

Variations

Omit the fennel seeds and garlic. Sauté 1 cup of finely chopped white part of fresh fennel in 2 tablespoons of olive oil. Cook until just tender, 2 to 5 minutes. Knead this into the dough after the first rising and proceed with the rest of the recipe.

Use fennel *focaccia* as a pizza crust. Top with ½ pound cubed Fontina cheese, 1 pound seeded fresh tomatoes, 5 to 6 fresh basil leaves, 2 tablespoons freshly grated Parmesan cheese, and a sprinkling of extra-virgin olive oil.

Note: The delicate dark green leaves of fennel make a nice garnish scattered on top of the bread before it is baked.

Focaccia alla Genovese (Genoan *Pesto* Bread)

Yield: Serves 6 to 8 as a side dish.

GENOA ABOUNDS WITH plentiful herbs and sharp Pecorino cheese, and these ingredients, in addition to golden olive oil, make up one of the most glorious sauces of the Italian repertoire—*Pesto*. But unlike the pasta sauce we are accustomed to, this mixture is not thickened with pignolis. It is quite simple: Fresh basil, mint, parsley, or any combination of the three are puréed together with some good olive oil to form a paste. Then Pecorino Romano cheese is added.

Focaccia alla genovese is best enjoyed at room temperature, because the flavor intensifies as it cools.

1. Preheat the oven to 400 degrees. Lightly coat a large pizza pan with vegetable oil and sprinkle it lightly with coarsely ground yellow cornmeal.

2. With your fingertips, press the dough into a 10- to 12-inch circle in the pan.

3. Smear the *Pesto* onto the dough with your fingers.

4. Bake for 30 minutes, or until the crust is just golden. Let the pie cool to room temperature before slicing.

1 **recipe Basic Pizza or Sicilian-style Dough (see pages 56–60), ready to use**

¾ **cup *Pesto* (see recipe page 82)**

Focaccia di Pumate (Sun-Dried Tomato Bread)

Yield: Serves 6 to 8 as a side dish.

WHEN YOU SEE how expensive sun-dried tomatoes are in specialty food stores, you would never think they were once a staple of peasant food. Fortunately, because their flavor is extremely intense, a little goes a long way. In this recipe, the tomatoes are shredded roughly or torn with the hands and spread over the dough. Use some of the marvelously flavored oil in which the tomatoes are sold to brush the top of the *focaccia*.

1. Preheat the oven to 400 degrees.

2. Lightly coat a large pizza pan with vegetable oil and sprinkle it lightly with coarsely ground yellow cornmeal.

3. With your fingertips, press the dough into a circle or square of about 12 inches in the pan.

4. Press the pieces of sun-dried tomato into the dough. Brush the tomato oil over the dough.

5. Bake for 30 minutes, or until the crust is just golden.

1 **recipe Basic Pizza or Sicilian-style Dough (see pages 56–60), ready to use**

10 **whole oil-packed sun-dried tomatoes, drained and roughly shredded**

2 **tablespoons tomato oil (from the jar) or olive oil**

Fresh Tomato Focaccia

Yield: Serves 6 to 8 as a side dish.

NO ONE KNOWS when the first Italian ate a fresh tomato. But I would speculate that his next thought was to put it on a piece of bread. This recipe is not the original version, but it is directly descended from the anonymous Italian cooks who picked fresh tomatoes from their gardens and plunked them down into their leftover bread dough.

Select only small, ripe cherry tomatoes for this recipe. Otherwise they will squirt at you when you bite down into them. Each bite of this simple yet heavenly *focaccia* should contain a mouthful of crusty bread, with just a hint of garlic and herbs, and half of a sweet, juicy tomato. It is delicious hot or cold.

1 **recipe Basic Pizza or Sicilian-style Dough (see pages 56–60), ready to use**

18 **ripe cherry tomatoes, cut in half**

36 **tiny slivers of fresh garlic (about 2 to 3 cloves)**

2 **tablespoons olive oil**

1 **teaspoon dried oregano, dried marjoram, fresh parsley leaves, or any combination of the three**
Coarse salt to taste

1. Lightly coat a large pizza pan with vegetable oil and sprinkle it lightly with coarsely ground yellow cornmeal.

2. With your fingertips press the dough out into a 12-inch circle or oval in the pan.

3. Preheat the oven to 400 degrees.

4. Place 2 to 3 tiny slivers of garlic together every inch or so in rows on top of the dough. Cover the garlic with a tomato half placed cut side down.

5. Cover the dough with a dish towel and let it rise for 30 minutes.

6. Before baking, push the tomato halves down into the risen dough so that they are partially embedded. Brush the dough with olive oil and sprinkle it with the herbs and a bit of salt.

7. Bake for 30 to 40 minutes, or until the crust is just golden.

Note: Fresh tomato *focaccia* is not suitable for the thinner style dough.

Fogatz with Gravy (Manhattan Focaccia)

Yield: Serves 6 to 8 as a side dish.

YEARS AGO, JUST about every Italian bakery in Manhattan sold generous slabs of hot, thick *fogatz* (as *focaccia* is known on this side of the Atlantic) with "gravy," just as pizza is sold by the piece today. Old-timers from Little Italy still recall the rich, meaty tomato sauce (gravy) that adorned those chewy breads of another era, and lament its disappearance.

However, we can still make *fogatz* at home. In fact, it's a perfect way to use those little ends of tomato sauce or meat sauce or even degreased pan drippings from roasts. *Fogatz* is easy to make, and I would venture to say that the kind you make at home will be every bit as good as the bakeries' in the old days.

1. Lightly coat a large pizza pan with vegetable oil and sprinkle it lightly with coarsely ground yellow cornmeal.

2. With your fingertips, push the dough into a 10- to 12-inch circle or square in the pan.

3. Preheat the oven to 400 degrees.

4. Let the dough rise in the pan for 30 minutes.

5. Spread the top of the dough with just enough of the sauce of your choice, to flavor the bread, not to saturate it.

6. Bake for 30 minutes, or until the crust is golden.

1 **recipe Basic Pizza or Sicilian-style Dough (see pages 56–60), ready to use**

½ **cup leftover homemade tomato or meat sauce or degreased pan drippings from a roast**

Fogatz di San Gennaro (San Gennaro Festival Pizza)

Yield: Serves 6 to 8 as a side dish.

IN THIS FLAVORFUL *fogatz* made for the feast of San Gennaro, onions and peppers are sautéed in olive oil and then spread on top of the dough. The olives are distributed over the surface during the final 10 minutes of baking so they don't dry out. Try breaking an egg over the top of the *focaccia* during the last 5 minutes or so of baking. I call this the breakfast of champions!

1 tablespoon olive oil
1 small sweet onion, peeled and diced
1 small sweet green pepper, seeded and diced
Salt and freshly ground black pepper to taste
1 recipe Basic Pizza or Sicilian-style Dough (see pages 56–60), ready to use
10 to 15 oil-cured black olives

1. Preheat the oven to 400 degrees.
2. Heat the tablespoon of olive oil in a medium-sized frying pan and sauté the onion and pepper for 2 to 3 minutes. Season with salt and pepper and set aside.
3. Lightly coat a large pizza pan with vegetable oil and sprinkle it lightly with coarsely ground yellow cornmeal.
4. With your fingertips, press the dough into a 12-inch circle in the pan.
5. Spread the onions and peppers on the dough. Let the dough rise in the pan for 15 minutes.
6. Bake for 20 minutes. Then distribute the olives over the pie, and bake for 10 minutes longer.

Variations

Distribute ½ cup raw sausage meat over the top of the *fogatz* before baking.

When the *fogatz* is golden, break 1 or 2 eggs over the pie and cook until they are set (about 5 minutes).

Antoinette Magnarelli Sacco's Fogatz di Zizi Sacco (Three-Onion *Focaccia*)

Yield: Serves 6 to 8 as a side dish.

THIS LIVELY COMBINATION was called to my attention by my friend and fellow pizza-lover, Paul Camardo. It is a favorite of his family, and it's easy to see why. The sweet onion-anchovy-olive combination reminds me of that distant French relative, *pissaladière*. Serve hot or cold.

4 tablespoons olive oil
1 small Bermuda onion, peeled and thinly sliced
1 small sweet yellow onion, thinly sliced
4 scallions, cut into ½-inch pieces
Salt and freshly ground black pepper to taste

1. Heat 2 tablespoons of the olive oil in a medium-sized frying pan. Sauté the onions and scallions for 2 to 3 minutes and season them with salt and pepper. Set aside until needed.
2. Lightly coat a 12- by 17-inch baking pan with vegetable oil and sprinkle it lightly with coarsely ground yellow cornmeal.
3. Press the dough out into the pan with your fingers.
4. Spread the onion mixture over the dough. Scatter the anchovies and olives over the onions and sprinkle with oregano and the remaining 2 tablespoons of olive oil.

5. Preheat the oven to 400 degrees.

6. Let the dough rise in the pan for 30 minutes.

7. Bake for about 30 minutes, or until the crust is golden.

Variation

For a main-dish pie, add ½ pound crumbled Italian sweet or hot sausage meat over the onions and add ½ pound coarsely shredded mozzarella during the final 5 to 10 minutes of baking.

1 recipe Sicilian-style Dough (see page 56), ready to use

1 2-ounce can anchovies, drained

15 oil-cured black olives

1 teaspoon dried oregano or dried marjoram

Fitascetta (Onion Ring)

Yield: Serves 6 to 8 as a side dish.

THIS DELICIOUS RING-SHAPED onion bread comes from the northern region of Lombardy. *Fitascetta* can be eaten warm or cold, simply spread with sweet butter, or, for a more substantial treat, with some mozzarella baked on top. Try splitting the ring like a sandwich and spreading the bottom half generously with some Gorgonzola cheese or salami slices. Replace the top half and cut the ring into thick wedges. This combination goes extraordinarily well with a bottle of Valtellina or Sassella.

1. Punch the dough down, knead it briefly, and shape it into a 12-inch circle. Push your fist into the center to form a 4-inch hole (like a doughnut).

2. Transfer the dough ring to a pizza pan that has been lightly coated with vegetable oil and lightly sprinkled with coarsely ground yellow cornmeal.

3. Sauté the *cippole* in the olive oil until they are translucent. Spread the onions over the dough and season them with salt and pepper.

4. Preheat the oven to 450 degrees. Let the pizza rise in the pan for 30 to 45 minutes.

5. Bake for 20 to 30 minutes. Add the cheese during the final 10 minutes of baking.

1 recipe Basic Pizza or Sicilian-style Dough (see pages 56–60), ready to use

1 pound *cippole* (small egg-shaped Italian red onions that sometimes resemble large shallots) or sweet red onions, peeled and thinly sliced

1 tablespoon olive oil
 Salt and freshly ground black pepper to taste

½ cup shredded or cubed mozzarella, optional

Schiacciata di Salsiccia (Sausage Bread)

Yield: Serves 6 to 8 as a side dish.

TRULY GOOD SAUSAGE is worth searching out. If you live near an Italian neighborhood, go to a pork store, *salumeria*, or butcher shop that makes its own pork sausages. Buying sausage from a reputable merchant usually means getting quality and great taste. Each place will have its own style of sausage, depending upon what part of Italy the owners come from. Some sausages have black pepper and sage or cinnamon and black pepper or parsley and cheese or just hot red pepper. My favorites are made with black pepper and fennel seeds. The character of the sausage you select will be important, for it is what flavors this *focaccia*.

There are two methods of making sausage *schiacciata*. The first involves pressing the raw sausage and onions right into the dough and letting them bake on top of the crust. In the second version, the sausage and onion are sautéed briefly and kneaded into the dough after the first rising. Both are delicious, but I prefer to knead the sausage and onion right into the dough because the result is more flavorful.

This *schiacciata* can be served on its own, but it also makes an excellent pizza crust, especially for *pizza bianca* and *pizza alla verdura*.

1 recipe Basic Pizza or Sicilian-style Dough (see pages 56–60), ready to use

½ pound good quality Italian sausage meat, removed from the casings and crumbled

1 small sweet onion, peeled and minced

1 tablespoon olive oil, optional

1. Preheat the oven to 400 degrees.

2. Lightly coat a 15-inch pizza pan with vegetable oil and sprinkle it lightly with coarsely ground yellow cornmeal.

3. With your fingertips, press the dough into a 10- to 12-inch circle in the pan.

4. Spread the onion and sausage meat over the dough.

5. Let the dough rise in the pan for about 20 minutes.

6. Bake for 30 minutes, or until the crust is golden.

Variation

Sauté the sausage meat and onion together in 1 tablespoon of olive oil until the sausage is no longer pink. After the dough has risen the first time, punch it down and knead in the sausage and onions. Fit the dough into a prepared pizza pan and let it rise another 30 minutes before baking.

Tortano (Prosciutto Bread)

Yield: Serves 6 to 8 as a side dish.

A NEAPOLITAN SPECIALTY, *prosciutto* bread has a rich, savory flavor that makes an excellent accompaniment to salads and cheese. I enjoy it with slices of mozzarella and fresh tomato as a kind of grilled cheese sandwich. Whether it is served as a side dish or all by itself, *tortano* disappears *fast!*

1 recipe Basic Pizza or Sicilian-style Dough (see pages 56–60), ready to use

2 tablespoons naturally rendered pork lard

½ teaspoon coarsely ground black pepper

4 ounces *prosciutto*, cut into ¼-inch cubes

1. Roll out the pizza dough into a 12- by 16-inch rectangle, dusting with flour to prevent sticking.

2. Spread the lard over the dough, leaving a ½-inch border all around.

3. Sprinkle the black pepper over the lard and layer the *prosciutto* over all.

4. Roll the dough into a tight roll. You should end up with a roll about 3 to 4 inches wide by 16 inches long.

5. Pinch the ends shut and transfer the roll to fit diagonally on a pan that has been lightly coated with vegetable oil and lightly sprinkled with coarsely ground yellow cornmeal.

6. Preheat the oven to 450 degrees.

6. Let the dough rise in the pan for 30 minutes.

8. Bake for 25 to 30 minutes, or until the roll is golden brown and crusty.

French Ashcakes

REMNANTS OF THE Roman occupation in parts of France and England are still evident in the many ruins scattered throughout their countrysides and cities. Along with the aqueducts, baths, and edifices of architectural fame, the Romans spread the legacy of *panus focus* over all of their ancient empire. Examples of these breads are known as *hearthcakes* in England. In France they're called *fougasse, fouasse, fouace, fouaches,* or *fouess,* depending upon the regional dialect.

Most *fougasse* derivatives have survived as sweet cakes. The *fouace* described by Rabelais was a rich cake redolent of spices. In the south of

France, *fougasse* is the name given to a number of different types of breads as well as cakes. Like their Italian counterparts, they are characterized as flat, crusty loaves, which, in some cases, are shaped like ladders or other fanciful forms. Here are some French contributions to the ashcake genre.

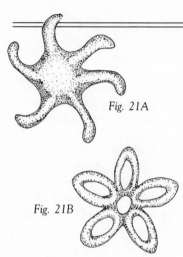

Fig. 21A

Fig. 21B

Fougasse

Yield: Serves 6 to 8 as a side dish.

MY FAMILY ALWAYS quarrels over who gets the crusty ends of Italian or French bread. The matter is usually resolved when the bread arrives from the baker's with one or both ends broken off—the family shopper having taken unfair advantage! *Fougasse* solves our problem in a different way, because the holes in this bread allow for maximum crust surface area. Crust-lovers may break off any number of choice pieces.

Flavored with nothing but oil, *fougasse* is just like *focaccia*, except that it is shaped. My favorite forms are the flower and the sun. They are crispy and delicious and make lovely additions to any buffet table or other festive occasion

1 recipe Basic Pizza or Sicilian-style Dough (see pages 56–60), ready to use

2 tablespoons olive oil, walnut oil, or peanut oil

1. Lightly coat a large pizza pan with vegetable oil and sprinkle it lightly with coarsely ground yellow cornmeal.

2. With your hands, press the dough out into a 4-inch circle on a smooth, clean surface. To make a sun, stretch out 6 points of dough from the center of the circle. The sun's "rays" should each be about 6 inches long (*Fig. 21A*). For a flower shape, make 6 slits with a knife in the dough to form a a a petal pattern. With your fingers, widen the slits so that they make a petal shape (*Fig. 21B*). Take care not to stretch the dough too thin, or it will tear. Carefully transfer the sun or the flower to the prepared baking pan.

3. Preheat the oven to 400 degrees.

4. Let the *fougasse* rise in the pan for 30 minutes.

5. Brush the bread with your choice of oil and bake for about 25 minutes, or until it is nicely browned.

Fouache d'Olives (Olive Bread)

Yield: Serves 6 to 8 as a side dish.

GOOD OIL-CURED black olives or tiny purple Niçoise olives are a must for this bread; its flavor and texture depend upon them. The oil released from the olives gives the bread a very rich taste and impart an almost flaky quality to the crust. The secret lies in kneading the chopped olives into the dough after the first rising. This enables the olive bits to be distributed throughout the dough without releasing too much oil before the bread is baked. The olives release their oil during the cooking time and form steam pockets in the dough. The layers are flaky and not unlike puff pastry.

By Hand

1. Follow the directions for the Basic Pizza Dough (page 56), using the proportions of ingredients indicated in this recipe.

2. Once the dough has been properly kneaded either by hand or in a processor, you will find that it is very soft and oily. This is the proper consistency; if it sticks to your hands, knead in only enough flour to stop the sticking.

3. Turn the dough out into an oiled bowl. Cover tightly with plastic wrap and let the dough double in bulk (35 to 45 minutes).

4. When the dough has doubled, punch it down and knead it briefly. If it sticks to your hands, knead in a sprinkling of flour to absorb some of the excess oil. Flatten the dough with your hands and knead in the chopped olives until they are evenly distributed.

5. Return the dough to the bowl. Cover with plastic wrap and let rise a second time (35 to 45 minutes).

6. Lightly coat a large pizza pan with vegetable oil.

7. After the dough has doubled a second time, punch it down. Knead it briefly and press it out into a 12-inch circle in the prepared pan. Make slashes with a sharp knife across the top, forming a lattice design.

8. Let it rise in the pan for 30 to 45 minutes.

9. Preheat the oven to 450 degrees

10. Bake for 20 minutes, or until it is just golden.

1 cup warm tap water (110 to 115 degrees)

2 packages active dry yeast

4 cups flour

½ cup extra-virgin olive oil

25 oil-cured black Mediterranean olives, or 35 purple Niçoise olives, pitted and roughly chopped

Food Processor Method (large capacity processor only)

1. Dissolve the yeast with the warm water in a bowl of the processor with a few on–off turns.

2. Add 1 cup of the flour to the dissolved yeast and the oil; process with 2 or 3 on–off pulses to mix.

3. Continue with the directions given in the Master Food Processor recipe (page 58), using the proportions in this recipe.

Variations

For a nice shine and a deeper color, brush with an egg white glaze (1 egg white beaten with 1 tablespoon of water) before baking.

Use this dough as the crust for a French *pissaladière*.

Fouace de Noix   (French Walnut Bread)

Yield: Serves 6 to 8 as a side dish.

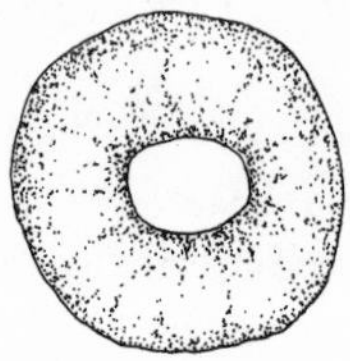

Fig. 21C

THE CONCEPT BEHIND *fouace de noix* is very similar to that of *fouache d'olives,* but in this recipe, the trick is to roast the walnuts in the oven until they are brown before using them in the recipe. Roasting brings out the oils in the nuts and produces a more intense flavor, and this is what gives *fouace de noix* its delicate taste. After baking, let the bread cool completely before serving, because its flavor improves as it cools. I enjoy *fouace de noix* spread with Roquefort cheese and served with a glass of good Sauternes—a decidedly Gallic approach to pizza but nonetheless a delectable one.

1 **cup warm tap water (110 to 115 degrees)**
1 **package active dry yeast**
3 **to 3½ cups flour**
½ **cup walnut oil, plus an additional 2 table- spoonsful for oiling the bowl and brushing on top of the bread before baking**

1. Follow the same methods as described in the preceding recipe for *fouache d'olives.* Use 1 tablespoon walnut oil to grease the bowl that the dough rises in. Knead the walnuts in after the first rising. Let the dough rise a second time and proceed with the recipe.

2. Lightly coat a pizza pan with vegetable oil.

3. When the dough has doubled a second time, punch it down and form a flat circle about 12 inches in diameter. Make a hole with your fist in the center and stretch the hole out to about 4 inches (*Fig. 21C*). With your fingertips, press the dough out to a thickness of ½ inch.

4. Preheat the oven to 400 degrees.

5. Arrange this doughnut shape on the prepared pan and let it rise for 30 minutes.

6. Brush with the remaining walnut oil before baking.

7. Bake for 35 to 40 minutes, or until it is lightly golden. Serve at room temperature.

½ teaspoon salt
½ cup chopped walnuts, roasted on a baking sheet at 350 degrees for 10 minutes

---

Fouasse à la Tapenade   (Anchovy and Olive Bread)

Yield: Serves 6 to 8 as a side dish.

THIS IS DELICIOUS hot or cold.

1. Once the dough has doubled, punch it down and knead it briefly.

2. Lightly coat a pizza pan with vegetable oil and fit the dough into it in a 12-inch circle.

3. Preheat the oven to 400 degrees.

4. Spread the *Tapenade* over the dough and let it rise for 30 minutes in the pan.

5. Bake for 30 minutes, or until the crust is golden.

1 recipe Basic Pizza or Sicilian-style Dough (see pages 56–60), ready to use
½ cup *Tapenade* (see recipe page 81)
2 tablespoons olive oil

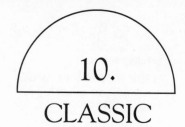

10.
CLASSIC ITALIAN PIZZA

Classic Italian pizza falls into two categories: regional ones, which vary from place to place, and general, ones which are more universally Italian.

The most well-known Italian pizzas come from the city of Naples, where a thin, crisp crust and tomatoes form the basis of every one of its approximately 30 variations. The names of these pies are easily recognized: *alla Napolentana* (just tomatoes), *alla Margherita*, or *della regina* (tomatoes with cheese), *con cozze* (tomatoes with mussels), *con funghi* (tomatoes with mushrooms), and so on.

In other regions, pizza doesn't necessarily go by the name pizza. Along the Italian Riviera it is known as *la sardinaira*. In Sicily, where there are more different kinds of pizza dishes than anywhere else, it's not called pizza, nor does it look like conventional pizza.

Sicilian pizza comes in a number of different forms. It can be thick and bready, as in *scacciata* or *sfincione*; encased between two crusts, as in *sfincuini*; or rolled up like a jelly roll, as in *bonata*. Pizza in Sicily can be anything from a snack to an entire feast rolled into one pie. There's a whole lot more to Sicilian pizza than the thick-crusted variation that we here in America are familiar with.

The most authentic examples of Sicilian pizza in this country come from the recipes of Italian-Americans who continue the tradition of pizza *casalinga* (home-style). Sicilian pizza, unlike Neapolitan, is really an art carried on in the home. Consequently, these recipes for *scacciata*, *sfincoine di San Vito*, and *pizza casalinga* will probably be very different from any Sicilian-style pizza you may have had before—unless, of course, you are Sicilian.

There are dozens of regional recipes for pizza *bianca*—white pizza. The pizza is "white" because no tomatoes or greens are used to make it. The primary ingredient of most *pizza bianca* is cheese, but there are also varieties that include onions, potatoes, and fish.

Another traditional genre of pizza in Italy is *pizza alla verdura* or *pizza alla erbazzone*. *Verdura* comes from the Italian for the color green, for leaf greens, and *erbazzone* means grass or herbs. These lush and savory pies are in the tradition of the old hearthcakes that were eaten with greens in broth or spread with herbs and oil. As time went on, and the concept of pizza as a meal in itself came about, the greens became the filling rather than the accompaniment.

A diminutive form of pizza, popular all over Italy and especially in the north, are *pizzette*. Usually sold in bakeries, *pizzette* are offered with a vast selection of toppings. These delicious little pizzas are extremely versatile and can be enjoyed as a snack, a light lunch, or as an appetizer.

Classic Neapolitan Pizza

Yield: 1 15- to 18-inch round pie.
Serves 4 as a main course or 6 to 8 as an appetizer.
Crust Suggestions: Basic Pizza, Sicilian-style, Semolina, Pepper-Lard, *Prosciutto*, Sausage, or Whole Wheat dough.
Method: Direct stone baking or a prepared pizza pan.

THIS IS SURELY one of man's most satisfying combinations—an impossibly thin, crisp, and light crust anointed with olive oil and topped with sweet ripe tomatoes and fresh basil. The classic Neapolitan pizza comes close to being a food made in heaven. The art of the *pizzaiolo* reaches its height in this simple dish for which only an expertly executed crust in communion with the ripest tomatoes will do.

1. Preheat the oven to 500 degrees for at least 30 minutes for a pizza pan and 60 minutes for pizza tiles and stones.

2. Lightly coat a pizza pan with vegetable oil and sprinkle it lightly with coarsely ground yellow cornmeal. Or lightly coat a large pizza screen with oil or a peel with flour.

3. Roll out or stretch the dough into a thin circle and fit it onto the prepared pan, screen, or peel.

4. Spread the tomatoes over the dough. Then add the garlic and anchovies, and finish with a sprinkling of herbs, salt and pepper, and olive oil.

5. Bake for 10 to 15 minutes, or until the crust is golden.

Note: For the most authentic results, classic Neapolitan pizza should be pressed or stretched out and baked directly on tiles or a stone with a pizza screen.

1 recipe pizza dough, ready to use
2 pounds ripe plum tomatoes, seeded and roughly chopped, or
1½ cups drained canned whole tomatoes, roughly chopped
2 garlic cloves, peeled and minced, optional
1 2-ounce can anchovies, drained, optional
6 to 7 fresh basil leaves, roughly shredded, or 1 teaspoon dried basil or dried oregano
Salt and freshly ground black pepper to taste
2 tablespoons olive oil

Pizza di Quattro Stagioni (Four-Season Pizza)

Yield: 1 15- to 18-inch round pie.
Serves 4 as a main course or 6 to 8 as an appetizer.
Crust Suggestions: Basic Pizza, Sicilian-style, Semolina, Pepper-Lard, or Whole Wheat dough.
Method: Direct stone baking or a prepared pizza pan.

PIZZA DI QUATTRO STAGIONI is the quintessential take-out pie, the granddaddy of pizza with everything on it. *Quattro stagioni* means the four seasons, and theoretically the pie is supposed to be divided into quarters with a different topping on each section to represent each season. But in Naples, birthplace of the take-out pie, these pizzas can reach lengths of almost a meter with as many different sections of topping as people eating the pie. In America, pizza enthusiasts go for the works. I often make this type of pizza for gatherings where I know there are diverse tastes. When you compose the pizza, take care to consider the juxtaposition of color and texture on the pie.

1 recipe pizza dough, ready to use
1 cup Basic Pizza Sauce (see recipe page 72)

Toppings (see Note)
½ pound mushrooms, cleaned and thinly sliced
1 teaspoon plus 2 tablespoons olive oil
¼ pound mozzarella, cut into 1-inch cubes
¼ pound hot or sweet Italian sausage meat, removed from the casings and crumbled

1. Preheat the oven to 500 degrees for at least 30 minutes for a pizza pan or 60 minutes for pizza tiles and stones.

2. Lightly coat a large pizza pan with vegetable oil and sprinkle it lightly with coarsely ground yellow cornmeal. Or lightly coat a large pizza screen with oil or a peel with flour.

3. If you are using the mushrooms, sauté them in a frying pan in 1 teaspoon of the olive oil until all of their liquid evaporates. Set them aside until needed.

4. Roll out or stretch the dough into a thin circle and fit it onto the prepared pan, screen, or peel.

5. Spread a thin layer of Pizza Sauce over the prepared dough. Divide the pie visually into wedges and arrange the toppings of your choice within them. (*Note:* If you are using any seafood, add it only during the final 5 minutes of baking time or it will become overcooked and rubbery.)

6. Sprinkle the pie with basil and the remaining 2 tablespoons of olive oil.

7. Bake for 10 to 15 minutes, or until the crust is golden.

Note: Choose any 4 or more of the following toppings. The proportions are figured on one quarter of the pie. If more toppings are added, they must be proportionally less.

2 ounces salami or sweet or hot dried sausage, thinly sliced

Half of a 2-ounce can of anchovies, drained

½ cup fresh shucked clams or drained canned clams

½ cup raw peeled and deveined shrimp

½ pound mussels, scrubbed clean and bearded

¼ pound squid, cleaned and cut into ¼-inch-thick rings

Half a sweet red or green pepper, seeded and thinly sliced

Half a small sweet onion, peeled and thinly sliced

1 tablespoon freshly grated Parmesan cheese

10 black, green, or Niçoise olives

6 to 7 fresh basil leaves, roughly shredded, or 1 teaspoon dried oregano

2 garlic cloves, peeled and thinly sliced

La Sardinaira (Italian Riviera-Style Pizza)

Yield: 1 15- to 18-inch round pie.
Serves 4 as a main course or 6 to 8 as an appetizer.
Crust Suggestions: Basic Pizza, Sicilian-style, Semolina, or Pepper-Lard dough.
Method: Direct stone baking or a prepared pizza pan.

THERE ARE SEVERAL variations of La Sardinaira, the pizza of the Italian Riviera. The dish varies from town to town, depending on what local specialties are available at the time: The olives may be different; sardines may be used instead of anchovies; and sometimes green peppers find their way in. This pie is good hot or cold.

1 **recipe pizza dough, ready to use**
½ **cup Basic Pizza Sauce (see recipe page 72)**
1 **pound fresh tomatoes, seeded and roughly chopped, or ½ cup additional Pizza Sauce, if fresh tomatoes are unavailable**
1 **small sweet red onion or other mild onion, sliced paper thin**
1 **2-ounce can anchovies, drained**
25 **oil-cured black olives or other Mediterranean olives**
¼ **cup drained capers**
1 **teaspoon dried marjoram or dried oregano**
2 **to 3 tablespoons olive oil**

1. Preheat the oven to 500 degrees for 30 minutes for a pizza pan or 60 minutes for pizza tiles or stones.

2. Lightly coat a large pizza pan with oil and sprinkle it lightly with coarsely ground yellow cornmeal. Or lightly coat a large pizza screen with oil or a peel with flour.

3. Roll out or stretch the dough into a thin circle and fit it onto the prepared pan, screen, or peel.

4. Spread the tomato sauce evenly over the dough. Arrange the fresh tomatoes, onion, anchovies, and capers over the sauce. Sprinkle with the marjoram and olive oil.

5. Bake for 10 to 15 minutes, or until the crust is golden.

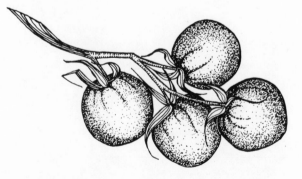

Pizza Margherita (Della Regina)

Yield: 1 15- to 18-inch round pie.
Serves 4 as a main course or 6 to 8 as an appetizer.
Crust Suggestions: Basic Pizza, Sicilian-style, Semolina, Pepper-Lard,
Herb, *Prosciutto*, or Sausage dough.
Method: Direct stone baking or a prepared pizza pan.

LITTLE DID RAFFAELE ESPOSITO know when he created this pizza for his Queen Margherita that it would become one of the most famous dishes of all time. In its original form, *pizza della regina* (of the queen) is classic Neapolitan tomato pizza plus mozzarella. The addition of mozzarella to the fabled pie was no less than a stroke of genius. Mozzarella was the one ingredient that Neapolitan pizza needed to bind together its herb-scented tomatoes and light, crisp crust.

1. Preheat the oven to 500 degrees for 30 minutes for a pizza pan and 60 minutes for pizza tiles or stones.

2. Lightly coat a large pizza pan with vegetable oil and sprinkle it lightly with coarsely ground yellow cornmeal. Or lightly coat a large pizza screen with oil or a peel with flour.

3. Roll out or stretch the dough into a thin circle and fit it onto the prepared pan, screen, or peel.

4. Spread the cheese over the dough. Then add the tomatoes, garlic, and basil. Sprinkle with the salt and pepper, Parmesan cheese, and olive oil.

5. Bake for 10 to 15 minutes, or until the crust is golden.

1 recipe pizza dough, ready to use

½ pound mozzarella, thinly sliced or cubed

1½ pounds fresh tomatoes, seeded and roughly chopped, or 1 cup drained canned whole tomatoes, roughly chopped

2 garlic cloves, minced

5 to 6 fresh basil leaves, roughly shredded, or 1 teaspoon dried basil or dried oregano
Salt and freshly ground black pepper to taste

2 tablespoons freshly grated Parmesan cheese, optional

2 tablespoons olive oil

Scacciata

Yield: Serves 6 to 8 as a main course or 10 to 12 as part of a buffet.

Crust Suggestions: Sicilian-style II dough.

Method: A prepared 14- by 17-inch jelly roll pan.

The CLASSIC SICILIAN *scacciata* is a thick, chewy crusted affair, topped with an abundance of ingredients: tomatoes, onions, anchovies, or sardines, black olives, and caciocavallo, scamorza, or mozzarella cheese. Sicilian pizza can be seasoned with oregano, fresh mint, and thyme.

1 recipe Sicilian-style Dough II, ready to use

1½ cups cubed caciocavallo, scamorza, or mozzarella

2 pounds fresh tomatoes, seeded and roughly chopped, or 2 cups well-drained whole canned tomatoes, roughly chopped

1 large onion, peeled, chopped, and sautéed in 1 tablespoon of olive oil

½ cup cubed boiled ham

1 2-ounce can anchovies, drained

20 oil-cured black olives
    Freshly ground black pepper to taste

2 to 3 sprigs fresh mint, chopped (Omit entirely if fresh is unavailable.)

1 teaspoon dried oregano

3 tablespoons olive oil

1. Lightly coat a 12- by 17-inch jelly roll pan with vegetable oil. Sprinkle it lightly with coarsely ground yellow cornmeal.

2. Press the dough into the pan evenly with your fingers and work up a 1-inch rim all around the pan.

3. In a large bowl, combine the cheese, tomatoes, onion, ham, and anchovies. Spread this mixture over the pizza dough. Garnish with black olives and season with pepper, mint, and oregano. Then sprinkle with the olive oil.

4. Let the pie rise in the pan for 30 minutes while you preheat the oven to 450 degrees.

5. Bake for 35 to 45 minutes, or until the crust is golden. Cut into thick squares to serve.

oregano

Sfincione di San Vito

Yield: Serves 6 to 8 as a side dish or light lunch.
Serves 12 to 14 as part of a buffet.
Crust Suggestions: Sicilian-style II dough.
Method: A prepared 12- by 17-inch jelly roll pan.

THE MOST RENOWNED of all Sicilian pizza is called *sfincione* or *sfincuini*, and it comes in two forms. One is a thick sauced bread which is considered a snack; the other is a hearty double-crust pie.

The *focacceria* is to the Sicilian capital of Palermo what the pizzeria is to Naples, but unlike a pizzeria, a *focacceria* serves many different kinds of bread or sandwich-like dishes. I learned about what a *focacceria* was from Vinnie Bondi, owner of La Focacceria, on the Lower East Side, the last place of its kind still operating in Manhattan. Open since 1914, La Focacceria is modeled exactly after those in Palermo. The best time to visit La Focacceria is on a Saturday afternoon. That's when Vinnie makes *panelli* (deep-fried chick-pea pancakes) and brings in his own *sfincione di San Vito*.

Here is an adaptation of Vinnie Bondi's special *sfincione di San Vito*.

1. Lightly coat the pan with vegetable oil and sprinkle the bottom with the sesame seeds.

2. Press the dough into the pan evenly, using your fingertips to form a 1-inch rim up the sides of the pan.

3. Spread the Gravy over the dough and let the pie rise in the pan for 30 minutes.

4. Preheat the oven to 450 degrees for 30 minutes.

5. Just before baking, combine the bread crumbs with the cheese and sprinkle the mixture over the top of the pie. Drizzle the olive oil over the crumb-cheese mixture.

6. Bake for 35 to 40 minutes, or until golden and crusty. Cut into squares to serve.

2 tablespoons sesame seeds
1 recipe Sicilian-style Dough II, ready to use
3 cups Gravy (see recipe page 74)
½ cup unseasoned bread crumbs
½ cup freshly grated Romano cheese
3 tablespoons olive oil

Pizza Casalinga alla Siciliana

(Sicilian Home-Style Pizza)

> Yield: Serves 6 as a main course or 10 to 12 as part of a buffet.
> Crust Suggestions: Sicilian-style II dough.
> Method: A prepared 12- by 17-inch jelly roll pan.

THIS DELECTABLE HOME-STYLE Sicilian pie features a filling made from a thick meaty sauce flavored with fresh mint. This sauce is a quintessential Sicilian pasta sauce, but for the moment, let it star on pizza.

1 **recipe Sicilian-style Dough II, ready to use**
3 **cups Sicilian Ragu (see recipe page 75)**
½ **pound scamorza or mozzarella, thinly sliced, optional**

1. Lightly coat the pan with vegetable oil and sprinkle it lightly with coarsely ground yellow cornmeal.

2. Press the dough out evenly into the pan, working up a 1-inch rim all around the pan.

3. Fill the dough shell with the sauce, using a slotted spoon to get rid of most of the liquid. (You should have ½ to 1 cup of leftover liquid.)

4. Let the pie rise in the pan while the oven heats for 30 minutes.

5. Preheat the oven to 400 degrees for 30 minutes.

6. Bake the pie for 30 minutes. Then add the cheese if you are using it. Bake the pie for 10 minutes longer, or until it is golden and the cheese is just bubbly. To reheat, bake the pie for 35 to 40 minutes and add the cheese while the pie reheats for 10 minutes in a 450-degree oven.

Pizza Bianca alla Romana

> Yield: 1 15- to 18-inch round pie.
> Serves 4 as a main course or 6 to 8 as an appetizer.
> Crust Suggestions: Basic Pizza, Sicilian-style, or Semolina dough.
> Method: Direct stone baking or a prepared pizza pan.

ROMANS LIKE THEIR PIZZA substantial, earthy—and with no tomatoes! This variety, with onions, bacon or *pancetta*, rosemary, and mozzarella doesn't merely sound divine, it is. In Rome, an individual-size variation often comes with an egg cooked on top. Try it as a satisfying light supper or for brunch, served hot or cold.

1. Heat the olive oil in a large frying pan and cook the bacon until it is crisp and golden. Remove the meat with a slotted spoon and set it aside.

2. Add the onions to the frying pan and cook over medium heat until they are translucent, about 10 minutes. While the onions are cooking, season them with the rosemary and black pepper. Stir in the bacon when the onions are done and set the mixture aside.

3. Preheat the oven to 500 degrees for 30 minutes for a pizza pan or 60 minutes for pizza tiles or stones.

4. Lightly coat a large pizza pan with vegetable oil and sprinkle it lightly with coarsely ground yellow cornmeal. Or lightly coat a large pizza screen with oil or a peel with flour.

5. Roll out or stretch the dough into a thin circle and fit it onto the prepared pan, screen, or peel.

6. Spread the mozzarella over the dough shell and lay the onions over the cheese.

7. Bake for 10 to 15 minutes, or until the crust is golden.

Variations

Add a handful of black olives to the topping.

Make 4 individual *pizzettes* and break an egg over each during the final 5 minutes of baking.

2 tablespoons olive oil
¼ pound slab bacon or *pancetta* in one piece, cubed
2 pounds sweet onions, thinly sliced
1½ teaspoons fresh rosemary leaves, or ¼ teaspoon dried whole rosemary leaves which have been coarsely crushed in a mortar with a pestle
Freshly ground black pepper to taste
1 recipe pizza dough, ready to use
½ pound mozzarella, thinly sliced

Pizza alla Romana II, For Luca

Yield: 1 14- by 17-inch pie.
Serves 6 to 8 as a main course or 10 to 12 as part of a buffet.

Crust Suggestions: Sicilian-style I or II, Pepper-Lard, *Prosciutto*, or Sausage dough.

Method: Use a deep-dish pizza pan that has been prepared with vegetable oil and cornmeal. (*Note:* Sicilian-style II will make a 12- by 17-inch large thick pie; any of the other doughs make a 15-inch round or 16-inch square thick-crusted pie.)

AUTHENTIC ROMAN PIZZA does not come from a pizzeria but from a bakery, where it is thick-crusted and baked in giant trays. There, the customer makes his selection and decides what size slab of pizza he wants;

then it is weighed and warmed in the oven. The final product comes out folded over like a book (*al libre*), hot and crusty. One of my official pizza-tasters, Luca del Borgo, was homesick for a particular kind of Roman pizza. He says it's the favorite of poor young students because it is the most substantial and the best tasting for the least money. I can see why; its combination of peppery, herb-scented, crunchy potatoes and thick chewy crust is incredibly satisfying and comforting. This is good hot or cold.

1 recipe pizza dough, ready to use
2 pounds thin-skinned waxy potatoes, such as Red Bliss, washed, dried, and sliced paper thin
2 garlic cloves, peeled and crushed through a press
⅓ cup olive oil
1 teaspoon fresh rosemary leaves, or ½ teaspoon dried rosemary leaves, roughly crumbled in a mortar
Salt and freshly ground black pepper to taste

1. Preheat the oven to 400 degrees for 30 minutes.

2. Lightly coat a large deep-dish pizza pan with vegetable oil and sprinkle the bottom of the pan lightly with coarsely ground yellow cornmeal.

3. Press the dough out into the pan with your fingertips and build up an outer edge of dough along the sides of the pan.

4. Let the dough rise in the pan for 30 minutes.

5. Combine the potato slices, garlic, olive oil, rosemary and salt and pepper in a large bowl. Mix everything together with your hands until each potato slice is well coated.

6. Arrange the potato slices in an overlapping layer either in a circle or in rows, depending on the shape of the pan. Pour any remaining oil from the bowl over the potatoes.

7. Bake for 45 to 50 minutes, or until the potatoes are brown and crusty.

Note: This is excellent with a soup made with greens, such as the *Pizza Minestre* on page 90.

Or try folding a slice of this pizza *al libre* around a piece of ham for a meal on the run, Roman style.

Genoan Pizza Bianca

Yield: 1 15- to 18-inch round pie.
Serves 6 to 8 as an appetizer or 10 to 12 in thin wedges as an hors d'oeuvre.
Crust Suggestions: Basic Pizza, Sicilian-style, Pepper-Lard, Sausage, or *Prosciutto* dough.
Method: Direct stone baking or a prepared pizza pan.

SERVE THIS PIZZA as a light lunch with a salad or in thin wedges hot or cold as part of an antipasto platter. This is good hot or cold.

1. Preheat the oven to 500 degrees for 30 minutes for a pizza pan or 60 minutes for pizza tiles or stones.

2. Lightly coat a large pizza pan with vegetable oil and sprinkle it lightly with coarsely ground yellow cornmeal. Or lightly coat a large pizza screen with oil or a peel with flour.

3. Roll out or stretch the dough into a thin circle and fit it onto the prepared pan, screen, or peel.

4. Bake the crust "blind" (without any topping) for 5 minutes.

5. Combine the *Pesto*, garlic, and cheeses in a bowl and spread the mixture over the partially baked crust.

6. Return the pizza to the oven and bake for 5 to 10 minutes longer, or until the cheese is just melted and bubbly.

1 recipe pizza dough, ready to use

¾ cup *Pesto* (see recipe page 82)

1 garlic clove, peeled and minced

¼ cup freshly grated locatelli or Romano cheese

1 pound mozzarella, cut into 1-inch cubes

Pizza Bianca I

Yield: 1 15- to 18-inch round pie.
Serves 6 to 8 as an appetizer or side dish.
Crust Suggestions: Basic Pizza, Sicilian-style, Pepper-Lard, Semolina, Sausage, *Prosciutto*, or Herb doughs.
Method: Direct stone baking or a prepared pizza pan.

THE CHEESE FORMS a thick chewy crust on the dough of this pizza. I particularly like to serve it warm, cut into thin wedges, or cold with an ice-cold red vermouth apéritif.

1. Preheat the oven to 500 degrees for 30 minutes for a pizza pan or 60 minutes for pizza tiles or stones.

2. Lightly coat a large pizza pan with vegetable oil and sprinkle it lightly with coarsely ground yellow cornmeal. Or lightly coat a pizza screen with oil. (This pizza cannot be assembled directly on a peel.)

3. Roll out or stretch the dough 2 inches larger than the pan or screen and fit it onto the pan of your choice.

4. Mix together the cheeses, eggs, and black pepper in a bowl. Spread the mixture over the dough shell. Fold the dough edges back over

1 recipe pizza dough, ready to use

½ cup freshly grated Parmesan cheese

1 cup freshly grated Gruyère cheese

½ cup freshly grated Provolone

3 extra large eggs, beaten

**Freshly ground black
pepper to taste**
2 tablespoons olive oil

the filling. Drizzle the olive oil over the pie and bake for 10 to 15 minutes, or until the cheese is just melted.

Variation

Half a pound of zucchini, grated and squeezed dry of all moisture can be added with the cheeses.

Pizza Bianca II

Yield: Serves 6 as a main course.
Crust Suggestions: Basic Pizza, Sicilian-style, Pepper-Lard, Sausage, *Prosciutto*, or Semolina dough.
Method: Use a 15-inch deep-dish round pizza pan prepared with oil and cornmeal.

THIS PIZZA ISN'T exactly *bianca*, because it contains cooked greens. No matter, though, this deep-dish pie makes a beautiful presentation.

½ **pound mushrooms,
cleaned and sautéed in
2 teaspoons olive oil
until all of their excess
liquid has evaporated**
1 **recipe Italian Greens,
such as broccoli rabe,
Swiss chard, spinach,
or escarole ready to use
(see recipe page 79)**
1 **recipe pizza dough,
ready to use**
1½ **pounds ricotta, sea-
soned with salt and
freshly ground black
pepper to taste**
½ **pound mozzarella,
thinly sliced**

1. Preheat the oven to 450 degrees for 30 minutes.
2. Lightly coat a 15-inch deep-dish pizza pan with oil and sprinkle cornmeal lightly over the bottom of the pan. Fit the dough into it forming a 1½-inch border up the sides of the pan.
3. Spread the seasoned ricotta over the dough shell and layer the mozzarella over the ricotta. Arrange the greens along the outer edge of the pie in a band about 3 inches wide. Layer the mushrooms along the inner border of the greens. Leave the center of the pizza white like a bull's eye.
4. Bake for 25 to 35 minutes, or until golden and puffy. For neater slices, wait at least 10 minutes before cutting into this pie.

Ligurian Pizza Bianca

Yield: 1 15- to 18-inch round pie.
Serves 4 as a main course or 6 to 8 as an appetizer.
Crust Suggestions: Basic Pizza, Sicilian-style, Pepper-Lard, Semolina, Sausage, or *Prosciutto* dough.
Method: Direct stone baking or a prepared pizza pan.

A DELIGHTFUL COMBINATION of sweet onions, salty anchovies, and black olives, this ancient variation is probably the source from which the famous French specialty, *pissaladière*, is derived.

1. Heat 2 tablespoons of the olive oil in a large frying pan. Add the onions and sauté them over medium heat for 10 minutes. Season the onions with salt and pepper while they are cooking. Stir the onions frequently to prevent them from sticking. When they are soft and golden, set the onions aside.

2. Preheat the oven to 500 degrees for 30 minutes for a pizza pan or 60 minutes for pizza tiles or stones.

3. Lightly coat a large pizza pan with vegetable oil and sprinkle it lightly with coarsely ground yellow cornmeal. Or lightly coat a large pizza screen with oil or a pizza peel with flour.

4. Roll out or stretch the dough into a thin circle and fit it onto the prepared pan, screen, or peel.

5. Spread the onions over the dough. Then distribute the anchovies and olives over the onions. Drizzle the remaining 2 tablespoons of olive oil over all.

6. Bake for 10 to 15 minutes, or until the crust is golden.

Variations

Lay ½ pound thinly sliced mozzarella down on the dough first and cover it with the onions and other toppings.

Or sprinkle on 2 tablespoons of drained capers.

---

4 tablespoons olive oil
2 pounds sweet onions, peeled and thinly sliced
Salt and freshly ground black pepper to taste
1 recipe pizza dough, ready to use
1 2-ounce can anchovies, drained
12 to 15 oil-cured black olives

Pizza Bianca alla Palmero

Yield: 1 15- to 18-inch round pie.
Serves 6 to 8 as an appetizer or side dish.
Crust Suggestions: Basic Pizza, Sicilian-style, Semolina, Pepper-Lard, Sausage, or *Prosciutto* dough.
Method: Direct stone baking or a prepared pizza pan.

HERE IS A RECIPE from the sunny south of Italy—deep in pizza country. The flavor and texture of the mozzarella are greatly improved by marinating it in olive oil and seasonings for a while before baking. This pizza is not a main-course pizza but more of a side dish, to be served along with salad or soup or cut into thin wedges as a snack or appetizer.

1 **pound mozzarella, cut into 1-inch cubes**
2 **tablespoons chopped fresh herbs, such as basil, parsley, or marjoram, or any one or combination**
4 **tablespoons olive oil Coarsely ground black pepper to taste**
1 **recipe pizza dough, ready to use**
1 **2-ounce can anchovies, drained**
10 **to 15 oil-cured black olives**

1. Combine the mozzarella, fresh herbs, olive oil, and black pepper in a small bowl. Let the mixture marinate at room temperature for 1 hour before using.

2. Preheat the oven to 500 degrees for at least 30 minutes for a pizza pan or 60 minutes for pizza tiles or stones.

3. Lightly coat a large pizza pan with vegetable oil and sprinkle it lightly with coarsely ground yellow cornmeal. Or lightly coat a large pizza screen with oil or a pizza peel with flour.

4. Roll out or stretch the dough into a thin circle and fit it onto the prepared pan, screen, or peel.

5. Spread the marinated mozzarella over the crust and distribute the anchovies and black olives over the cheese.

6. Bake for 10 to 15 minutes, or until the crust is golden and the cheese is bubbly.

Pizza con Quattro Formaggio (Four-Cheese Pizza)

Yield: 1 15-inch round pie.
Serves 4 to 6 as a main course or 6 to 8 as an appetizer.
Crust Suggestions: Basic Pizza, Sicilian-style, Semolina, Pepper-Lard, Sausage, *Prosciutto*, or Herb doughs.
Method: Use a prepared pizza pan.

PROBABLY BASED ON the pasta dish with four cheeses, this variation comes from the northern part of Italy near the Piedmont region. Try varying the cheese on this pie. It is equally good with Bel Paese, Gorgonzola, and Gouda.

1. Preheat the oven to 400 degrees for 30 minutes.

2. Lightly coat a large pizza pan with vegetable oil and sprinkle cornmeal lightly over the bottom of the pan.

3. Roll out or stretch the dough into a circle and fit it onto the prepared pan. Let the dough rise in the pan while you prepare the filling.

4. Combine the ricotta, Parmesan, locatelli, mozzarella, pepper, herbs, and eggs together in a large bowl. *Do not overmix or the filling will turn green!*

5. Spread the filling out onto the crust leaving a 2-inch border of dough around the pizza. Fold the border back over the filling. (This will prevent the filling from leaking out.)

6. Bake for 25 to 30 minutes, or until the crust and filling are golden.

1 **recipe pizza dough, ready to use**
1 **pound ricotta**
¼ **cup freshly grated Parmesan cheese**
¼ **cup freshly grated locatelli or Romano cheese**
½ **pound mozzarella, roughly grated**
Freshly ground black pepper to taste
2 **tablespoons chopped fresh herbs, such as parsley, basil, mint, marjoram, or any combination of two herbs (Substitute 1 teaspoon of the dried herb for any fresh.)**
2 **eggs, lightly beaten with a fork**

Pizza Verdura Master Recipe

Yield: 1 15- to 18-inch round pie.

Serves 4 as a main course or 6 to 8 as an appetizer.

Crust Suggestions: Basic Pizza, Sicilian-style, Semolina, Pepper-Lard, Sausage, or *Prosciutto* dough.

Method: Direct stone baking or a prepared pizza pan.

THESE TASTY PIES, flavored with cheese and bits of ham, sun-dried tomatoes, and the like, are a feast for the eyes as well as the mouth. Good hot or cold, they are one of the best ways to get children to eat their greens.

1. Preheat the oven to 500 degrees for 30 minutes for a pizza pan or 60 minutes for pizza tiles or stones.

2. Lightly coat a large pizza pan with vegetable oil and sprinkle it lightly with coarsely ground yellow cornmeal. Or lightly coat a large pizza screen with oil or a peel with flour.

3. Roll out or stretch the dough into a thin circle and fit it onto the prepared pan, screen, or peel.

4. Spread the sliced or cubed cheese over the dough shell. Then spread the cooked greens over the cheese and sprinkle the remaining ingredients over the greens.

5. Bake for 10 to 15 minutes, or until the crust is golden and the topping is bubbly.

Pizza alla Verdura I (Spinach-Cheese Pizza)

1 recipe pizza dough, ready to use

½ pound mozzarella, thinly sliced

1 recipe well-drained Italian Greens made with spinach (see recipe page 80)

¼ cup freshly grated Parmesan cheese

2 tablespoons olive oil

Variations

Substitute ½ pound Fontina or Gouda cheese for the mozzarella and break 2 or 3 extra large eggs over the pie during the final 5 minutes of baking.

Add 5 oil-packed sun-dried tomatoes to the filling and ½ pound peeled and deveined shrimp during the final 5 minutes of baking.

Pizza alla Verdura II

1 recipe pizza dough,
ready to use
½ pound smoked
mozzarella, thinly sliced
1 recipe well-drained Italian Greens made with
broccoli rabe (see rec-
ipe page 80)
½ pound mushrooms,
cleaned, thinly sliced,
and sautéed in 1 table-
spoon of olive oil until
all of their excess liquid
has evaporated
2 tablespoons olive oil

Pizza Erbazzone alla Romana

1 recipe pizza dough,
ready to use
½ pound mozzarella,
thinly sliced
1 recipe well-drained Italian Greens made with
escarole (see recipe
page 80)
1 2-ounce can anchovies,
drained
1 tablespoon drained
capers
15 oil-cured black olives
2 tablespoons olive oil

Pizza alla Erbazzone

1 recipe pizza dough,
ready to use
1½ cups caciocavallo,
Gruyère, Gouda, or Bel
Paese cheese cut into
1-inch cubes
1 recipe well-drained Italian Greens (see recipe
page 80)
4 ounces *prosciutto*, cut
into ½-inch cubes
2 tablespoons olive oil

Pizza alla Verdura d'Abruzzi

1 recipe pizza dough,
ready to use
½ pound scamorza or
mozzarella, thinly sliced
1 recipe well-drained Italian Greens made with
broccoli and adding 1
whole partially crushed
red pepper to the initial
cooking (see recipe
page 80)
2 tablespoons olive oil

Pizzette Master Recipe

Yield: 6 6-inch appetizer size or 10 to 12 4-inch party size *pizzette*.

Crust Suggestions: Basic Pizza, Sicilian-style, Semolina, Pepper-Lard, Sausage, *Prosciutto*, Herb, or Onion dough.

Method: A large prepared baking sheet will bake the *pizzette* in batches like cookies.

PIZZETTE ARE NOT just miniature pizzas, they have their own identity. Their toppings are light, with a decidedly northern Italian flavor, and they are almost never made of more than three or four main ingredients. (More than that would offer too complex a mouthful of tastes, and since *pizzette* are meant to be savored in just a few bits, the flavors must be succinct and concentrated.) Color and arrangement of toppings on *pizzette* are very important, for the effect must be enticing. Because they can be made in advance and easily reheated, *pizzette* are usually offered on a tray with many different combinations.

In their smallest size, *pizzette* are savory tidbits that are perfect for buffets or cocktail parties. The larger size makes an original appetizer. Where you might once have served a wedge of quiche or even a pasta course, a *pizzette* is an unusual and delicious substitute.

1. Preheat the oven to 500 degrees for at least 30 minutes.
2. Lightly coat a baking sheet with vegetable oil.
3. Assemble all of the toppings.
4. Divide 1 recipe of pizza dough into 6 or 10 to 12 equal pieces and roll or press out each ball to the desired size.
5. Arrange the pizzettes on one or more prepared baking sheets and top with the filling of your choice.
6. Bake for 10 to 15 minutes, or until golden and crusty. If you wish to prepare them in advance, bake them for only 5 minutes, or until the crust puffs up and begins to color, and remove them to a wire rack to cool. They may be refrigerated for a day or two before being reheated but I do not recommend freezing, as this destroys their fresh taste. To reheat, preheat the oven to 500 degrees and bake them for 5 to 10 minutes. Serve hot or at room temperature.

Variations

All of the following fillings make great full size pizza, too. Just follow the Basic Pizza Dough recipe on page 56, for assembling a pizza and use any one of these fillings on it. Likewise any other topping can be substituted for *pizzette* by dividing it among them. Choose the simpler combinations for the best effect.

Mushroom, Béchamel, and Cheese Pizzette

THE CUISINE OF Piedmont in Italy has a decidedly French undertone. Where else would you eat pizza with Béchamel Sauce? If you think this combination is a bit rich, Waverley Root, in *The Food of Italy*, describes a similar *pizzette* to which freshly grated white truffle was added. Extravagant, yes, but absolutely scrumptious. Dried *porcini* or fresh golden oak mushrooms would also make an excellent and less expensive variation.

1. Proceed with the Master *Pizzette* Recipe for crust type, shaping, and baking, following steps 1 through 5.

2. Spread each *pizzette* with some Béchamel Sauce. Distribute the mushrooms over the sauce and top with the cheeses.

3. Dot each *pizzette* with butter and bake for 10 to 15 minutes, or until golden.

Variations

Soak 2 ounces of *porcini* in boiling water to cover for 10 minutes. Rinse them well to rid them of their sand. Chop them roughly and sauté them in 2 tablespoons of sweet butter for 3 minutes. Add the mushrooms to the Béchamel and proceed with the recipe.

Fresh golden oak (also known as shiitake mushrooms) or other wild mushrooms can be substituted for cultivated mushrooms. Halve the amount indicated in the recipe and prepare them in the same manner as regular mushrooms.

1 recipe pizza dough, ready to use

1 pound mushrooms, cleaned, thinly sliced, and sautéed in 2 tablespoons of butter until all their excess liquid has evaporated
Salt and freshly ground black pepper to taste

½ recipe Béchamel Sauce (see recipe page 78)

½ pound Gruyère cheese, freshly grated

2 tablespoons freshly grated Parmesan cheese

2 tablespoons sweet butter

Mozzarella Pizzette I

TENDER STRINGS OF fresh mozzarella, seasoned with fresh herbs and fruity green olive oil, offer sensations with every bite. Choose the best fresh cow's milk mozzarella or, if it's available, splurge on some creamy, authentic Italian buffalo milk mozzarella for these *pizzette*.

1 recipe pizza dough, ready to use

½ pound mozzarella, cut into ½-inch cubes

¼ cup freshly grated Parmesan cheese

2 tablespoons of any 1 or combination of fresh parsley, basil, mint, or marjoram leaves, or 1 pinch of dried herbs for each *pizzette*

2 tablespoons extra-virgin olive oil

1. Proceed with the Master *Pizzette* Recipe for crust type, shaping, and baking, following steps 1 through 5.

2. Lay the mozzarella on first, followed by a sprinkling of Parmesan and herbs on each *pizzette*. Drizzle a bit of the olive oil on each *pizzette* before baking.

3. Bake for 10 to 15 minutes, or until the cheese just melts into tender pools.

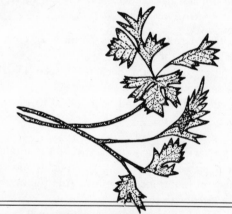

Mozzarella Pizzette II

HERE'S A MOZZARELLA *pizzette* with the salty accents of anchovies and olives. Try to find some imported Italian anchovies, such as Rizzoli Emanuelli & Co. from Parma, which are packed in extra-virgin olive oil and herbs. They are expensive but superb. Substitute the delicious oil in which the anchovies were packed for the green olive oil in the recipe to drizzle on top of each *pizzette* before baking.

1. Proceed with the Master *Pizzette* Recipe for crust type, shaping, and baking, following steps 1 through 5.

2. Lay the mozzarella on first, followed by the anchovies and olives on each *pizzette*.

3. Drizzle the olive oil over each *pizzette* and bake for 10 to 15 minutes.

1 **recipe pizza dough, ready to use**
½ **pound mozzarella, cut into ½-inch cubes**
1 **2-ounce can anchovies, drained**
24 **oil-cured black olives**
2 **to 3 tablespoons extra-virgin olive oil**

Mushroom, Fontina, and Parmesan Pizzette

THIS IS A MUCH lighter *pizzette* than the recipe on page 125.

1. Proceed with the Master *Pizzette* Recipe for crust type, shaping, and baking, following steps 1 through 5.

2. Distribute the mushrooms over each *pizzette* first. Then season them with salt and pepper and finish with layers of the Fontina and Parmesan cheese.

3. Dot each *pizzette* with butter and bake for 10 to 15 minutes.

Variation

Substitute ½ pound fresh wild mushrooms for the 1 pound of mushrooms in the recipe. The stronger flavor of fresh wild mushrooms makes a little go a long way.

1 **recipe pizza dough, ready to use**
1 **pound mushrooms, cleaned, thinly sliced, and sautéed in 2 tablespoons of butter until their excess liquid has evaporated**
 Salt and freshly ground black pepper to taste
½ **pound imported Italian Fontina or Gouda or other Fontina-type cheese, cut into ½-inch cubes**
2 **tablespoons freshly grated Parmesan cheese**
2 **tablespoons sweet butter**

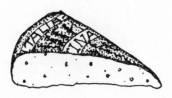

Gorgonzola, Ricotta, and Basil Pizzette

1 recipe pizza dough,
   ready to use
¼ pound Gorgonzola or
   other blue cheese,
   crumbled
½ pound ricotta
   Freshly ground black
   pepper to taste
¼ cup freshly grated Par-
   mesan cheese
10 to 12 tiny fresh basil
   leaves or fresh Italian
   parsley leaves
2 tablespoons sweet
   butter

1. Proceed with the Master *Pizzette* Recipe for crust type, shaping, and baking, following steps 1 through 5.

2. Mix together the Gorgonzola, ricotta, and black pepper in a medium-sized bowl with a fork and spread this mixture over each *pizzette*.

3. Sprinkle with the Parmesan. Garnish each *pizzette* with a basil leaf and dot with butter.

4. Bake for 10 to 15 minutes.

Tomato Pizzette Variations

Here are five variations on the *pizzette* theme that do honor to the tomato.

Tomato Pizzette Base

1 recipe pizza dough,
   ready to use
1 to 1½ pounds ripe to-
   matoes, seeded and
   roughly chopped, or 1
   cup well drained
   canned tomatoes,
   roughly chopped, or 10
   to 12 oil-packed sun-
   dried tomatoes, drained
   and roughly shredded

1. Proceed with the Basic Pizza Recipe on page 56 for crust type, shaping and baking, following steps 1 through 5.

2. Spread the tomatoes on each *pizzette* and the toppings of your choice in the order they are written. Dot each *pizzette* with either butter or drizzle with olive oil, depending on the variation.

3. Bake for 10 to 15 minutes.

Tomato Pizzette #1

1 cup Bel Paese, or other
semi-soft cheese, cut
into ½-inch cubes
2 tablespoons finely
minced fresh herbs,
such as parsley, basil,
mint, chervil, chives, or
marjoram, separately or
in combination
3 tablespoons sweet
butter

Tomato Pizzette #2

¼ cup freshly grated Par-
mesan cheese
2 garlic cloves, peeled
and minced
2 tablespoons finely
minced fresh herbs,
such as parsley, basil,
mint, chervil, chives, or
marjoram, separately or
in combination
2 tablespoons extra-virgin
olive oil

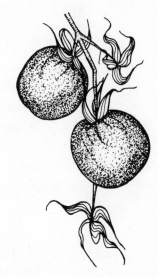

Tomato Pizzette #3

1 small sweet green pep-
per, seeded and thinly
sliced
1 2-ounce can anchovies,
drained
1 pinch marjoram per
pizzette
2 tablespoons extra-virgin
olive oil

Tomato Pizzette #4

1 2-ounce can anchovies,
drained
10 to 12 oil-cured black
olives
2 tablespoons extra-virgin
olive oil

Tomato Pizzette #5

1 small sweet red onion,
sliced paper thin
2 tablespoons drained
capers
2 tablespoons extra-virgin
olive oil

11.

MORE CLASSIC
PIZZA

The following pizza variations have no particular namesakes. Some of them are combinations which were described to me, but most of the others are my own contributions to the genre. For convenience's sake, I have grouped these recipes by main ingredient, so if you are in the mood for, say, zucchini pizza, look up the zucchini variations.

Sausage, Cheese, Tomato, and Onion Pizza

Yield: 1 15- to 18-inch round pie.
Serves 4 as a main course or 6 to 8 as an appetizer.
Crust Suggestions: Basic Pizza, Sicilian-style, Semolina, Pepper-Lard, or Whole Wheat I or II dough.
Method: Direct stone baking or a prepared pizza pan.

THIS IS A THOROUGHLY satisfying pizza, with chewy pieces of sausage, crisp onions, gooey cheese, and just a dash of sharp Romano cheese to give it a charge.

1 recipe pizza dough, ready to use
½ pound mozzarella, thinly sliced
1 cup Basic Pizza Sauce (see recipe page 72)
½ pound hot or sweet Italian sausage meat, removed from the casings and crumbled
1 small sweet onion, sliced paper thin
2 tablespoons freshly grated Romano cheese
2 tablespoons olive oil

1. Preheat the oven to 500 degrees for 30 minutes for a pizza pan or 60 minutes for pizza tiles or stones.

2. Lightly coat a large pizza pan with vegetable oil and sprinkle it lightly with coarsely ground yellow cornmeal. Or lightly coat a large pizza screen with oil or a pizza peel with flour.

3. Roll out or stretch the dough into a thin circle and fit it onto the prepared pan, screen, or peel.

4. Lay the mozzarella over the dough shell. Spoon the sauce over the cheese and then distribute the sausage meat and onion over the sauce. Sprinkle with the Romano and olive oil before baking.

5. Bake for 10 to 15 minutes.

Sausage, Onion, Pepper, and Egg Pizza

(Italian Breakfast Pizza)

> Yield: 1 15-inch round pie, *or* 1 12- by 17-inch rectangular pie.
> Serves 4 as a main course or 6 to 8 as a side dish.
>
> Crust Suggestions: Basic Pizza, Sicilian-style, Pepper-Lard, Semolina, Herb, Cheese, or Whole Wheat II dough.
>
> Method: Use a prepared pizza pan with a rim.

PIZZA-LOVERS EVERYWHERE have been known to eat cold pizza for breakfast, but few are aware that they are carrying on an age-old custom. The Roman legions, who had originally adapted the dish of "bread with a relish" from the Greeks, also started their day by eating pizza. If pizza for breakfast provided the Romans with enough energy to build an empire, think what it can do for you! Breakfast pizza does *not* have to be last night's leftover anchovy-onion pie, though. It can be a whole new kind of meal.

A pizza brunch makes perfect sense. It's delicious and an extremely easy way of dealing with a crowd. Have you ever tried to make sausages, eggs, toast, and hashbrowns for a large group of people? Pizza can be made up of any number of traditional breakfast components, all baked right in one dish. Sausage, peppers, onions, tomatoes, spinach, cheese, and eggs might all go on breakfast pizza. The dough can be prepared the night before and left to rise overnight in the refrigerator. The fillings can also be prepared in advance, but the eggs must be added at the last moment. Eating this pizza is rather like eating a thick filled omelet on top of a crusty slab of homemade bread.

1. Heat the oil in a large frying pan and sauté the onion and peppers over medium-high heat for about 5 minutes, or until they are tender. Set aside until needed.

2. Preheat the oven to 500 degrees for 30 minutes.

3. Lightly coat a large pizza pan with a rim with vegetable oil and sprinkle it lightly with coarsely ground cornmeal. Press the dough out in the pan with your fingertips, building up an edge about 1½ inches high along the sides of the pan.

4 tablespoons olive oil
1 medium-sized sweet onion, peeled and chopped
2 sweet green peppers, seeded and chopped
1 recipe pizza dough, ready to use
½ pound Fontina cheese, cut into ½-inch cubes

1 **pound Italian or other
sausage meat, removed
from the casings and
roughly crumbled**
6 **extra large eggs, lightly
beaten
Salt and freshly ground
black pepper to taste**

4. Mix the onion and peppers with the Fontina, sausage meat, and eggs together in a large bowl. Season the mixture with salt and pepper.
5. Bake the pie for 15 to 20 minutes, or until it is golden and puffy.

Other Breakfast Pizzas

Fogatz di San Gennaro
Sausage, Onion, Pepper, and Egg Pizza
Pizza Primavera
Spanish Tortilla Pizza
Ham, Cheese, and Sun-Dried Tomato Calzone
Manhattan Breakfast Calzone
Western Breakfast Calzone
Riviera Breakfast Calzone
Eppi Roll
Spinach-Fontina-Ham Roll
Prosciutto, Smoked Mozzarella, and Sun-Dried Tomato Roll
Torta Rustica
Pizza with Smoked Salmon and Golden Caviar

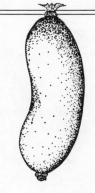

Bucci's Homemade Sausage Pizza

Yield: 1 12- by 17-inch pie.
Serves 4 to 6 as a main course.
Crust Suggestions: Sicilian-style II dough.
Method: A prepared 12- by 17-inch pizza pan.

BUCCI'S SAUSAGE PIZZA was the first pizza I ever had of its kind, and it has been the model against which I have measured all homemade pies ever since. This combination of thick, chewy crust, hearty meat sauce and thick cheese seems to have a similar effect on whoever tastes it. It is far and away the most popular pizza among my students at the pizza workshop.

1. Preheat the oven to 450 degrees for 30 minutes.
2. Lightly coat a jelly roll pan with vegetable oil and sprinkle it lightly with coarsely ground yellow cornmeal.
3. Press the dough into the pan with your fingertips and make sure it comes up the sides of the pan about 1 inch.
4. Use a slotted spoon to ladle the sauce over the dough. (You will have a little liquid leftover. Use it on pasta or on *foccacia*.)
5. Let the dough rise in the pan for 30 minutes before baking.
6. Bake the pie for 20 to 25 minutes in all. Add the cheese during the final 5 minutes of baking.

1 recipe Sicilian-style II Dough, ready to use
4 cups Bucci's Sausage Sauce (see recipe page 76)
12 ounces mozzarella, thinly sliced

Spicy Eggplant Pizza

Yield: 1 15- to 18-inch round pie.
Serves 4 as a main course or 6 to 8 as an appetizer.
Crust Suggestions: Basic Pizza, Sicilian-style, Semolina, Pepper-Lard, or Whole Wheat I dough.
Method: Use a prepared 15-inch pizza pan.

EGGPLANT IS TERRIFIC on pizza. Its smoky flavor and meaty texture make it a viable replacement for meat, at a considerable savings in cost and calories.

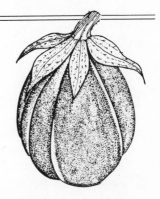

1. Heat ¼ cup of the olive oil in a medium-sized frying pan. Add the eggplant cubes and hot red pepper and sauté over medium heat for about 10 minutes, or until the eggplant is just tender but not mushy. Discard the hot red pepper and set the eggplant aside until needed.
2. Preheat the oven to 500 degrees for 30 minutes.
3. Lightly coat a large pizza pan with vegetable oil and sprinkle it lightly with coarsely ground yellow cornmeal.
3. Roll out or stretch the dough into a thin circle and fit it onto the prepared pan.
4. Lay the cheese over the dough shell. Spoon the Pizza Sauce over the cheese and then distribute the garlic and reserved eggplant over the pie. Sprinkle the remaining 2 tablespoons of olive oil over the pie.
5. Bake for 10 to 15 minutes, or until the crust is golden.

¼ cup plus 2 tablespoons olive oil
1 pound unpeeled eggplant, trimmed and cut into 1-inch cubes
1 whole dried hot red pepper, broken in half
1 recipe pizza dough, ready to use
½ pound mozzarella, thinly sliced
1 cup Basic Pizza Sauce (see recipe page 72)
2 garlic cloves, minced

Deep-Dish Eggplant-Sausage Pizza

Yield: 1 15- to 16-inch pie.
Serves 6 as a main course.
Crust Suggestions: Basic Pizza, Sicilian-style I or II, Pepper-Lard, Semolina, or Whole Wheat II dough.
Method: Use a deep dish pizza pan that has been prepared with vegetable oil and cornmeal. The Sicilian-style II dough will make a 12- by 17-inch large pie; any of the others will make a 15-inch round or 16-inch square, thick-crusted pie.

IN THIS RECIPE, the eggplant is cooked in a rich meaty sauce, and the result is a hearty, stew-like consistency. This substantial filling requires a deep-dish crust.

1 **recipe pizza dough, ready to use**
4 **cups Eggplant-Sausage Sauce (see recipe page 76)**
12 **ounces mozzarella, thinly sliced**

1. Preheat the oven to 400 degrees. Lightly coat a deep-dish pizza pan with vegetable oil and sprinkle it lightly with coarsely ground yellow cornmeal.

2. Press the dough out into the pan with your fingertips and build up an edge along the sides of the pan. This edge will act as a wall to hold the topping.

3. Spread the sauce over the dough and let the pie rise in the pan for 20 minutes before baking.

4. Bake for 35 to 40 minutes. Then make a layer of the mozzarella on top of the sauce and bake the pie for 5 to 10 minutes longer. Let the pie sit for 5 to 10 minutes before cutting it.

Note: For Deep-Dish Eggplant-Zucchini Pizza see the sauce variation on page 76.

Eggplant Pizza Parmigiana

Yield: 1 15- to 16-inch pie.
Serves 4 as a main course or 6 to 8 as an appetizer.
Crust Suggestions: Basic Pizza, Sicilian-style, Pepper-Lard, Semolina, Sausage or *Prosciutto*, or Whole Wheat II dough.
Method: Use a prepared pizza pan

THE ORIGINAL IDEA for this recipe came from eggplant Parmigiana. Here I have skipped the egg-and bread-crumb coating in favor of frying the eggplant slices directly in olive oil for a much lighter effect. The slices are sautéed very briefly and finished on top of the pie until they are tender. The trick here is not to add the cheese until the eggplant is just cooked or, it will get overbrowned and tough.

1. Heat the olive oil in a heavy frying pan and fry the eggplant slices over medium heat until they are tender, about 5 to 7 minutes. Turn the slices once as they cook. Add additional oil to the pan, if necessary, to fry all the eggplant slices. Remove the cooked eggplant slices to a plate and sprinkle them with salt and pepper. Set the eggplant slices aside until needed. (See Note.)

2. Preheat the oven to 500 degrees for 30 minutes. Lightly coat a large pizza pan with vegetable oil and sprinkle it lightly with coarsely ground yellow cornmeal.

3. Roll out or stretch the dough and fit it onto the prepared pan.

4. Sprinkle with herbs and cheese.

5. Spread the pizza sauce over the dough and arrange the eggplant slices in a single layer over the sauce.

6. Bake for 15 to 20 minutes. Then make a layer of the mozzarella over the eggplant slices and bake for 5 to 10 minutes longer, or until the cheese is just melted.

Note: If you want, you can avoid frying the eggplant slices, and bake them instead. Coat a baking pan large enough to hold the eggplant slices in 1 layer with 2 tablespoons of the olive oil. Lay the eggplant slices in the pan and brush them equally with the remaining oil. Bake in a preheated 400-degree oven for 20 minutes, or until just tender. Then proceed with the recipe.

4 tablespoons olive oil
1 pound unpeeled eggplant, trimmed and cut into ¼-inch thick slices
Salt and freshly ground black pepper to taste
1 recipe pizza dough, ready to use
1 cup Basic Pizza Sauce (see recipe on page 72)
5 to 6 fresh basil leaves, or ½ teaspoon dried marjoram or dried oregano
3 tablespoons freshly grated Parmesan cheese
½ pound mozzarella, thinly sliced

Smoked Mozzarella and Tomato Pizza

Yield: 1 15- to 18-inch round pizza.
Serves 4 as a main course or 6 to 8 as an appetizer.
Crust suggestions: Basic Pizza, Sicilian-style, Semolina, Pepper-Lard, or Herb dough.
Method: Direct stone baking or a prepared pizza pan.

ONE OF THE MOST frequent questions put to me is, "What is your favorite pizza?" I generally reply, "Whichever one I happen to be eating," but smoked mozzarella and tomato pizza is one of my favorites. The combination of mozzarella and tomato on pizza is heavenly bliss! The secret is to marinate the mozzarella in extra-virgin olive oil with crushed garlic, fresh basil, and black pepper for a few hours.

12 ounces smoked mozzarella or plain mozzarella, cut into ¼-inch-thick slices
¼ cup extra-virgin olive oil
6 large fresh basil leaves, shredded, or 1 teaspoon mixed dried *herbes de Provence*
2 garlic cloves, peeled and crushed
Freshly ground black pepper to taste
1 recipe pizza dough, ready to use
1½ pounds fresh tomatoes, seeded and roughly chopped, or 1 28-ounce can whole tomatoes, well drained and roughly chopped

1. Mix the mozzarella with the olive oil, basil, garlic, and black pepper in a shallow bowl. Let the mixture marinate at room temperature for 1 to 2 hours or more.

2. Preheat the oven to 500 degrees for 30 minutes for a pizza pan and 60 minutes for pizza tiles or stones.

3. Lightly coat a large pizza pan with vegetable oil and sprinkle it with coarsely ground yellow cornmeal. Or lightly coat a large pizza screen with oil or a peel with flour.

4. Roll out or stretch the dough into a thin circle and fit it onto the prepared pan screen, or peel.

5. Spread the marinated mozzarella over the dough first and cover it with the tomatoes. Drizzle any oil from the bowl over the pie before baking.

6. Bake for 10 to 15 minutes.

Deep-Dish Mushroom Pizza

Yield: Serves 6 as a main course.
Crust Suggestions: Basic Pizza, Sicilian-style II, Pepper-Lard, or Whole Wheat II dough.
Method: Use a 15- or 16-inch deep-dish round pizza pan or a 12- by 17-inch rectangular pan for Sicilian-style II.

1. Heat 4 tablespoons of the olive oil in a large frying pan and add the mushrooms and onion. Sauté over medium heat until the mushroom liquid has evaporated and the onion is translucent. Remove the vegetables to a bowl and set aside until needed.

2. Heat 4 more tablespoons of the olive oil in the same frying pan. Add the eggplant cubes and sauté them for about 10 minutes, or until the eggplant is tender. Transfer the eggplant cubes to the bowl with the mushrooms and onion and stir in the Basic Pizza Sauce. Set aside until needed.

3. Preheat the oven to 400 degrees for 30 minutes.

4. Lightly coat a large pizza pan with vegetable oil and sprinkle it lightly with coarsely ground yellow cornmeal. Press the dough into the prepared pan with your fingertips and build up an outer edge about 1 inch high along the sides of the pan. This edge will help to hold in the topping.

5. Spread the vegetable-sauce mixture over the dough shell and sprinkle with the Parmesan cheese. Drizzle the remaining 2 tablespoons of olive oil over the pie before baking.

6. Bake for 20 to 25 minutes. Then distribute the Fontina cheese on top of the pie and bake for 5 to 10 minutes longer. Let the pie rest for 5 to 10 minutes before slicing for a neater presentation.

10 tablespoons olive oil
2 pounds fresh mushrooms, cleaned and thinly sliced
1 small sweet onion, peeled and minced
½ pound unpeeled eggplant, cut into 1-inch cubes
1½ cups Basic Pizza Sauce (see recipe page 72)
1 recipe pizza dough, ready to use
2 tablespoons freshly grated Parmesan cheese
½ pound Italian Fontina cheese, cut into 1-inch cubes

Mushroom, Salami, and Mozzarella Pizza

Yield: 1 15- to 18-inch round pie.

Serves 4 as a main course or 6 to 8 as an appetizer.

Crust Suggestions: Basic Pizza, Sicilian-style, Semolina, Pepper-Lard, Whole Wheat I, or Onion dough.

Method: Direct stone baking or a prepared pizza pan.

HERE'S ANOTHER CLASSIC. For this pie, use only excellent-grade salami—Genoa, Sicilian, or Soprasatta style.

3 tablespoons olive oil
1 pound fresh mush-
  rooms, cleaned and
  thinly sliced
1 recipe pizza dough,
  ready to use
½ pound mozzarella,
  thinly sliced
1 cup Basic Pizza Sauce
  (see recipe page 72)
1 cup salami or any other
  kind of dried sausage,
  cut into ½-inch cubes

1. Heat 1 tablespoon of the olive oil in a large frying pan. Add the mushroom slices and sauté until all the mushroom liquid has evaporated. Transfer the mushrooms to a plate and set them aside until needed.

2. Preheat the oven to 500 degrees for 30 minutes for a pizza pan or 60 minutes for pizza tiles and stones.

3. Lightly coat a large pizza pan with vegetable oil and sprinkle it lightly with coarsely ground yellow cornmeal. Or lightly coat a large pizza screen with oil or a peel with flour.

4. Roll out or stretch the dough into a thin circle and fit it onto the prepared pan, screen, or peel.

5. Lay the cheese over the dough shell. Then spoon the sauce over the cheese. Distribute the mushrooms and salami cubes over the sauce. Drizzle the remaining 2 tablespoons of olive oil over the pie.

6. Bake for 10 to 15 minutes, or until the crust is golden.

Mushroom-Tomato Pizza

Yield: 1 15- to 18-inch round pie.

Serves 4 as a main course or 6 to 8 as an appetizer.

Crust Suggestions: Basic Pizza, Sicilian-style, Semolina, Pepper-Lard, Sausage, *Prosciutto*, or Cheese dough.

Method: Direct stone baking or a prepared pizza pan.

MUSHROOMS TOSSED WITH lemon, garlic, and parsley make a sensational combination. If you omit the olive oil and use a nonstick pan to cook the mushrooms, this pizza becomes a low-calorie treat.

1. Toss the cleaned, sliced mushrooms with the lemon juice in a bowl and set aside.

2. Heat 3 tablespoons of the olive oil in a large frying pan and sauté the mushrooms over high heat, until all of their excess liquid has evaporated. Season with salt and pepper and chopped parsley and remove from the heat.

3. Preheat the oven to 500 degrees for a pizza pan or 60 minutes for pizza tiles or stones.

4. Lightly coat a large pizza pan with vegetable oil and sprinkle it lightly with coarsely ground yellow cornmeal. Or lightly coat a large pizza screen with oil or a peel with flour.

5. Roll out or stretch the dough into a thin circle and fit it onto the prepared pan, screen, or peel.

6. Spread the tomato sauce over the dough shell. Then lay the mushrooms over the sauce. Sprinkle the garlic and remaining 2 tablespoons of olive oil over the pie.

7. Bake for 10 to 15 minutes, or until the crust is golden.

Variation:

Lay ½ pound of mozzarella or Fontina cheese, cut into ½-inch cubes down before the sauce and continue with the recipe.

2 **pounds fresh mushrooms, cleaned and thinly sliced**
 Juice of ½ lemon
5 **tablespoons olive oil**
 Salt and freshly ground black pepper to taste
2 **tablespoons chopped fresh parsley leaves or basil leaves**
1 **recipe pizza dough, ready to use**
1 **cup Basic Pizza Sauce (see recipe 72)**
2 **garlic cloves, peeled and minced**

Green Pepper, Tomato, and Cheese Pizza

Yield: 1 15- to 18-inch round pie.
Serves 4 as a main course or 6 to 8 as an appetizer.
Crust Suggestions: Basic Pizza, Sicilian-style, Semolina, Pepper-Lard, or Whole Wheat I dough.
Method: Direct stone baking or a prepared pizza pan.

SWEET, CRISP GREEN PEPPERS star on this pizza.

1. Preheat the oven to 500 degrees for 30 minutes for a pizza pan or 60 minutes for pizza tiles or stones.

2. Lightly coat a large pizza pan with vegetable oil and sprinkle it lightly with coarsely ground yellow cornmeal. Or lightly coat a large pizza screen with oil or a peel with flour.

3. Roll out or stretch the dough into a thin circle and fit it onto the prepared pan, screen, or peel.

1 **recipe pizza dough, ready to use**
½ **pound mozzarella, thinly sliced**
1 **cup Basic Pizza Sauce (see recipe page 72)**
2 **garlic cloves, peeled and minced**

1 tablespoon drained
   capers
2 tablespoons freshly
   grated Romano cheese
1 large sweet green pep-
   per, seeded and thinly
   sliced
1 teaspoon dried oregano
2 tablespoons olive oil

4. Lay the mozzarella over the dough shell and spoon the Pizza Sauce over the cheese. Then distribute the garlic, capers, Romano cheese, and green peppers over the sauce. Sprinkle the oregano and olive oil over the pie.

5. Bake for 10 to 15 minutes, or until the crust is golden.

Roasted Red Pepper and Bel Paese Pizza

Yield: 1 15- to 18-inch round pie.

Serves 4 as a main course or 6 to 8 as an appetizer.

Crust Suggestions: Basic Pizza, Sicilian-style, Semolina, or Pepper-Lard dough.

Method: Direct stone baking or a prepared pizza pan.

THIS COMBINATION OF tangy red peppers and smooth Bel Paese cheese is inspired. The process of roasting brings out the complex flavors of the red peppers, rendering them sweet and smoky, and their flavor is further enhanced by being marinated in olive oil and black pepper. Enjoy this pizza piping hot from the oven.

3 pounds sweet red
   peppers
4 tablespoons extra-virgin
   olive oil
   Freshly ground black
   pepper to taste
1 recipe pizza dough,
   ready to use
1 pound Bel Paese
   cheese, cut into 1-inch
   cubes

1. Roast the red peppers in a low pan, 6 inches below a high broiler flame for approximately 20 minutes, or until the peppers are black. Keep turning the peppers over with tongs as the skin blisters until they are evenly blackened on all sides. Transfer the peppers to a large mixing bowl, cover tightly with plastic wrap, and let them stand for 10 minutes before peeling. The peppers will steam a bit in the bowl, making it easier to remove their skins. Peel the skins off with a small paring knife or with your fingers.

2. Mix the peeled peppers with the olive oil and season them with the black pepper. Marinate at room temperature for at least 2 hours before using. The peppers will keep for up to a month in the refrigerator if they are completely covered with oil and stored in an airtight container.

3. Preheat the oven to 500 degrees for 30 minutes for a pizza pan or 60 minutes for pizza tiles or stones.

4. Lightly coat a large pizza pan with vegetable oil and sprinkle it lightly with coarsely ground yellow cornmeal. Or lightly coat a large pizza screen with oil or a peel with flour.

5. Roll out or stretch the dough into a thin circle and fit it onto the prepared pan, screen, or peel.

6. Lay the cheese over the dough shell. Then spread the peppers and their marinade over the shell. Sprinkle the garlic over the pie.

7. Bake for 10 to 15 minutes, or until the crust is golden.

2 **garlic cloves, peeled and minced**

Tomato, Salami, Onion, Olive, and Caper Pizza

Yield: 1 15- to 18-inch round pie.
Serves 4 as a main course or 6 to 8 as an appetizer.
Crust Suggestions: Basic Pizza, Sicilian-style, Semolina, Pepper-Lard, Herb, or Whole Wheat I dough.
Method: Direct stone baking or a prepared pizza pan.

1. Preheat the oven to 500 degrees for 30 minutes for a pizza pan or 60 minutes for pizza tiles or stones.

2. Lightly coat a large pizza pan with vegetable oil and sprinkle it lightly with coarsely ground yellow cornmeal. Or lightly coat a large pizza screen with oil or a peel with flour.

3. Roll out or stretch the dough into a thin circle and fit it onto the prepared pan, screen, or peel.

4. Spread the sauce over the dough shell with a spoon and lay the salami, onion, olives, and capers over the sauce. Sprinkle the herbs and olive oil over the pie before baking.

5. Bake for 10 to 15 minutes.

Variations

Add 1 2-ounce can anchovies, drained, or 1 4-ounce can sardines, drained, or 1 4-ounce can Italian-style tuna packed in olive oil, drained and roughly crumbled.

1 **recipe pizza dough, ready to use**
1 **cup Basic Pizza Sauce (see recipe page 72)**
1 **cup diced salami**
1 **small sweet onion, sliced paper thin**
15 **oil-cured black olives**
2 **tablespoons drained capers**
1 **teaspoon dried marjoram or dried oregano**
2 **tablespoons olive oil**

Tomato, Cheese, and Hot Pepper Pizza

Yield: 1 15- to 18-inch round pie.
Serves 4 as a main course or 6 to 8 as an appetizer.
Crust Suggestions: Basic Pizza, Sicilian-style, Semolina, Pepper-Lard, Sausage, or Whole Wheat I or II dough.
Method: Direct stone baking or a prepared pizza pan.

Some like it hot. If you do, this is the pizza for you. Don't seed the peppers, or they will lose much of their potency. Two whole, fresh hot peppers ring two alarms, and three mean fiery pizza!

1 **recipe pizza dough, ready to use**
½ **pound mozzarella, thinly sliced**
1 **cup Basic Pizza Sauce (see recipe page 72)**
2 **to 3 hot green chile peppers, minced**
2 **garlic cloves, peeled and minced**
½ **small sweet onion, sliced paper thin**
12 **to 15 oil-cured black olives**
2 **tablespoons olive oil**

1. Preheat the oven to 500 degrees for 30 minutes for a pizza pan or 60 minutes for pizza tiles or stones.

2. Lightly coat a large pizza pan with vegetable oil and sprinkle it lightly with coarsely ground yellow cornmeal. Or lightly coat a large pizza screen with oil or a peel with flour.

3. Roll out or stretch the dough into a thin circle and fit it onto the prepared pan, screen, or peel.

4. Lay the mozzarella down on top of the dough shell first. Then spread spoonfuls of the sauce over the cheese. Distribute the hot peppers, garlic, onion, and olives over the sauce. Drizzle with the olive oil.

5. Bake for 10 to 15 minutes, or until the crust is golden.

Tomato-Pesto Pizza

Yield: 1 15- to 18-inch round pie.
Serves 4 as a main course or 6 to 8 as an appetizer.
Crust Suggestions: Basic Pizza, Sicilian-style, Pepper-Lard, Sausage, *Prosciutto*, or Onion dough.
Method: Direct stone baking or a prepared pizza pan.

PESTO-INFUSED MOZZARELLA is the heart of this pizza. When fresh basil is not available, try fresh mint or parsley for a very different flavor.

1. Mix the *Pesto*, Parmesan cheese, garlic, and black pepper together in a shallow bowl. Then add the mozzarella. Mix all the ingredients together and marinate at room temperature for at least 1 hour.

2. Preheat the oven to 500 degrees for 30 minutes for a pizza pan or 60 minutes for pizza tiles or stones.

3. Lightly coat a large pizza pan with vegetable oil and sprinkle it lightly with coarsely ground yellow cornmeal. Or lightly coat a large pizza screen with oil or a peel with flour.

4. Roll out or stretch the dough into a thin circle and fit it onto the prepared pan, screen, or peel.

5. Spread the marinated cheese over the dough and cover the cheese with the tomatoes.

6. Bake for 10 to 15 minutes, or until golden and crusty.

¾ cup **Pesto** (see recipe page 82)

4 tablespoons freshly grated Parmesan cheese

1 garlic clove, peeled and crushed
Freshly ground black pepper to taste

½ pound mozzarella, cut into ¼-inch-thick slices

1 recipe pizza dough, ready to use

1½ pounds fresh tomatoes, seeded and roughly chopped, or 1 28-ounce can whole tomatoes, well drained and roughly chopped

Tomato-Gorgonzola Pizza

Yield: 1 15- to 18-inch round pie.

Serves 4 as a main course or 6 to 8 as an appetizer.

Crust Suggestions: Basic Pizza, Sicilian-style, Semolina, Sausage, *Prosciutto,* or Pepper-Lard dough.

Method: Direct stone baking or a prepared pizza pan.

PUNGENT GORGONZOLA CHEESE adds just the right amount of zest to this pizza. Any blue-veined cheese will give excellent results.

1 recipe pizza dough, ready to use

1 cup crumbled Gorgonzola cheese or other blue cheese

2 pounds fresh tomatoes, seeded and roughly chopped, or 1 28-ounce can whole tomatoes, well drained and roughly chopped

7 fresh basil leaves, shredded

1. Preheat the oven to 500 degrees for 30 minutes for a pizza pan or 60 minutes for pizza tiles or stones.

2. Lightly coat a large pizza pan with vegetable oil and sprinkle it lightly with coarsely ground yellow cornmeal. Or lightly coat a large pizza screen with oil or a peel with flour.

3. Roll out or stretch the dough into a thin circle and fit it onto the prepared pan, screen, or peel.

4. Spread the cheese over the dough and lay the tomatoes over the cheese. Garnish the pie with the basil and bake for 10 to 15 minutes.

Variation

A combination of ¼ pound cubed mozzarella plus ¼ pound crumbled Gorgonzola produces a more mellow taste.

Sun-Dried Tomato and Mozzarella Pizza

Yield: 1 15- to 18-inch round pie.

Serves 6 to 8 as an appetizer.

Crust Suggestions: Basic Pizza, Sicilian-style, Semolina, Pepper-Lard, Sausage, *Prosciutto,* or Whole Wheat I dough.

Method: Direct stone baking or a prepared pizza pan.

WHEN YOU CAN'T get good fresh tomatoes, bring back the bright taste of summer with sun-dried tomatoes. Their sun-sealed goodness give pizza a unique flavor. Pair them with tender zucchini and rich Fontina cheese and you have another taste delight.

1. Preheat the oven to 500 degrees for 30 minutes if using a pizza pan or 60 minutes for pizza tiles or stones.

2. Lightly coat a large pizza pan with vegetable oil and sprinkle it lightly with coarsely ground yellow cornmeal. Or lightly coat a large pizza screen with oil or a pizza peel with flour.

3. Roll out or stretch the dough into a thin circle and fit it onto the prepared pan, screen, or peel.

4. Lay the cheese over the dough shell. Spread the tomatoes (and/or zucchini) over the cheese and sprinkle the herbs, garlic, and olive oil over the pie.

5. Bake for 10 to 15 minutes, or until the pie is golden and bubbly.

1 recipe pizza dough, ready to use

12 ounces mozzarella, thinly sliced

10 whole oil-packed sun-dried tomatoes, drained and coarsely shredded

5 to 6 fresh basil leaves, or 1 teaspoon dried basil

2 garlic cloves, peeled and minced

3 tablespoons oil from the sun-dried tomatoes or olive oil

Variation

For Sun-Dried Tomato, Zucchini, and Fontina Pizza, use the following ingredients and the instructions above:

1 recipe pizza dough, ready to use

½ pound Italian Fontina cheese, cut into 1-inch cubes

2 small zucchini, washed, trimmed, and thinly sliced

7 whole oil-packed sun-dried tomatoes, drained and coarsely shredded

10 fresh basil leaves, or 1 teaspoon dried basil
Freshly ground black pepper to taste

2 garlic cloves, peeled and minced

3 tablespoons oil from the sun-dried tomatoes or olive oil

basil

Tomato, Shrimp, and Pesto Pizza

Yield: 1 15- to 18-inch round pie.

Serves 4 as a main course or 6 to 8 as an appetizer.

Crust Suggestions: Basic Pizza, Sicilian-style, Pepper-Lard, or Herb dough.

Method: Direct stone baking or a prepared pizza pan.

THIS SHRIMP AND *Pesto* pizza is superb. Tiny bay scallops or shelled clams are equally good in this recipe in this way. Remember, add the marinated seafood only during the last 5 minutes of cooking time, or it will be overcooked and rubbery.

¾ cup *Pesto* (see recipe page 82)

1 pound medium-sized shrimp, peeled, deveined, washed, and dried

1 garlic clove, peeled and minced

1 recipe pizza dough, ready to use

½ pound mozzarella, thinly sliced

½ pound fresh tomatoes, seeded and roughly chopped, or 1 cup well-drained canned whole tomatoes, roughly chopped

1. Preheat the oven to 500 degrees for 30 minutes for a pizza pan or 60 minutes for pizza tiles or stones.

2. Lightly coat a large pizza pan with vegetable oil and sprinkle it with coarsely ground yellow cornmeal. Or lightly coat a large pizza screen with oil or a peel with flour.

3. Combine the *Pesto* with the shrimp and garlic and marinate at room temperature for a short while.

4. Roll out or stretch the dough into a thin circle and fit it onto the prepared pan, screen, or peel.

5. Spread the cheese over the dough and lay the tomatoes over the cheese.

6. Bake for 10 minutes. Then distribute the *Pesto*-shrimp mixture over the cheese and bake for 5 minutes longer.

Variation

Substitute 1 heaping cup of tiny bay scallops, shucked drained clams, or sliced squid for the shrimp.

Note: Pizzas baked directly on tiles should not take more than 10 minutes to cook. Therefore, spread the shrimp mixture on top of the tomatoes during the initial baking time.

Grated Zucchini-Pesto Pizza

Yield: 1 15- to 16-inch round pie.

Serves 4 as a main course or 6 to 8 as an appetizer.

Crust Suggestions: Basic Pizza, Sicilian-style, Semolina, Pepper-Lard, Sausage, *Prosciutto*, or Whole Wheat I dough.

Method: Direct stone baking or a prepared pizza pan.

1. Preheat the oven to 500 degrees for 30 minutes for a pizza pan or 60 minutes for pizza tiles or stones.

2. Lightly coat a large pizza pan with vegetable oil and sprinkle it lightly with coarsely ground yellow cornmeal. Or lightly coat a large pizza screen with oil or a peel with flour.

3. Roll out or stretch the dough into a thin circle and fit it onto the prepared pan, screen, or peel.

4. Combine the zucchini, *Pesto*, garlic, and mozzarella in a large bowl. Spread the mixture over the dough shell.

5. Bake for 10 to 15 minutes, or until the crust is golden. This pie is delicious hot or cold.

1 **recipe pizza dough, ready to use**

2 **pounds zucchini, washed, trimmed, grated or shredded, and squeezed dry in a dish towel**

¾ **cup *Pesto* (see recipe page 82)**

2 **garlic cloves, peeled and minced**

½ **pound mozzarella, roughly shredded**

Pizza Primavera

Yield: 1 15- to 18-inch round pie.

Serves 4 as a main course or 6 to 8 as an appetizer.

Crust Suggestions: Basic Pizza, Sicilian-style, Semolina, Pepper-Lard, *Prosciutto*, Herb, or Onion dough.

Method: Direct stone baking or a prepared pizza pan.

PRIMAVERA MEANS SPRINGTIME in Italian. The essence of primavera is in its use of tiny, fresh vegetables—the smallest zucchini, the firmest white button mushrooms, the smallest, sweetest tomatoes, and the most tender scallions. Use only fresh parsley, basil, or mint and only creamy cheeses such as Fontina or Bel Paese instead of mozzarella. Sometimes pencil-thin asparagus spears that have been barely steamed to a crisp consistency also find their way on this pie. Try snow peas, tiny bits of *prosciutto*, yellow zucchini, or artichoke hearts. But keep the dish light and don't crowd in too many toppings or it will end up tasting like pizza salad.

3 tablespoons olive oil
½ pound fresh mush-
   rooms, cleaned and
   sliced
1 recipe pizza dough,
   ready to use
½ pound Italian Fontina
   or Bel Paese cheese,
   cut into ½-inch cubes
1 pound ripe tomatoes,
   seeded and roughly
   chopped
2 very small zucchini,
   washed, trimmed, and
   thinly sliced
2 scallions, including
   white and green parts,
   sliced
1 garlic clove, peeled and
   minced
1 tablespoon freshly
   grated Parmesan cheese
10 fresh basil leaves,
   shredded, or 1 table-
   spoon chopped fresh
   herbs, such as parsley,
   mint, marjoram, or
   oregano

1. Heat 1 tablespoon of olive oil in a large frying pan and sauté the mushrooms until all their liquid has evaporated. Set them aside.

2. Preheat the oven to 500 degrees for 30 minutes for a pizza pan or 60 mintues for pizza tiles or stones.

3. Lightly coat a large pizza pan with vegetable oil and sprinkle it lightly with coarsely ground yellow cornmeal. Or lightly coat a large pizza screen with oil or a peel with flour.

4. Roll out or stretch the dough into a thin circle and fit it onto the prepared pan, screen, or peel.

5. Distribute the cheese cubes over the dough shell. Then make layers of the tomatoes, zucchini, and mushrooms. Sprinkle on the scallions, garlic, Parmesan cheese, and the remaining 2 tablespoons of oil.

6. Bake for 10 to 15 minutes, or until the crust is golden.

Zucchini-Tomato Pizza

Yield: 1 15- to 18-inch round pie.
Serves 4 as a main course or 6 to 8 as an appetizer.
Crust Suggestions: Basic Pizza, Sicilian-style, Pepper-Lard, or Whole
Wheat I dough.
Method: Direct stone baking or a prepared pizza pan.

ZUCCHINI NEED LITTLE preparation to be used on pizza. Sliced paper thin, they cook right on top of the pie. In this pizza, a sweet onion-based tomato sauce coupled with the salty and tart accents of the black olives and capers complements the crisp zucchini.

1. Preheat the oven to 500 degrees for 30 minutes for a pizza pan or 60 minutes for pizza tiles or stones.

2. Lightly coat a large pizza pan with vegetable oil and sprinkle it lightly with coarsely ground yellow cornmeal. Or lightly coat a large pizza screen with oil or a peel with flour.

3. Roll out or stretch the dough into a thin circle and fit it onto the prepared pan, screen, or peel.

4. Spread the tomato sauce evenly over the dough shell. Then lay the zucchini slices over the sauce. Sprinkle the pie with the capers, olives, and oregano. Drizzle the olive oil over the pie.

5. Bake for 10 to 15 minutes, or until the crust is golden.

1 recipe pizza dough, ready to use
1 cup Basic Pizza Sauce with Onions (see recipe page 72)
2 medium-sized zucchini, washed, dried, trimmed, and cut into paper-thin slices
1 tablespoon drained capers
15 to 20 oil-cured black olives
1 teaspoon dried oregano
2 tablespoons olive oil

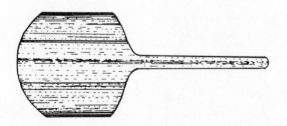

Rich Zucchini-Ricotta Pizza

Yield: 1 15-inch round pie.

Serves 4 to 6 as a main course.

Crust Suggestions: Basic Pizza, Sicilian-style, Semolina, Pepper-Lard, Sausage, *Prosciutto*, and Herb dough.

Method: Use a 15-inch round pizza pan.

HERE'S ANOTHER VARIATION on the *pizza bianca* theme, this time with zucchini. Be sure to use a pan for this pie. The amount of filling will be much too heavy for any direct stone method of cooking.

1 recipe pizza dough, ready to use

1 pound ricotta

¼ cup freshly grated Parmesan cheese

Freshly ground black pepper to taste

1 tablespoon finely minced fresh parsley leaves

1 pound zucchini, washed, trimmed, and thinly sliced

2 garlic cloves, peeled and minced

½ pound mozzarella, thinly sliced

1. Preheat the oven to 500 degrees for 30 minutes.

2. Lightly coat a large pizza pan with vegetable oil and sprinkle it lightly with coarsely ground yellow cornmeal.

3. Roll out or stretch the dough into a thin circle and fit it onto the prepared pan.

4. Mix the ricotta, Parmesan cheese, black pepper, and parsley together in a bowl. Spread the cheese mixture over the dough shell. Make a layer of the zucchini on top of the cheese mixture and sprinkle the garlic on top of the zucchini.

5. Bake for 10 to 15 minutes. Then lay the sliced mozzarella on top of the pie. Bake for 5 minutes longer, or until the cheese is just melted. Let the pie rest for 5 to 10 minutes before cutting; the slices will be neater if you do.

Zucchini, Tomato, Pesto, and Smoked Mozzarella Pizza

Yield: 1 15- to 18-inch round pie.
Serves 4 as a main course or 6 to 8 as an appetizer.
Crust Suggestions: Basic Pizza, Sicilian-style, Semolina, Pepper-Lard, Herb, Sausage, or *Prosciutto* dough.
Method: Direct stone baking or a prepared pizza pan.

IF ZUCCHINI, PESTO, fresh tomatoes, and smoked mozzarella cheese sound good enough to make your mouth water, just wait until you smell this combination baking in the oven!

1. Preheat the oven to 500 degrees for 30 minutes for a pizza pan or 60 minutes for pizza tiles or stones.

2. Lightly coat a large pizza pan with vegetable oil and sprinkle it lightly with coarsely ground yellow cornmeal. Or lightly coat a large pizza screen with oil or a peel with flour.

3. Roll out or stretch the dough into a thin circle and fit it onto the prepared pan, screen, or peel.

4. Make a layer of the mozzarella on the dough shell and distribute the tomatoes over the mozzarella.

5. Combine the zucchini with the *Pesto* and spread the mixture over the tomatoes.

6. Bake for 10 to 15 minutes, or until the crust is golden and the topping bubbly.

1 recipe pizza dough, ready to use

½ pound smoked or regular mozzarella, thinly sliced

1 pound ripe tomatoes, seeded and roughly chopped or 1 cup drained whole canned tomatoes, roughly chopped

½ pound tiny zucchini, washed, trimmed, and cut into ½- by 3-inch strips

¾ cup **Pesto** made with 1 crushed garlic clove (see recipe page 82)

Greek Pizza

Yield: 1 15- to 18-inch round pie.

Serves 4 as a main course or 6 to 8 as an appetizer.

Crust Suggestions: Basic Pizza, Sicilian-style, Semolina, or Pepper-Lard dough.

Method: Direct stone baking or a prepared pizza pan.

GREEK VENDORS MAKE these in saucer-size pans and sell them as a quick take-out treat.

1 recipe pizza dough, ready to use

½ pound feta cheese, crumbled

1½ pounds ripe tomatoes, seeded and roughly chopped, or 1 cup canned whole drained tomatoes, roughly chopped

1 sweet green pepper, thinly sliced

6 pickled hot peppers, halved

10 green or purple Greek olives

1 teaspoon dried oregano

2 tablespoons olive oil

1. Preheat the oven to 500 degrees for 30 minutes for a pizza pan or 60 minutes for pizza tiles or stones.

2. Lightly coat a large pizza pan with vegetable oil. Or lightly coat a large pizza screen with oil or a peel with flour.

3. Roll out or stretch the dough into a thin circle and fit it onto the prepared pan, screen, or peel.

4. Distribute the feta cheese over the dough shell. Then make layers of the tomatoes, green peppers, hot peppers, and olives over the cheese. Sprinkle the pie with the oregano and olive oil.

5. Bake for 10 to 15 minutes, or until the crust is golden.

Variation

Anchovies and capers can be added to the topping.

Greek Spinach Pizza

Yield: 1 15- to 16-inch round pie.

Serves 4 as a main course or 6 to 8 as an appetizer.

Crust Suggestions: Basic Pizza, Sicilian-style, Semolina, or Pepper-Lard dough.

Method: Direct stone baking or a prepared pizza pan.

MOST OF US ARE familiar with *spanakopeta*, that delectable Greek spinach-cheese-filo dough creation. But what kind of crust do you think was used on this pie before the Greeks discovered the secret of light, flaky multilayered filo dough? You guessed it—pizza dough. Pizza dough makes an admirable substitute for filo. It is easier to handle and contains far less fat than the buttery filo. You may make this pie with or without a double crust. Serve this pizza hot or cold.

1. Preheat the oven to 500 degrees for 30 minutes for a pizza pan or 60 minutes for pizza tiles or stones.

2. Lightly coat a large pizza pan with vegetable oil and sprinkle it lightly with coarsely ground yellow cornmeal. Or lightly coat a large pizza screen with oil or a peel with flour.

3. Roll out or stretch the dough into a thin circle and fit it onto the prepared pan, screen, or peel.

4. Put the spinach, feta cheese, mint, and eggs into a large bowl. Combine well and spread this mixture over the dough shell.

5. Bake for 15 to 20 minutes, or until the crust is golden and the topping is puffy.

Variation

For a double crust-style pie, use this filling and follow the directions in the Stuffed Pizza Master Recipe on page 192.

1 **recipe pizza dough, ready to use**

2 **pounds fresh spinach, washed, cooked, squeezed dry, and finely chopped, or 2 10-ounce packages frozen chopped spinach, cooked and squeezed dry**

1 **pound feta cheese, crumbled**

2 **tablespoons chopped fresh mint leaves or fresh dill**

2 **extra large eggs, lightly beaten**

Middle Eastern Pizza *(Lahma Bi Ajim or Ajeen)*

Yield: 1 15-inch round pie.
Serves 4 to 6 as a main course.
Crust Suggestions: Basic Pizza, Sicilian-style, Pepper-Lard, or Semolina dough.
Method: Use a prepared 15-inch round pizza pan omitting the cornmeal.

A SAVORY AND RICH combination of ground lamb, raisins, pignolis, tomatoes, and spices, *Lahma Bi Ajim* is the Lebanese answer to pizza. Serve this hearty pie along with a yogurt-cucumber-mint salad and a grated carrot salad.

The preferred technique here is to roll the dough out with a rolling pin, fit it into a pizza pan and crimp the edges as you would for a common piecrust. For individual presentations, follow the divisions and rolling techniques given for *pizzette*. Make sure you crimp all of the edges to give them their characteristic shape. This pie is very good hot or cold.

2 tablespoons sweet butter
1 pound ground lean lamb or beef
2 small sweet onions, finely minced
1 12-ounce can whole tomatoes in purée or juice
1 tablespoon tomato paste
2 tablespoons raisins
Pinch of ground cinnamon
Pinch of grated nutmeg
Salt and freshly ground black pepper to taste
1 recipe pizza dough, ready to use
2 tablespoons pignolis

1. Melt the butter in a large frying pan and sauté the meat and onions over medium heat for about 5 to 8 minutes, or until the onions are limp and the meat is browned.

2. Add the tomatoes, tomato paste, raisins, cinnamon, nutmeg, and salt and pepper and stir. Simmer for 10 minutes and set aside. (The recipe may be made in advance to this point.)

3. Preheat the oven to 450 degrees for at least 30 minutes.

4. Lightly coat a round 15-inch pizza pan with vegetable oil.

5. Roll out the dough into a thin circle with a rolling pin. Fit it onto the prepared pizza pan and crimp the outer edges as you would for a pie.

6. Fill the dough shell with the meat mixture and sprinkle with pignolis.

7. Bake for 45 minutes to 1 hour, or until the crust is golden.

Note: This filling is also good paired with leftover rice as a stuffing for baked tomatoes or green peppers.

Spanish Tortilla Pizza

Yield: 1 15-inch round pie.

Serves 4 as a main course or 6 to 8 as an appetizer.

Crust Suggestions: Basic Pizza, Sicilian-style, Semolina, or Pepper-Lard dough.

Method: Use a 15-inch round prepared pizza pan.

I'VE NEVER HAD pizza in Spain, but I've read that the Spanish soldiers occupying Naples in the eighteenth century were some of its first devotées. And the Spanish were responsible for bringing back the tomato from the New World. This makes a wonderful breakfast pizza.

1. Preheat the oven to 500 degrees for 30 minutes.

2. Lightly coat a large pizza pan with vegetable oil and sprinkle it lightly with coarsely ground yellow cornmeal.

3. Heat the oil in a medium-sized frying pan. Add the onions and peppers and sauté over medium heat for about 5 minutes. Remove them from the heat and stir in the tomatoes, ham, and parsley. Set aside until needed.

4. Roll out or stretch the dough into a thin circle and fit it onto the prepared pan.

5. Mix the eggs into the cooled vegetable-ham mixture and season it with salt and pepper. Spread the mixture over the dough shell.

6. Bake for 10 to 15 minutes, or until the crust is golden.

3 tablespoons olive oil

½ pound sweet onions, thinly sliced

1 large sweet green pepper, seeded and thinly sliced

1 large sweet red pepper, seeded and thinly sliced

1 pound ripe tomatoes, seeded and roughly chopped, or 1 cup drained canned tomatoes roughly chopped

¼ pound boiled ham, cut into bite-sized pieces

1 recipe pizza dough, ready to use

4 extra large eggs, lightly beaten
Salt and freshly ground black pepper to taste

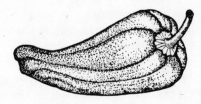

12.

FRENCH PIZZA

I think you'll find the lively combination of French-style pizza a refreshing change. They're not very far from their Italian roots, but they do seem to give credence to the French saying, *vive la différence!*

Pissaladière

The most commonly held notion is that *pissaladière* is a Frenchification of the word pizza. The two do sound similar, but pissaladière derives from the Provençale *pissala* or *pissalat*. *Pissala* is a condiment made of crushed anchovies or olives or a combination of the two, and it is the base flavoring of several Provençale preparations, including *tapenade* and *anchoiade*. *Pissaladière*'s unique flavoring is based on the same anchovy-olive combination. There are even some variations of *pissaladière* that call for flavoring the onions with *pissala* while they cook before the filling is used on the pie. Origins aside, today *pissaladière* has as many variations as there are cooks in the south of France.

The most French of all pizza comes in three basic types: *pissaladière à l'ancienne* or *du boulanger*, *pissaladière du pâtissier*, and *pissaladière de mènage*.

The first kind, *à l'ancienne*, means as in the old days, and *du boulanger* means the baker's. Both refer to yeast-risen doughs. This kind of *pissaladière* could have a thick bready crust, an eggy brioche-like crust, or a thin, crisp pizza crust. In France it's sold in large trays from a *boulangerie* (bakery), and the onion toppings are usually on the plain side because the purchaser is expected to add to them before reheating the bread.

The next category, *pissaladière du pâtissier*, refers to a much more refined product, which is sold as a savory in a pastry shop. These delicately seasoned onion tarts are made with flaky puff pastry and sold by weight. Some of these more elegant versions of *pissaladière* include sun-dried tomatoes, pignolis, and capers, as well as the traditional olive-anchovy topping.

Pissaladière de mènage means homemade, and it is invariably made with a pastry crust. It resembles a tart more than a pizza.

True *pissaladière* contains only cooked-down seasoned onions, anchovies, and black olives—no tomatoes or cheese. The onions are highly seasoned with herbs, black pepper, and garlic, and their natural sweetness is brought out through long cooking until they almost melt.

This sweet purée contrasts with the saltiness of the anchovies and black olives and affords one of the most unusual and delicious of all pizza combinations. Here's a recipe for that classic and some other delicious variations.

Pissaladière de Ménage (Comme Chez Nous)

Yield: Serves 4 as a main course or 6 to 8 as an appetizer.
Crust Suggestions: Provençale Olive Oil Pastry Crust, Basic Pizza, Sicilian-style, Semolina, or Pepper-Lard dough.
Method: Use a 12-inch tart or pizza pan lightly coated with vegetable oil.

THIS CREATION IS more like a creamy quiche than a standard pizza. But the creamy custard of onions and tomatoes or cheese on top is equally as good on a pizza crust. Try both variations.

1. Preheat the oven to 400 degrees at least 20 minutes before baking.

2. Heat the olive oil and butter in a medium-sized frying pan. Add the onions and seasonings and sauté for 10 minutes, or until the onions are tender. Remove from the heat and let cool.

3. Roll out or stretch the dough and fit it onto the prepared tart or pizza pan. (Make sure the rim is high enough on the pizza dough to hold in the custard.)

4. Mix together the eggs, milk, and cheese in a medium-sized bowl. Stir in the cooled onions. Pour the onion custard onto the prepared crust.

5. Bake for 45 minutes to 1 hour, or the crust is golden and the custard is set. (A knife inserted in the center should come out clean.)

Variation

Arrange 2 medium-sized peeled and thickly sliced tomatoes decoratively over the onion custard before baking.

1 recipe Provençale Olive Oil Pastry, or ½ a recipe pizza dough, ready to use
1 tablespoon olive oil
1 tablespoon sweet butter
1 pound sweet Bermuda onions, or other mild onions, thinly sliced
½ teaspoon dried thyme, or 1 teaspoon fresh thyme leaves
Salt and freshly ground black pepper to taste
3 extra large eggs, lightly beaten
1 cup milk or cream
¼ cup grated Gruyère or Parmesan cheese (or a combination), optional

Pissaladière Master Recipe

Yield: 1 12- by 17-inch rectangular pie, *or* 1 15- to 18-inch thin crusted round pie.

Serves 6 to 8 as a main course.

Crust Suggestions: Basic Pizza, Sicilian-style, Pepper-Lard, Rich Egg, or Flaky Pizza dough.

Method: Will vary according to which dough you choose.

Variation #1—Traditional

- 1 recipe pizza dough, ready to use
- 1 recipe *Pissaladière* Onion Base (see recipe page 79)
- 4 ounces anchovy fillets, drained
- 20 oil-cured black or Niçoise olives

Variation #2—du Pâtissier

- 1 recipe pizza dough, ready to use
- 1 recipe *Pissaladière* Onion Base (see recipe page 79)
- 4 ounces anchoyy fillets, drained
- 15 oil-cured black or Niçoise olives
- 5 oil-packed sun-dried tomatoes, roughly shredded
- 1 tablespoon drained capers
- 1 tablespoon pignolis

1. Spread the onion base over the dough shell. Arrange the anchovies in a lattice pattern over the onion base and arrange the olives and other toppings within the lattice pattern. If you wish, you can drizzle 1 or 2 tablespoons of extra-virgin olive oil over the pie before you bake it.

2. Bake for 15 to 20 minutes, or until the crust is golden.

Pizza au Fruits de Mer (Provençale Seafood Pizza)

Yield: 1 15- to 18-inch round pie.

Serves 4 as a main course or 6 to 8 as an appetizer.

Crust Suggestions: Basic Pizza, Sicilian-style, Pepper-Lard, or Semolina dough.

Method: Direct stone baking or a prepared pizza pan.

IN THE HILLS of Provence, away from the tourists and sun worshippers, the social life revolves around the village café. The selections there are fairly standard: *grillades,* smoky, freshly baked pizza of some kind, *plat de charcuterie or de crudités, steak au pommes frites,* some local wine, and, perhaps, some fruit for dessert. At one such place I had this incredible seafood pizza.

1. Spread the Tomato *Coulis* over a prepared dough shell. Layer on the garlic, anchovies, shrimp, squid, mussels, and olives. Finish with a sprinkling of thyme and olive oil.

2. Bake for 10 to 15 minutes, or until the crust is golden. Before serving, discard any mussels which do not open during cooking.

Note: This pie needs a minimum support, therefore a screen is recommended if the direct stone method is used.

1 recipe pizza dough, ready to use

1 cup Tomato *Coulis* (see recipe page 74)

2 garlic cloves, minced

1 2 ounce can anchovies, drained

½ pound shrimp, peeled and deveined

½ pound squid, cleaned and cut into ¼-inch-thick rings

½ pound mussels, scrubbed clean and bearded

15 to 20 oil-cured black or Niçoise olives

6 to 7 sprigs fresh thyme, or ½ teaspoon dried thyme

2 tablespoons extra-virgin olive oil

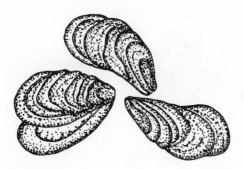

Pizza à la Tapenade

Yield: 1 15- to 18-inch round pie.
Serves 4 as a main course or 6 to 8 as an appetizer.
Crust Suggestions: Basic Pizza, Sicilian-style, Semolina, Pepper-Lard, or Flaky Pizza dough.
Method: Direct stone baking, a prepared pizza pan, or special instructions for Flaky Pizza Dough.

1 recipe pizza dough, ready to use
⅔ cup *Tapenade* (see recipe page 81)
½ pound mozzarella, thinly sliced
1 pound fresh tomatoes, seeded and roughly chopped, or 1 cup drained canned tomatoes, roughly chopped
½ small sweet onion, cut into paper-thin slices
1 teaspoon dried marjoram, dried oregano or dried thyme
2 tablespoons olive oil

1. Spread the *Tapenade* over a prepared pizza shell. Layer the cheese over the *Tapenade* and then the tomatoes. Finish with a layer of onions and a sprinkling of herbs and olive oil. on top of the pie.

2. Bake for 10 to 15 minutes, or until the crust is golden.

Variation

Omit the mozzarella and the raw onion. Spread the dough with *Tapenade* and cover with 1 recipe of *Pissaladière* Onion Base. Then add the tomatoes, herbs, and olive oil as in the recipe.

Pizza à l'Anchoiade

Yield: 1 15- to 18-inch round pie.

Serves 4 as a main course or 6 to 8 as an appetizer.

Crust Suggestions: Basic Pizza, Sicilian-style, Semolina, or Pepper-Lard dough.

Method: Direct stone baking or a prepared pizza pan.

1. Combine the garlic, anchovies, vinegar, ¼ cup of the olive oil, and black pepper in the bowl of a blender or food processor and blend until smooth.

2. Spread this mixture over the prepared dough shell. Lay the tomatoes, green pepper, onion, capers, and olives on top. Finish with a sprinkling of fresh herbs and some olive oil before baking.

3. Bake for 10 to 15 minutes, or until the crust is golden.

2 **garlic cloves, peeled**

2 **2-ounce cans anchovy fillets, drained**

1 **tablespoon red wine vinegar**

¼ **cup plus 1 to 2 tablespoons olive oil Freshly ground black pepper to taste**

1 **recipe pizza dough, ready to use**

1 **pound fresh tomatoes, seeded and roughly chopped, or 1 cup drained canned tomatoes roughly crushed**

1 **small sweet green pepper, thinly sliced**

½ **small sweet onion, peeled and thinly sliced**

2 **tablespoons drained capers**

15 **oil-cured black or Niçoise olives**

2 **tablespoons finely minced fresh parsley leaves or basil leaves**

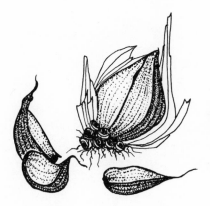

Ratatouille Pizza

Yield: 1 15-inch round pie.

Serves 6 as a main course.

Crust Suggestions: Basic Pizza, Sicilian-style, Pepper-Lard, or Whole Wheat I or II dough.

Method: Use a prepared 15-inch pizza pan.

CERTAIN PROVENÇALE DISHES not commonly associated with pizza seem made for it. One of those dishes is *Ratatouille*, that hearty Provençale vegetable stew. *Ratatouille* is simple to make, and it is good hot or cold as an appetizer, a side dish, and on pasta. And of course, it's wonderful on pizza.

4 cups **Ratatouille, ready to use** (see recipe page 81)

1 **recipe pizza dough, ready to use**

2 **tablespoons freshly grated Parmesan cheese**

½ **pound mozzarella, thinly sliced**

1. Spread the *Ratatouille* over a prepared dough shell and sprinkle it with the Parmesan cheese.

2. Bake for 10 to 15 minutes. Add the mozzarella cheese during the final 5 minutes of baking.

Chèvre Pizza

Yield: 1 15- to 18-inch pie.

Serves 4 as a main course or 6 to 8 as an appetizer.

Crust Suggestions: Basic Pizza, Sicilian-style, Pepper-Lard, Semolina, Herb, Sausage, or Flaky Pizza dough

Method: Direct stone baking, a prepared pizza pan, or special instructions for Flaky Pizza Dough.

CHÈVRE—FRENCH GOAT CHEESE—seems now destined for fame and glory atop the world's most popular pie. And why not? Goat cheese's natural creaminess and light sharpness combine with other pizza makings in the most wonderful way.

Chèvre Pizza #1—Goat Cheese, Mozzarella, and Sun-Dried Tomatoes

1. Combine the chèvre, mozzarella, garlic, herbs, and black pepper in a small bowl.

2. Spread the cheese mixture over the prepared dough shell. Lay the sun-dried tomatoes over the cheese mixture and finish with a sprinkling of olive oil.

3. Bake for 10 to 15 minutes, or until the crust is golden and the topping is bubbly.

8 ounces chèvre (goat cheese), coarsely crumbled

8 ounces mozzarella, coarsely shredded

2 garlic cloves, peeled and minced

1 teaspoon dried *herbes de Provence,* or 1 teaspoon of a combination of dried marjoram, dried oregano, dried thyme, and dried rosemary
Freshly ground black pepper to taste

1 recipe pizza dough, ready to use

10 whole oil-packed sun-dried tomatoes, coarsely shredded

2 tablespoons extra-virgin olive oil or oil from the tomatoes

11 to 12 ounces
Montrachet goat cheese
(or similiar variety),
coarsely crumbled
2 garlic cloves, peeled
and minced
1 teaspoon *herbes de
Provence,* or a com-
bination of marjoram,
oregano, thyme, or
rosemary
Freshly ground black
pepper to taste
1 recipe pizza dough,
ready to use
1½ pounds fresh tomatoes,
seeded and roughly
chopped, or 1 cup
drained canned to-
matoes, roughly
crushed
2 tablespoons extra-virgin
olive oil

Chèvre Pizza #2—Herbed Goat Cheese and Fresh Tomatoes

1. Mash together the chèvre, garlic, herbs, and pepper with a fork in a small bowl.

2. Spread the cheese mixture over the prepared dough shell. Lay the tomatoes over the cheese and finish with a sprinkling of olive oil.

3. Bake for 10 to 15 minutes, or until the crust is golden and the topping is bubbly.

Chèvre Pizza #3—Goat Cheese, Fresh Herbs, Sweet Garlic Purée, and Walnut Oil

1 large whole head garlic
(about 20 to 25
cloves), separated into
cloves but unpeeled
1 pound chèvre (goat
cheese), crumbled
4 ounces mozzarella,
coarsely shredded

1. Cook the garlic in water to cover at a simmer for about 45 to 60 minutes, or until it is soft. Drain and squeeze the soft flesh from the peels into a bowl.

2. Add the chèvre, mozzarella, herbs, and pepper to the same bowl and mix together.

3. Spread this mixture over a prepared dough shell and drizzle the walnut oil over the pie.

4. Bake for 10 to 15 minutes, or until the pie is golden and puffed.

Variation

Add a few coarsely shredded oil-packed sun-dried tomatoes and some peeled raw shrimp to the top of this pie and bake on a pizza screen or in a pan.

1 tablespoon finely minced fresh parsley leaves
1 tablespoon minced chives
  Freshly ground black pepper to taste
1 recipe pizza dough, ready to use
2 tablespoons walnut oil

Chèvre Pizza #4—Herbed Goat Cheese with Spinach and Prosciutto

1. Mix the chèvre, mozzarella, garlic, herbs, and black pepper together in a small bowl.

2. Spread the cheese mixture over the prepared dough shell. Lay the spinach and *prosciutto* over the cheese mixture and finish with a sprinkling of some walnut oil.

3. Bake for 10 to 15 minutes, or until the crust is golden.

11 to 12 ounces chèvre (goat cheese), coarsely crumbled
4 ounces mozzarella, coarsely shredded
2 garlic cloves, peeled and minced
2 teaspoons *herbes de Provence*, or a combination of marjoram, oregano, thyme and rosemary
  Freshly ground black pepper to taste
1 recipe pizza dough, ready to use
1 pound fresh spinach, wilted and drained, or 1 10-ounce package frozen spinach, cooked and squeezed dry
4 ounces *prosciutto*, cut into ½-inch cubes
2 tablespoons walnut oil

rosemary

Chèvre Pizza #5—Herbed Goat Cheese and Walnut Oil-Dressed Bitter Greens

1 pound arugola or watercress or other bitter greens, tough stems removed, washed, and dried
1 tablespoon red wine vinegar
5 tablespoons walnut or olive oil
2 garlic cloves, peeled and minced
11 to 12 ounces chèvre (goat cheese), coarsely crumbled
4 ounces mozzarella, coarsely shredded
Freshly ground black pepper to taste
1 recipe pizza dough, ready to use

1. Toss the arugola with the vinegar, 3 tablespoons of the walnut oil, and the garlic in a large frying pan over high heat until the greens are just wilted. Drain off the excess liquid and set aside.

2. Mix the chèvre, mozzarella, and black pepper together in a small bowl and set aside.

3. Spread the cheese mixture over the prepared dough shell. Layer the arugola over the cheese mixture and finish with a sprinkling of walnut oil.

4. Bake for 10 to 15 minutes, or until the crust is golden.

Pizza Provençale I

Yield: 1 15- to 18-inch round pie, or 1 12- by 17-inch rectangular pie.
Serves 4 as a main course or 6 to 8 as an appetizer.
Crust Suggestions: Basic Pizza, Sicilian-style, Pepper-Lard, Semolina, Rich Flaky Pizza dough.
Method: Direct stone baking, a prepared pizza pan, or special instructions for Flaky Pizza Dough.

THIS VERSION OF Pizza Provençale absolutely requires good ripe tomatoes. Fresh bite-sized cherry tomatoes, generally available most of the year, are fine for this pizza. A word of caution, though: This pie is for garlic lovers. This pizza is excellent hot or cold.

1. Arrange the tomatoes cut side up on a prepared dough shell. Sprinkle with salt and pepper, garlic, Parmesan cheese, and parsley. Drizzle the olive oil over all.

2. Bake for 15 to 20 minutes, or until the tomatoes are just soft, but not mushy, and the crust is golden.

1 **recipe pizza dough, ready to use**
2 **pounds ripe cherry tomatoes, halved and seeded**
 Salt and freshly ground black pepper to taste
8 **garlic cloves, peeled and minced**
6 **tablespoons freshly grated Parmesan cheese**
4 **tablespoons finely chopped fresh parsley leaves, or 2 teaspoons dried** *herbes de Provence*
4 **tablespoons extra-virgin olive oil**

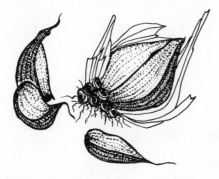

Pizza Provençale II

Yield: 1 15- to 18-inch round pie.
 Serves 4 as a main course or 6 to 8 as an appetizer.
Crust Suggestions: Basic Pizza, Sicilian-style, Pepper-Lard, Semolina, Rich Egg, or Flaky Pizza dough.
 Method: A prepared pizza pan or special instructions for Flaky Pizza Dough.

IN RECENT YEARS, Pizza Provençale has become very popular in and around Nice. In this variation, the familiar *pissaladière* is crowned with ruby red tomatoes and topped with Gruyère cheese. Sometimes the pizza is divided in half, with the traditional *Pissaladière* topping on one side and the tomatoes on the other. Provençale pizza makes a lovely presentation and is delicious hot or cold.

1. Spread the onion base evenly over a prepared dough shell and arrange the tomatoes cut side up over the onions. Distribute the an-

1 **recipe pizza dough, ready to use**

1 recipe *Pissaladière* Onion Base, ready to use
  (see recipe page 79)
2 pounds ripe Italian
  plum-style tomatoes,
  cut in half
1 2-ounce can anchovies,
  drained
10 to 15 oil-cured black
  olives
1½ cups freshly grated
  Gruyère cheese

chovies and olives between the tomatoes. Sprinkle the Gruyère cheese over all.

2. Bake for 10 to 15 minutes, or until the crust is golden brown.

Pizza Provençale III

Yield: 1 15- 18-inch round pie.

Serves 4 as a main course or 6 to 8 as an appetizer.

Crust Suggestions: Basic Pizza, Sicilian-style, Pepper-Lard, Semolina, or Rich Egg dough.

Method: Direct stone baking or a prepared pizza pan

1 recipe pizza dough,
  ready to use
½ pound Gouda cheese,
  cut into ½-inch cubes
2 pounds ripe tomatoes,
  seeded, drained, and
  roughly sliced
2 garlic cloves, minced
½ teaspoon dried thyme,
  or 1 teaspoon fresh
  thyme leaves
½ teaspoon fennel seeds
15 oil-cured black or Niçoise olives
2 tablespoons extra-virgin
  olive oil

1. Layer the cheese over the prepared dough shell. Then follow it with the tomatoes, garlic, thyme, fennel, and olives. Sprinkle the olive oil over the pie before baking.

2. Bake for 10 to 15 minutes or until the crust is golden.

In many ways, *calzoni*—folded pizza—are a more versatile and convenient form of pizza to make than the familiar openstyle pie. *Calzoni* can be large enough to feed a family or divided into individual-sized portions. They can be baked or deep-fried and eaten hot or cold. They are perfectly suited to advance preparation, because they reheat and freeze beautifully. One of the advantages of folding the dough over the filling is that it allows for the maximum amount of crisp outer crust and keeps the stuffing moist. A *calzone* makes a neat, portable package for a complete meal, and because it can be eaten without a knife and fork, it is a perfect item for the picnic basket.

At the same time, *calzoni* can measure up to more formal occasions. *Calzoni* are usually thought of as earthy, peasant fare, to be eaten like sandwiches, but, depending upon their size, filling, and crust, they can be remarkably elegant as a unique appetizer, first course, or main dish. If telling your guests they're eating *calzone* seems too mundane, call it the fancier sounding *mezzaluna*.

Mezzaluna is exactly like a *calzone* except that its filling is largely composed of sautéed greens. I have heard the name *mezzaluna* applied to other fillings and even to other kinds of stuffed pizza, and it is difficult to say whether or not the name connotes a particular filling. My guess is that the term *mezzaluna* is interchangeable with *calzone* and that the recipes passed on to me are coincidentally all filled with greens of some kind.

Panzerotti, the smallest member of the pizza turnover family, are usually made with a pastry crust and deep-fried. But this is not a hard and fast rule, as there are also a number of recipes that call for baking them with a traditional yeast-risen dough. Size is what distinguishes *panzerotti* from *calzoni* or *mezzalunas*.

This scaled-down form of folded *pizzette* is considered finger food. *Panzerotti* are usually not served as a main dish; they are considered mainly a snack or a hot hors d'oeuvres. They are absolutely delicious when served with drinks and make extremely versatile party fare.

The French make filled pastry turnovers called *chaussons*, which are very much akin to Italian *calzoni*. The most well known example of this dish, *chausson aux pommes*, is an apple-filled turnover that is served for dessert. Most written recipes for *chaussons* contain apple or fruit fillings, but they have been known to be made with savory fillings as well.

13.
FOLDED PIZZA

Master Calzone Recipe

Yield: 1 15-inch full-size *calzone* (see special instructions on page 171)
          6 8-inch main-course size *calzone*
          8 6-inch luncheon-size *calzone*
          10 4-inch appetizer or snack-size *calzone*

Some General Notes on Calzone

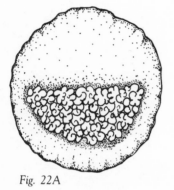

Fig. 22A

1. The filling proportions in each recipe are based on the amount necessary to fill a full-size *calzone*. As you divide the recipe into 6, 8, or 10 *calzoni*, you'll need proportionally less filling. Don't try to use up all of the filling or it will leak. Go by the amounts indicated in the Method section below for each *calzone* and expect to have some leftover filling.
2. Avoid fillings that are too wet. They make a *calzone* soggy.
3. Keep the fillings bite-sized. Too-large pieces are difficult to chew.
4. Virtually any pizza topping can be used as a *calzone* filling.

Method

Fig. 22B

1. Preheat the oven to 500 degrees for 30 minutes for a pizza pan or 60 minutes for pizza tiles or stones.
2. Have one recipe of pizza dough ready to use.
3. Divide the dough into 6, 8, or 10 portions (depending on what sizes you want to make).
4. Roll out each piece of dough with a rolling pin, dusting it with flour if necessary. You should have even 8-, 6-, or 4-inch circles.
5. Lay some filling on the lower half of each circle, leaving a border around. Use ½ cup filling for an 8-inch circle, ⅓ cup for a 6-inch circle, and 1 tablespoon for a 4-inch circle (*Fig. 22A*).
6. Fold the top half of the circle over the mixture. Then fold the border over and crimp the edge with the tines of a fork or with your fingers (*Fig. 22B*).
7. Carefully transfer each *calzone* with a spatula to a prepared pizza pan or screen.
8. Brush each *calzone* lightly with some additional olive oil or with a glaze made from 1 egg yolk beaten with 4 tablespoons of water.

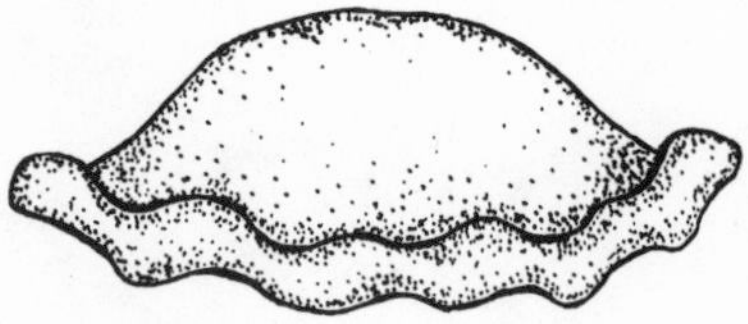

9. Bake for 20 to 30 minutes, or until puffed and golden brown.

Special Instructions for Full-Size Calzoni

1. Flatten the dough out to a 1-inch thickness and roll out a circle to 16 inches.

2. Assemble the pie by draping half of the dough over the side of a prepared baking pan.

3. Fill the dough shell following the same proceedure as for the smaller ones, except that you'll need all of the filling called for in the recipe. Crimp the edges and brush with olive oil or the optional egg glaze. (Assembling the *calzone* in the pan eliminates the problem of transferring a large heavy pie from the work surface to a baking pan.)

4. Bake the full-size *calzone* in a preheated 450-degree oven for 45 to 50 minutes.

5. When the *calzone* is golden brown, it is done. Let it sit for 5 minutes before slicing.

Deep Frying

1. Deep-fry only appetizer or snack-size *calzoni, panzerotti,* or *chaussons* in 2 inches of vegetable oil heated to 375 degrees on a deep-fry thermometer.

2. Don't crowd too many in the pan at a time or they won't puff up and brown.

3. As the turnovers brown, remove them with a slotted spoon to a cooling rack lined with a double layer of paper towels.

4. Serve as soon as possible, or reheat in a 350-degree oven for 10 to 15 minutes.

Freezing

1. Cook the *calzoni* only until they are lightly colored and puffed. Let them cool completely before wrapping them in aluminum foil and freezing.

2. To reheat the frozen *calzoni,* preheat the oven to 400 degrees and bake them wrapped in foil for 30 minutes. Remove the foil and return the *calzoni* to a pan to finish baking for 20 minutes longer, or until they are browned.

Simple Cheese Calzone

Crust Suggestions: Basic Pizza, Sicilian-style, Herb, Onion, *Prosciutto*, Sausage, Pepper-Lard, or Semolina dough.

THE DELICACY OF this basic filling is best appreciated when you use fresh ricotta.

1½ pounds ricotta, preferably freshly made
½ pound mozzarella,
coarsely shredded
Freshly ground coarse
black pepper to taste

1. Combine all the ingredients in a medium-sized bowl with a wooden spoon and mix well.

2. Proceed with step 3 of the Master *Calzone* Recipe.

Variation

For an Herb and Cheese *Calzone*, add ¼ cup freshly grated Parmesan cheese and 2 to 3 tablespoons finely minced herbs, such as a combination of parsley, mint, basil, chives, marjoram, or thyme to the cheese mixture.

Note: Fold leftover filling into an omelet or toss it with some tomatoes for a pasta sauce.

Four-Cheese Calzone

Crust Suggestions: Basic Pizza, Sicilian-style, Herb, Onion, *Prosciutto*, Sausage, Pepper-Lard, or Semolina dough.

HERE'S YET ANOTHER interpretation of the pasta-with-four-cheeses idea. Gouda and Fontina add a mellow flavor to this combination, but other cheeses, such as Bel Paese or other Fontinas (Swedish and the like) or Edam cheese, are all equally as good.

1 pound ricotta
½ pound Fontina cheese,
cut into ½-inch cubes
½ pound Gouda cheese,
cut into ½-inch cubes
¼ cup freshly grated Par-
mesan cheese
Freshly ground black
pepper to taste

1. Combine all the ingredients in a medium-sized bowl and mix well with a wooden spoon.

2. Proceed with step 3 of the Master *Calzone* recipe.

Note: Any leftover filling is good tossed with pasta or used as an omelet filling. It can also be used to stuff hollowed out zucchini or eggplant.

Pesto-Cheese Calzone

Crust Suggestions: Basic Pizza, Sicilian-style, Onion, *Prosciutto*, Sausage, Pepper-Lard, or Semolina dough.

THE LOVELY FRAGRANCE of fresh basil and the crunch of toasted pignolis make this *calzone* particularly different. Try using parsley or mint instead of basil if it is not available; either herb makes an admirable substitute. This is delicious hot or cold.

1. Combine all of the ingredients in a medium-sized bowl and mix well with a wooden spoon. (Don't worry, the filling is supposed to turn green!)

2. Proceed with step 3 of the Master *Calzone* Recipe.

Note: Any leftover filling is very good tossed with pasta. The filling can also be frozen for up to 2 months.

1½ **pounds ricotta**
½ **pound mozzarella, coarsely shredded**
½ **cup pignolis, toasted for 10 minutes in a 350-degree oven**
1 **recipe *Pesto* (see recipe page 82)**

Gorgonzola Calzone

Crust Suggestions: Basic Pizza, Sicilian-style, Herb, Onion, *Prosciutto*, Sausage, Pepper-Lard, or Semolina dough.

TANGY GORGONZOLA CHEESE livens up this *calzone*, but, any blue-veined cheese will work just as well—the stronger, the better.

1. Combine all the ingredients in a medium-sized bowl and mix well with a wooden spoon.

2. Proceed with step 3 of the Master *Calzone* Recipe.

Variation

Add 8 to 10 shredded fresh basil leaves to the base.

Note: Any leftover filling is good tossed with pasta or used as an omelet filling. It can also be used to stuff hollowed out zucchini or eggplant.

1 **pound ricotta**
½ **pound mozzarella, coarsely shredded**
½ **pound Gorgonzola cheese, crumbled**
¼ **cup pignolis, toasted for 10 minutes in a 350-degree oven**

Cheese and Meat Calzone

Crust Suggestions: Basic Pizza, Sicilian-style, Herb, Onion, *Prosciutto*, Sausage, Pepper-Lard, or Semolina dough.

1 **pound ricotta**
½ **pound mozzarella, coarsely shredded**
½ **pound sweet Italian meat, removed from the casings and crumbled, or ¼ pound *prosciutto* or salami, roughly chopped**

1. Combine all the ingredients in a mixing bowl and blend well with a wooden spoon.
2. Proceed with step 3 of the Master *Calzone* Recipe.

Variation

Substitute 1 2-ounce can anchovies, drained and roughly chopped for the meat.

Spoon 2 to 3 tablespoons of homemade tomato sauce over the filling of each *calzone* before sealing it. (Note: This is not suitable for the 4-inch size *calzoni*.)

Note: Any leftover filling can be used to fill manicotti or large pasta shells. It can also be used to stuff hollowed out zucchini or eggplant.

Ham, Cheese, and Sun-Dried Tomato Calzone

Crust Suggestions: Basic Pizza, Sicilian-style, Herb, Onion, *Prosciutto*, Sausage, Pepper-Lard, or Semolina dough.

1 **pound ricotta**
½ **pound mozzarella, coarsely shredded, or Fontina or imported Swiss cheese, cubed**
¼ **pound boiled ham, cut into ½- by 2-inch strips**
4 **whole oil-packed sun-dried tomatoes, drained, cut into bite-sized pieces**

1. Combine all the ingredients in a mixing bowl and blend well with a wooden spoon.
2. Proceed with step 3 of the Master *Calzone* Recipe.

Note: Any leftover filling can be used as a filling for omelets. It can also be frozen for up to 2 months.

Goat Cheese Calzone

Crust Suggestions: Basic Pizza, Sicilian-style, Herb, Onion, *Prosciutto*,
Sausage, Pepper-Lard, or Semolina dough.

GOAT CHEESE CALZONI are making quite a splash on the West Coast,
and they seem destined to become the new darlings of the gourmet
scene. Fortunately, you don't have to fly to California to enjoy one; you
can make the best goat cheese calzone ever with this basic recipe. These
calzoni are good hot or cold.

1. Combine the ricotta, mozzarella, and chèvre and garlic in a bowl.

2. Proceed with step 3 of the Master *Calzone* Recipe.

3. After completing step 5 of the Master Recipe, sprinkle each with a
helping of black pepper and herbs. Drizzle each *calzone* filling with a
small amount of olive oil, and then follow the Master Recipe from step 6
on.

Variations

Add ¼ pound of chopped *prosciutto* to the cheese base.

Add 5 roughly chopped whole oil-packed sun-dried tomatoes to the
cheese base and use 2 tablespoons fresh basil chopped leaves instead of
thyme.

Use 1 pound of imported Italian buffalo milk mozzarella instead of the
ricotta. Omit the domestic mozzarella, and add 5 roughly chopped whole
oil-packed sun-dried tomatoes to the base.

Note: Any leftover filling can be tossed with pasta or used to stuff
baked zucchini, onions, or acorn squash.

1 **pound ricotta**

½ **pound mozzarella,
coarsely shredded**

12 **ounces chèvre (goat
cheese), without rind
or ash coating,
crumbled**

2 **garlic cloves, peeled
and minced
Coarsely ground black
pepper to taste**

2 **tablespoons fresh
thyme, or enough dried
thyme or *herbes de
Provence* to sprinkle
about ¼ teaspoon in
every calzone**

3 **tablespoons extra-virgin
olive oil to drizzle over
the filling and to brush
over the crust to pro-
mote browning**

Fiadone

Crust Suggestions: Basic Pizza, Sicilian-style, Herb, Onion, *Prosciutto*, Sausage, Pepper-Lard, or Semolina dough.

IN THE ITALIAN REGION of Abruzzi, *fiadone* is the equivalent of their own particularly delicious variation of cheese *calzone*. Scamorza and caciocavallo are two regional cheeses that lend a distinctive touch to this folded pizza. Traditionally this dish is served as a main course napped with a tomato sauce, in a manner similar to pasta.

1 **pound ricotta**
½ **pound caciocavallo or imported Provolone, grated**
½ **pound scamorza or mozzarella, coarsely shredded**
2 **extra large eggs, beaten Freshly ground black pepper to taste**

1. Combine all the ingredients in a mixing bowl and blend well with a wooden spoon.
2. Proceed with step 3 of the Master *Calzone* Recipe.
Note: Any leftover filling can be used to make a delicious vegetable gratin. Try it over alternating slices of fried eggplant and fresh tomatoes. Bake in a 350-degree oven until golden and bubbly.

Calzone Pugliesi

Crust Suggestions: Basic Pizza, Sicilian-style, Herb, Onion, Cheese, *Prosciutto*, Sausage, Pepper-Lard, or Semolina dough.

THIS IS A TRADITIONAL *calzone* from Apulia, the "heel" of the Italian boot. Try it hot or cold.

1 **cup Basic Pizza Sauce (see recipe page 72)**
2 **cans anchovies, drained, or 2 cans sardines, drained**

1. Follow the Master *Calzone* Recipe from step 3 through step 5.
2. Spread a few spoonfuls of sauce over each *calzone*. Lay some anchovies over the sauce. Then add some black olives and cheese. Sprinkle each *calzone* filling with a few grindings of black pepper and proceed with the Master Recipe from step 6 on.

Variation

Substitute drained canned oil-packed tuna fish for the anchovies or sardines.

Note: Any leftover filling may be tossed with pasta.

25 **oil-cured black olives, pitted**
¾ **pound scamorza or mozzarella, coarsely shredded**
Freshly ground black pepper to taste

Meat Calzone

Crust Suggestions: Basic Pizza, Sicilian-style, Herb, Onion, Cheese, Pepper-Lard, or Semolina dough.

FOR A HEARTY, thoroughly satisfying, complete meal all wrapped up in a neat crust, try this meat *calzone*. Filled with chunks of sausage, hearty tomato sauce, and thick cheese, this is a dish that you can truly sink your teeth into! It's excellent hot or cold.

Proceed with the Master *Calzone* Recipe up to step 5 and lay the filling in the following order: Sausage, followed by a few spoonfuls of sauce, and finished with a generous sprinkling of cheese. Then follow the Master Recipe from step 6 on.

Variations

Use 1 recipe for Meatballs (page 199) instead of the sausage.

Add pitted black olives, coarsely chopped onions or peppers, or sautéed mushrooms—any one or combination to taste. (Don't overfill the *calzone* or it will burst.)

Note: Any leftover filling may be tossed with cooked ziti or cooked spaghetti squash and then baked in a 400-degree oven for about 20 minutes, or until heated through. The filling is also good as a stuffing for baked eggplant.

1½ **pounds sweet or hot Italian sausage, cut into bite-sized pieces**
1 **cup Basic Pizza Sauce (see recipe page 72) or other tomato sauce**
½ **pound mozzarella, coarsely shredded**

Hearty Eggplant and Sausage Calzone

Crust Suggestions: Basic Pizza, Sicilian-style, Herb, Onion, Cheese, Pepper-Lard, or Semolina dough.

HERE IS ANOTHER *Calzone* adaptation borrowed from the stew-like filling of *Deep-Dish Eggplant Pizza*. These *calzoni* are good hot or cold.

4 cups Eggplant-Sausage Sauce (see recipe page 76)

½ pound mozzarella, coarsely shredded

2 tablespoons freshly grated Parmesan cheese

1. Follow the Master *Calzone* Recipe starting with step 3 through step 5 and lay a few spoonfuls of the Eggplant-Sausage Sauce down first on each *calzone*. Then add some mozzarella and a sprinkling of Parmesan.

2. Then follow the Master Recipe from step 6 on.

Variations

Use ½ of one recipe *Ratatouille* (page 81) plus ½ pound of Italian sausage cut into bite-sized chunks and ½ pound Fontina cheese, cut into ½-inch cubes. Put some of the *Ratatouille* down first, then some sausage meat, and top with some Fontina.

Substitute ½ pound of zucchini, cut into rough chunks and sautéed in 1 tablespoon of olive oil for 2 to 3 minutes (until they are just crunchy) for the sausage meat in the Eggplant-Sausage Sauce on page 76.

Note: Any leftover filling may be tossed with cooked ziti or cooked spaghetti squash and then baked in a 400-degree oven for about 20 minutes, or until heated through.

Shrimp and Pesto Calzone

Crust Suggestions: Basic Pizza, Sicilian-style, Herb, Onion, Pepper-Lard, or Semolina dough.

IF THE FRESH AROMA of *Pesto* doesn't charm you, the colors in this *calzone* will. It makes a unique and elegant first course for a special meal or as a luncheon entrée. Serve them at room temperature.

1 pound (30 to 35) fresh shrimp, peeled, deveined, washed, and well dried

1. Combine the shrimp, tomatoes, and *Pesto* in a mixing bowl.

2. Follow the Master *Calzone* Recipe from step 3 through step 5.

3. Divide the shrimp equally among the *calzoni* and lay some mozzarella on top of the shrimp.

4. Proceed with the Master Recipe from step 6 on.
Variation
Substitute 1 pound of bay scallops for the shrimp or a mixture of half shrimp and half scallops.
Note: Any leftover filling may be used to fill an omelet or tossed quickly with pasta.

1 **pound fresh tomatoes, seeded, drained, and roughly chopped**
¾ **cup** *Pesto* **(see recipe page 82)**
½ **pound mozzarella, coarsely shredded**

Savory Goat Cheese and Onion Calzone

Crust Suggestions: Basic Pizza, Sicilian-style, Herb, Pepper-Lard, or Semolina dough.

THIS CALZONE FILLING was adapted from Madeleine Kamman's recipe for *Torteau Fromage aux Oignons* (cheese and onion pie) in *When French Women Cook*. The combination of goat cheese, sour cream, herbs, and onions is so superb that you may want to try this filling out on top of a pizza, too, just to taste it browned and puffed from the oven. Inside pizza or on top, this is a winner. This *calzone* is good hot or cold.

1. Combine the onions, goat cheese, sour cream, eggs, and pepper in a mixing bowl.
2. Proceed with step 3 of the Master *Calzone* Recipe.
3. After completing step 5 of the Master Recipe, sprinkle each helping of the cheese filling with some thyme before continuing with the recipe from step 6.
Note: Any leftover filling is excellent mixed with julienned zucchini and baked in a shallow baking dish in a 350-degree oven for about 45 minutes, or until the zucchini is tender.

1 **pound sweet onions, peeled, roughly sliced, and cooked down to the translucent stage in 4 tablespoons of sweet butter or olive oil (about 10 minutes)**
12 **ounces chèvre (goat cheese), without rind or ash coating, crumbled**
½ **cup sour cream**
2 **extra large eggs, beaten Freshly ground black pepper to taste Dried or fresh thyme**

Riviera Breakfast Calzone

Crust Suggestions: Basic Pizza, Sicilian-style, Herb, Onion, Cheese, Pepper-Lard, or Semolina dough.

I DON'T KNOW IF anyone on the Riviera actually eats this *calzone* for breakfast, but, whenever I have it, images of the Riviera dance in my head. Whatever time of the day you choose to enjoy this heady Mediterranean mixture of flavors, the effect will please your palate. These *calzoni* are good hot or cold, but I prefer them at room temperature.

2 pounds ripe tomatoes, seeded, well drained, and roughly chopped

¼ pound smoked mozzarella, grated

4 ounces *prosciutto*, cut into ½-inch cubes

20 oil-cured black olives, pitted and roughly chopped

1 small sweet red onion, peeled and thinly sliced

2 tablespoons drained capers

2 garlic cloves, peeled and minced

Generous sprinklings of fresh or dried herbs, such as marjoram, oregano, thyme, or a mixture of *herbs de Provence*

Coarsely ground black pepper to taste

Extra-virgin olive oil to taste

1. Combine all of the ingredients in a bowl, except the herbs, pepper, and oil, with a few swift strokes.

2. Proceed with the Master *Calzone* Recipe starting from step 3 through step 5.

3. After filling each *calzone* with the mixture, sprinkle the herbs and pepper over each one and drizzle with some olive oil. Continue with the Master Recipe from step 6 on.

Note: Any leftover filling makes a great omelet filling or is delicious tossed with hot pasta.

Western Breakfast Calzone

Crust Suggestions: Basic Pizza, Sicilian-style, Herb I and II, Onion,
Cheese, Pepper-Lard, or Semolina dough.

1. Combine all the ingredients in a mixing bowl.

2. Proceed with step 3 of the Master *Calzone* Recipe.

Note: Any leftover filling makes a great omelet filling or is delicious tossed with hot pasta.

1½ pounds ripe tomatoes, seeded and roughly chopped, or 10 oil-packed sun-dried to-matoes, drained and chopped

1 pound fresh mush-rooms, quartered and sautéed in 1 tablespoon of olive oil for 10 minutes

½ pound boiled ham, cut into ½-inch cubes

½ pound Fontina cheese, cut into ½-inch cubes

4 extra large eggs, beaten
Coarsely ground black pepper to taste
Sprinkling of fresh parsley, basil, or *herbes de Provence* (about 1 tablespoon of fresh herbs, or 2 teaspoons of dried)

Manhattan Breakfast Calzone

Crust Suggestions: Basic Pizza, Sicilian-style, Herb, Onion, Cheese, Pepper-Lard, or Semolina dough.

HAVE YOU EVER HAD a picnic breakfast? It's really a great way to start off a lazy spring or summer Sunday.

1 **pound sweet or hot Italian sausage, cut into bite-sized pieces**
1 **cup onions, peeled, roughly chopped, and sautéed in 1 tablespoon of olive oil for 5 minutes**
1 **large sweet green pepper, seeded and roughly chopped (The pepper can be added to the onions to cook off some of its rawness.)**
½ **pound mozzarella, grated**
4 **extra large eggs, beaten**

1. Combine all of the ingredients in a mixing bowl.
2. Proceed with the Master *Calzone* Recipe from step 3 on. Work quickly with this filling as it tends to spread and leak; try to seal the *calzoni* as quickly as possible.

Variation

Any sausage can be substituted for the Italian sausage. Other cheeses, such as Fontina, Gouda, Gruyère, or even Cheddar cheese, also add different touches.

Note: Any leftover filling can be used to fill an omelet.

Fresh Tomato and Smoked Mozzarella Calzone

Crust Suggestions: Basic Pizza, Sicilian-style, Herb, Onion, *Prosciutto*, Sausage, Pepper-Lard, or Semolina dough.

THESE CALZONI LEND THEMSELVES particularly well to hot-weather cooking, as they can be made early in the day and enjoyed at room temperature in the evening.

1. Combine all of the ingredients in a medium-sized bowl.

2. Follow the Master *Calzone* Recipe starting with step 3 and on to the end.

Note: Any leftover filling may be tossed with pasta.

1 **pound ripe tomatoes, seeded, well drained, and roughly chopped**

4 **extra large eggs, beaten**

½ **pound smoked mozzarella, coarsely shredded**

¼ **cup freshly grated Parmesan cheese**

2 **garlic cloves, peeled and minced**

8 **to 10 fresh basil leaves, shredded**
   Coarsely ground black pepper to taste

Calzoni con Tonno

Crust Suggestions: Basic Pizza, Sicilian-style, Herb, Onion, Pepper-Lard, or Semolina dough.

1. Follow the Master *Calzone* Recipe from step 3 through step 5.

2. Lay some tomatoes, tuna, anchovies, olives, and capers on each *calzone*. Sprinkle each *calzone* filling with a few drops of lemon juice and finish with a layer of hard-boiled eggs.

3. Proceed with the Master *Calzone* Recipe from step 6 on.

Note: Mash any leftover filling with a fork and use it as a spread for crackers or as a sandwich filling or as a filling for raw vegetables, such as cucumbers and tomatoes.

2 **pounds ripe tomatoes, seeded, drained, and roughly chopped**

1 **7-ounce can tuna in olive oil, drained and roughly flaked**

1 **2-ounce can anchovy fillets, drained**

2 **tablespoons drained capers**
   Juice of 1 lemon

3 **hard-boiled extra large eggs, peeled and sliced**

Broccoli-Cheese Mezzaluna

Crust Suggestions: Basic Pizza, Sicilian-style, Onion, *Prosciutto*, Sausage, Pepper-Lard, or Semolina dough.

A CALZONE BY any other name is a *mezzaluna*. Call them what you will, these lushly verdant, stuffed "half moons" are delicious hot or cold and will make a welcome addition to your repertoire of recipe favorites.

1 **pound mushrooms, cleaned and thinly sliced**
2 **tablespoons olive oil**
 Salt and freshly ground black pepper to taste
1 **recipe well-drained Italian Greens (page 80), using 1 pound broccoli rabe cut into bite-sized pieces**
½ **pound smoked mozzarella, coarsely shredded**

1. Sauté the mushrooms in the olive oil until all their excess liquid has evaporated. Season with salt and pepper.

2. Combine the mushrooms and greens in a mixing bowl and proceed with step 3 of the Master *Calzone* Recipe.

3. After completing step 5 of the Master Recipe, sprinkle mozzarella on each of the *calzone* and continue with step 6.

Variations

Omit the mushrooms and smoked mozzarella and add 2 cans tuna packed in olive oil, drained and roughly flaked, and 2 tablespoons drained capers.

Omit the mushrooms and smoked mozzarella and substitute ½ pound *prosciutto*, cut into ½-inch cubes, and ½ pound Fontina cheese, cut into ½-inch cubes.

Note: Any leftover filling may be used to fill an omelet or tossed with pasta.

Sausage, Spinach, and Cheese Mezzaluna

Crust Suggestions: Basic Pizza, Sicilian-style, Onion, *Prosciutto*, Sausage, Pepper-Lard, or Semolina dough.

FOR A MAIN DISH PIZZA that has it all, try this luscious *mezzaluna*. Its combination of lively greens, creamy cheeses, and bits of sausage throughout are enough to drive you to third helpings! These are good hot or cold.

1. Combine the spinach, cheeses, sausage meat, and black pepper in a mixing bowl.

2. Proceed with the Master *Calzone* Recipe from step 3 on.

Note: This filling makes a good filling for manicotti. It can be frozen for up to 2 months.

1 recipe well-drained Italian Greens (page 80), using 1 pound fresh spinach or 2 10-ounce packages frozen spinach, defrosted, and squeezed dry
½ pound ricotta
½ pound mozzarella, coarsely shredded
½ pound Italian sausage meat, removed from the casings and crumbled
Freshly ground black pepper to taste

Rolled Calzone

For this last variety of *calzone*, the dough is folded over or rolled around a filling, and the result looks very much like its namesake—a trouser leg. This shape makes it perfect for eating pizza on the run, as it fits neatly in the hand.

But the form also has its limitations. Fillings that give off liquid and those that are particularly soft are not suited to this type of *calzone*, because the ends of the roll are not sealed.

The Eppi Roll

Crust Suggestions: Basic Pizza, Sicilian-style, *Prosciutto*, Sausage, Onion, Cheese, Herb, Pepper-Lard, or Semolina dough.

IN MANHATTAN, LAND of pizza by the slice and eating on the run, these calzoni are known as sausage rolls, and they are very popular.

How did the name *eppi roll* evolve? Ask any pizza-maker in New York City, and you'll probably get the same answer I did, "I just make pizza. I don't name 'em." Someday I will get to the bottom of the name, but for the time being, try any one of these *calzoni* and you'll see why New Yorkers are so fond of them.

2 tablespoons olive oil

2 medium-sized sweet onions, peeled and thickly sliced (in vertical slices)

2 sweet green peppers, seeded and cut into thick slices

10 hot or sweet Italian sausages, pricked all over with a fork

1. Heat the oil in a large frying pan. Add the onions, peppers, and sausages and sauté over medium heat for 10 minutes, or until the onions are golden, and the peppers are tender, and the sausages begin to color. Let cool for about 10 minutes.

2. Proceed with step 3 of the Master *Calzone* Recipe through to step 5. Roll the dough out into oval shapes rather than circular ones. Place one sausage and some peppers and onions at the top of one oval piece of dough and roll the dough around them (*Figs. 23A, B, and C*).

3. Continue with the Master Recipe through step 6.

4. Bake the sausage rolls in a pan as they do tend to leak.

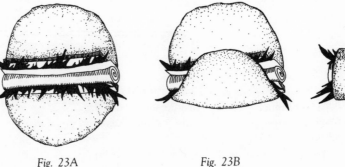

Fig. 23A   Fig. 23B   Fig. 23C

Prosciutto, Smoked Mozzarella, and Sun-Dried Tomato Roll

1. Proceed with step 3 of the Master *Calzone* Recipe through step 5, but roll the dough out into oval shapes rather than circular ones. Place one rolled slice of *prosciutto*, some mozzarella, and a sun-dried tomato at the top of one oval piece of dough and roll the dough around them.

2. Continue with the Master Recipe through step 6.

3. Bake the *calzoni* in a pan to prevent their leaking onto the oven.

10 thin slices *prosciutto*, rolled up

½ pound smoked mozzarella, cut into thin slices

10 whole oil-packed sun-dried tomatoes

Spinach-Fontina-Ham Roll

1. Proceed with step 3 of the Master *Calzone* Recipe through step 5. Roll the dough out into oval shapes rather than circular ones. Place some spinach and some cheese and ham strips at the top of one oval piece of dough and roll the dough around them.

2. Continue with the Master Recipe through step 6.

3. Bake the *calzoni* in a pan to prevent their leaking onto the oven.

1 pound leaf spinach, stemmed, washed, cooked, and squeezed dry

½ pound Fontina cheese cut into 1- × ¼-inch strips

½ pound boiled ham in one piece (approx. ¼ inch thick), cut into 1- × ¼-inch strips

Panzerotti

ALTHOUGH DEEP-FRIED *panzerotti* are quite a treat, for reasons of health and convenience, I much prefer to bake them in the oven. Baked *panzerotti* are infinitely lighter and less troublesome to cook, and they freeze and reheat well. These features can matter a great deal if you are preparing a large number of them for a party or if you like to keep some on hand in the freezer for unexpected guests.

Here are a few traditional fillings to get you started. If you'd like to improvise different ones, bear in mind that a *panzerotti* is meant to be eaten in two or three bites, like *pizzette*, so keep the fillings simple. Don't overcomplicate flavors by adding too many different elements. The best *panzerotti* are those made with one or two strong flavors.

Panzerotti Master Recipe

Yield: Roman Pepper Pastry will make approximately 30 to 35 3-inch *panzerotti*. Any of the other yeast doughs will yield approximately 40 to 45 3-inch *panzerotti*.

Crust Suggestions: Roman Pepper Pastry Crust, Basic Pizza, Sicilian-style, Semolina, Herb, or Pepper-Lard dough.

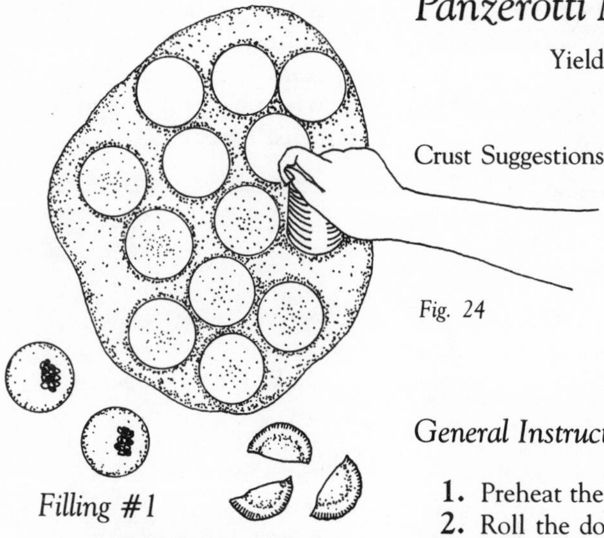

Fig. 24

Filling #1

⅓ cup Basic Pizza Sauce (page 72) or homemade tomato sauce

½ cup scamorza or mozzarella, coarsely shredded

1 garlic clove, peeled and minced

2 fresh basil leaves, finely minced, or ¼ teaspoon dried thyme, oregano, or marjoram

Freshly ground black pepper to taste

General Instructions for Panzerotti

1. Preheat the oven to 450 degrees for 30 minutes.

2. Roll the dough of your choice out to an even ⅛-inch thickness with a rolling pin. If necessary, use dustings of flour to prevent the dough from sticking.

3. Cut out as many *panzerotti* as possible using a 3-inch glass as a cutter (*Fig. 24*).

4. Combine all of the ingredients together in a bowl for any of the 6 filling suggestions.

5. Put a scant teaspoon of filling on one half of each of the circles of dough. (There will be leftover filling if using Roman Pepper Pastry Dough; use it in an omelet.)

6. Fold the dough over into little crescent shapes, pressing down to seal the edges with your fingers. Place each one on an oiled baking sheet.

7. Bake for 15 to 20 minutes, or until lightly colored. Or deep-fry in 2 inches of vegetable oil until golden. (See Master *Calzone* Recipe, page 170 for deep-frying instructions.) *Panzerotti* are best served piping hot.

Freeze the raw *panzerotti* in one layer on a baking sheet.

   Once they are frozen solid, they can be transferred to plastic bags (which should be tightly closed). They can be frozen for up to 4 months.

Reheating

To reheat *panzerotti*, simply put them on a baking sheet and warm them up in a 350-degree oven for 10 to 15 minutes.

   To bake frozen *panzerotti*, preheat the oven to 450-degrees. Lay the *panzerotti* on a baking sheet and cover them tightly with aluminum foil. Bake for 15 minutes. Then remove the foil and continue baking until the turnovers are golden brown.

   Note: Fillings 3 to 6 make exceptional first courses when served with a fresh tomato sauce. The suggested serving size is 3 *panzerotti* per person plus approximately ½ cup of sauce.

Filling #2

- ⅓ cup Basic Pizza Sauce (page 72) or homemade tomato sauce
- ½ cup mozzarella, coarsely shredded
- 1 2-ounce can anchovies, drained and finely chopped
- 1 teaspoon finely minced fresh parsley leaves
  Freshly ground black pepper to taste

Filling #3

- ½ cup cooked spinach, squeezed dry and finely chopped
- ½ cup ricotta
- 2 tablespoons freshly grated Parmesan cheese
- ½ cup finely minced *prosciutto*
  Freshly ground black pepper to taste

Filling #4

- ½ cup cooked spinach, squeezed dry and finely chopped
- 1 2-ounce can anchovies, drained and finely chopped
- 2 tablespoons drained capers
- 2 tablespoons ricotta
  Freshly ground black pepper to taste

Filling #5

- ½ cup shredded Fontina cheese
- ½ cup finely chopped onion, sautéed in 2 teaspoons olive oil until wilted
- 1 teaspoon dried *herbes de Provence*, or 1 tablespoon assorted fresh herbs
- 10 oil-cured black olives, pitted and finely chopped
  Freshly ground black pepper to taste

Filling #6

- ½ cup ricotta
- ¼ cup finely chopped salami
- ½ cup smoked mozzarella, coarsely shredded

Chaussons

Yield: 4 8-inch main-course *chaussons*
6 6-inch appetizer or luncheon *chaussons*
30 to 35 3-inch hors d'oeuvre *rissoles* (the French name for the diminutive form of *chaussons*)

Crust Suggestions: Provençale Olive Oil or Roman Pepper Pastry Crust.

CHAUSSONS ARE A VIVID part of my earliest food experiences, for they were the first thing I was allowed to make in the kitchen. Whenever my mother made a tart, there was always enough leftover dough and filling so that I could make my own *chaussons*. I remember my delight in rolling out the dough with my mother's large rolling pin to form the turnovers, and in decorating them with leaves and flowers cut from the last tiny scraps of dough. But the best thing about making *chaussons* was eating them. Perhaps because I made them myself, they always seemed to taste much better than the tart itself.

Like *calzoni*, *chaussons* were invented because thrifty housewives wanted to use up leftovers. But they are so delightful that they deserve to be made from scratch. Their thin crisp pastry crust is considerably lighter than a yeast dough, and their fillings—simple Provençale interpretations—are elegant enough to serve as a first course or luncheon entrée.

Chaussons are good hot or cold and especially delicious when paired with a small bit of dressed salad greens.

General Instructions for Chaussons

1. Prepare 1 recipe of either Provençale Olive Oil Pastry (page 68) or Roman Pepper Pastry (page 68) through step 5.

2. While the dough is resting, prepare the filling of your choice.

3. Mix the ingredients together in a bowl until they are just combined, using any one filling suggestion.

4. Preheat the oven to 450 degrees.

5. Lightly oil a baking sheet.

6. Divide the dough into 4 or 6 pieces.

Filling #1

11 or 12 ounces chèvre (goat cheese) without rind or ash coating
2 garlic cloves, peeled and minced
A few generous grindings of black pepper

7. Roll out either 4 8-inch or 6 6-inch circles and place some filling on the lower half of each *chausson*. (Don't overstuff the *chaussons* or they'll leak.)

8. Lightly moisten the edges of each *chausson* with a pastry brush dipped in water. Fold the top half over and crimp the edges with the tines of a fork.

9. Transfer each *chausson* with a spatula to the prepared baking sheet and bake for 25 to 35 minutes, or until golden brown. Serve hot or at room temperature.

Note: *Chaussons* can be adapted to *panzerotti*-sized portions for finger food. The French call these tiny turnovers *rissoles anciennes* and deep-fry them exactly as the Italians do for *panzerotti*. Use the *Panzerotti* Master Recipe as your guide for rolling, shaping and cooking the *rissoles*.

The same reheating and freezing directions given for *panzerotti* (page 188) can be applied to *chaussons*; only they will take 5 to 10 minutes longer to reheat than the smaller-sized turnovers do.

Variation

Omit the Gruyère and use ½ cup crumbled Roquefort or other blue cheese.

3 to 4 tablespoons fresh (or 3 teaspoons dried) assorted herbs, such as thyme, marjoram, basil, mint, parsley, oregano, chives, sage, or rosemary

Filling #2

1½ cups *Pissaladière* Onion Base (see recipe page 79)

1 2-ounce can anchovies, drained and roughly chopped

15 oil-cured black olives, pitted and roughly chopped

Filling #3

1 cup ripe tomatoes, seeded, drained, and roughly chopped

2 garlic cloves, peeled and minced

2 tablespoons finely minced fresh parsley leaves or other fresh herb

½ cup shredded Gruyère cheese

Filling #4

1 cup ripe tomatoes, seeded, drained, and roughly chopped

½ cup shredded Gruyère cheese

2 tablespoons chopped walnuts

Filling #5

1 cup ripe tomatoes, seeded, drained, and roughly chopped

½ cup *Tapenade* (see recipe page 81)

½ 2-inch onion, peeled and sliced paper thin

3 tablespoons fresh (or 3 teaspoons dried) assorted herbs, such as thyme, marjoram, basil, parsley, rosemary, or fennel seeds

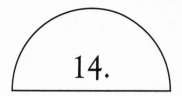

14.

S tuffed pizzas are among the most versatile of all pizzas. They can enclose any pizza topping or *calzone* filling; they can be prepared in advance and frozen or reheated; and they are substantial enough to feed 6 hungry people. The same size double-crust pie can be served in neat wedges as a main course, a luncheon dish, an appetizer, or as part of a buffet dinner.

STUFFED PIZZA

Stuffed Pizza Master Recipe

1. One recipe pizza dough, ready to use.

2. Preheat the oven to 450 degrees for 15 minutes before baking.

3. Lightly coat a 15-inch round, preferably black, pizza pan with vegetable oil and sprinkle it lightly with coarsely ground yellow cornmeal.

4. Divide the dough into 2 portions, making one slightly larger than the other.

5. Dust the work surface lightly with flour and roll out the larger portion of dough into a thin 15-inch circle and carefully transfer it to the prepared pizza pan.

6. Layer the fillings in the order given for each recipe, leaving a 2-inch border of dough.

7. Roll out the second piece of dough into a 14-inch circle and fit it over the filling.

8. Fold the bottom edge of the dough over the top all around the pie and finish by crimping the edge decoratively with your fingers or with a fork. (See Note.)

9. Before baking, brush the top and edges of the stuffed pizza lightly with some olive oil.

10. Bake for 30 to 40 minutes, or until golden brown.

11. Remove the pizza from the pan and let it cool on a wire rack for 5 to 10 minutes before slicing. (This will ensure neater slices.) Use a serrated bread knife to cut the slices.

Note: For a thicker, more bread-like crust, let the pie rise in the pan for 30 to 45 minutes before baking.

Freezing

Half-cook the pie for about 15 to 20 minutes, or until it just begins to color. Let it cool completely before wrapping in foil and freezing.

These pies are excellent cold but they can be reheated for 15 minutes in a 400-degree oven.

To reheat frozen pies, put the foil-wrapped pie in a preheated 400-degree oven for 30 minutes. Remove the pie from its foil cover and transfer it to a baking pan. Turn the oven temperature up to 450 degrees and bake the pie for another 15 or 20 minutes, or until it is well browned.

Note: Substitute any pizza topping or *calzone* stuffing for any of the fillings on the following pages.

Keep the filling pieces bite-sized and remember to pit any olives before you add them to the stuffing.

Pitta Calabrese I (Calabrian Meat Pie)

Yield: 1 12- to 14-inch pie.
Serves 4 to 6 as a main course.
Crust Suggestions: Basic Pizza, Sicilian-style, Herb, Pepper-Lard, or Semolina dough.

CALABRIA, THAT SMALL REGION located at the toe of the Italian boot, is the home of a group of stuffed pies known as *pitte*. This hearty dish of the people is the Calabrese version of pizza, and like its Neapolitan cousin, it is inexpensive and utterly delicious. Both the word *pitta* and the dish itself can be traced back to the Greeks, who colonized that area during antiquity and who introduced similar pizza prototypes to other southern Italian colonies.

1. Preheat the oven to 450 degrees. Lightly coat a 15-inch pizza pan with vegetable oil and sprinkle it lightly with coarsely ground yellow cornmeal.

2. Heat the 2 tablespoons of the olive oil in a medium-sized frying pan. Add the onions and sauté over moderate heat for about 3 minutes, or until they became translucent.

3. Add the chopped meat and break up the lumps with a fork. When the meat is no longer pink, add the garlic and fennel seeds and season with salt and pepper. Stir to prevent sticking and continue to cook over moderate heat for 3 minutes longer.

1 **recipe pizza dough, ready to use**
2 **tablespoons olive oil**
1 **medium-sized sweet onion, peeled and roughly chopped**
1 **pound lean chopped beef or pork**
2 **garlic cloves, peeled, crushed and minced**

1 teaspoon fennel seeds
 Salt and freshly ground
 black pepper to taste
½ cup dry red wine
1 tablespoon chopped
 fresh parsley leaves
2 cups roughly crushed,
 seeded, and drained
 whole tomatoes
½ pound scamorza or
 mozzarella, thinly sliced

4. Add the wine to the pan, turn the heat up to high, and cook until the wine evaporates completely. Stir in the parsley and remove from the heat. Let cool while preparing the *pitta*.

5. Follow steps 4 through 6 of the Stuffed Pizza Master Recipe.

6. Spread the meat over the dough. Top with the tomatoes and then with the cheese.

7. Continue with the Master Recipe from step 7 through to completion.

Variation

Substitute hot Italian sausage meat, remove from the casings and crumbled, for the chopped meat. Omit the fennel.

Pitta Calabrese II

Yield: 1 12- to 14-inch pie.
Serves 4 to 6 as a main course.
Crust Suggestions: Basic Pizza, Sicilian-style, Herb, Pepper-Lard, or Semolina dough.

1 recipe pizza dough,
 ready to use
5 tablespoons olive oil
3 pounds sweet onions,
 peeled and thinly sliced
4 ounces diced bacon,
 pancetta, prosciutto, or
 pork cracklings
1 bay leaf
 Salt and freshly ground
 black pepper to taste
1 tablespoon chopped
 fresh parsley leaves
½ pound caciocavallo,
 coarsely shredded

1. Heat 4 tablespoons of the olive oil in a large frying pan and sauté the onions, bacon, and bay leaf over moderate heat for about 20 minutes, stirring to prevent sticking, or until the onions are soft and the excess liquid has evaporated.

2. Remove the pan from the heat and remove the bay leaf. Season the onion mixture with salt and pepper and stir in the fresh parsley.

3. Follow steps 4 to 6 of the Stuffed Pizza Master Recipe.

4. Spread the onions over the bottom crust and lay the cheese over the onions.

5. Continue with the Master Recipe from step 7 through completion.

Pitta Imbottite (Stuffed Pizza)

Yield: 1 12- to 14-inch pie.
Serves 4 to 6 as a main course.
Crust Suggestions: Basic Pizza, Sicilian-style, Herb, Pepper-Lard, or
Semolina dough.

THIS POPULAR VEGETARIAN version of pizza is even better when it is
served at room temperature or warmed up.

1. Follow steps 4 through 6 of the Stuffed Pizza Master Recipe.
2. Mix the greens together with the ricotta in a large bowl.
3. Spread the greens and cheese mixture on the bottom crust. Then
lay the anchovies, black olives, and, finally, the mozzarella over all.
4. Continue with the Master Recipe from step 7 through to completion.

Variation

Add 5 whole oil-packed sun-dried tomatoes, drained and coarsely
shredded with the anchovies and black olives before finishing with the
shredded cheese.

1 recipe pizza dough,
 ready to use
1 recipe spinach or other
 similar greens prepared
 according to the Italian
 Greens Recipe, page
 80, well drained
1½ pounds ricotta
1 2-ounce can anchovies,
 drained
15 oil-cured black olives,
 pitted and roughly
 chopped
½ pound mozzarella,
 coarsely shredded

Sfincuini di Palermo

Yield: 1 15-inch pie.

Serves 4 to 6 as a main course.

Crust Suggestions: Basic Pizza, Sicilian-style, Herb, Pepper-Lard, or Semolina dough.

PALERMO, THE CAPITAL of Sicily, is known for its version of stuffed pizza, the *sfincuini*, which is very similar to *pitta Calabrese*. Both dishes owe more to ancient Greek heritage than to their Italian lineage. Like a *pitta*, *sfincuini* can encase any pizza or *calzone* filling, but the following combinations are especially Sicilian.

1 recipe pizza dough, ready to use

3 hard-boiled eggs, peeled and sliced

2 cups seeded, well-drained, roughly chopped fresh or canned tomatoes

2 garlic cloves, peeled and minced

1 tablespoon chopped fresh parsley leaves

1 teaspoon dried oregano

1 teaspoon chopped fresh mint leaves (Omit if fresh is not available.)

10 oil-cured olives, pitted and roughly chopped

1 2-ounce can anchovies, drained

½ pound caciocavallo, shredded

1. Follow steps 4 through 6 of the Stuffed Pizza Master Recipe.

2. Lay the hard-boiled eggs on the bottom crust first. Then spread the tomatoes over the eggs and sprinkle on the garlic and herbs. Lay the anchovies and olives on next and finish with a thick layer of cheese over all.

3. Continue with the Master Recipe from step 7 through completion.

Sfincuini Trapanese

Yield: 1 15-inch pie.

Serves 4 to 6 as a main course and 8 to 10 as an appetizer.

Crust Suggestions: Basic Pizza, Sicilian-style, Herb, Pepper-Lard, or Semolina dough.

EACH SPRING THE ports of the Trapanese region are the final destination of the fishing boats returning from *la mattanza,* the Sicilian ritual of the tuna kill. Entire schools of tuna are caught in nets and speared with harpoons when they rise to the surface. The tuna kill is a deeply rooted Sicilian tradition, and it attracts a fair number of tourists.

This recipe, from the port town of Trapani, makes lavish use of tuna. Only tuna packed in olive oil will do for this dish; anything else would be too bland. Serve this pizza cool or at room temperature and do try it with a semolina crust.

1. Follow steps 4 to 6 of the Stuffed Pizza Master Recipe.

2. Combine the eggs, tuna, anchovies, capers, lemon juice, and black pepper in a bowl. Mix with a fork.

3. Lay this mixture over the bottom crust and then spread the tomatoes over all.

4. Continue with the Master Recipe from step 7 through to completion.

1 recipe pizza dough, ready to use

3 hard-boiled eggs, peeled and chopped

2 7-ounce cans Italian-style tuna packed in olive oil, drained and flaked

1 2-ounce can anchovies, drained

⅓ cup drained capers
  Juice of 2 lemons
  Freshly ground black pepper to taste

1 pound ripe tomatoes, seeded and roughly chopped

Sfincuini con Polpette

Yield: 1 15-inch pie.

Serves 4 to 6 as a main course.

Crust Suggestions: Basic Pizza, Sicilian-style, Pepper-Lard, or Semolina dough.

WHO INVENTED THE MEATBALL? Although the Sicilians claim parentage, the true originators are the ancient Greeks.

One of the major influences on ancient cuisine had to do with the fact that people ate in a reclining position. Dining in this fashion created certain limitations on the kinds of dishes served; the foods had to be eaten with one hand while the other was engaged in supporting the diner's head propped up on one elbow. Thus, the meatball was originally conceived of as a finger food, which could be eaten without utensils.

But if the Greeks came up with the original concept for the dish, it is the Sicilians who made *polpette* (meatballs) world famous. Sicilian meatballs come in all shapes and sizes and are served dozens of different ways: stuffed, fried, baked, stewed in sauces, added to broth, and, of course, in pizza.

I had always thought that meatball pizza was an American invention until I came across this recipe for the original Sicilian version. Stuffing a pie with meatballs makes much more sense than cooking them on top of pizza, where they become tough and dry. Enclosed in a crisp crust, smothered in zesty tomatoes and cheese, *sfincuini con polpette* is terrific.

1 recipe pizza dough, ready to use

1 recipe for Meatballs (see following recipe)

1 cup homemade tomato sauce or well-drained coarsely crushed whole tomatoes

½ pound mozzarella, coarsely shredded

1. Follow steps 4 to 6 of the Stuffed Pizza Master Recipe.

2. Lay the meatballs over the bottom crust. Cover them with the tomato sauce and sprinkle the cheese over all.

3. Continue with the Master Recipe page 192 from step 7 through to completion.

Meatballs

1. Preheat the oven to 450 degrees.
2. Combine the meats, garlic, onion, bread crumbs, cheese, parsley, eggs, salt, pepper, and the nutmeg in a bowl. Blend well using your hands to knead everything together.
3. Shape the mixture into 1-inch balls and place on an oiled baking pan.
4. Bake the meatballs for 30 to 45 minutes, turning them frequently, until they are evenly browned.

Note: These meatballs freeze very well. Therefore, try doubling or tripling the recipe whenever possible so that you can always have a supply on hand.

½ **pound lean ground beef**
½ **pound lean ground pork**
½ **pound ground veal**
1 **clove garlic, peeled and finely minced**
1 **medium-sized onion, finely chopped**
1 **cup unseasoned bread crumbs**
¼ **cup grated Romano cheese**
2 **tablespoons chopped fresh parsley leaves**
½ **teaspoon salt**
1 **teaspoon freshly ground black pepper**
Pinch of grated nutmeg

Pizza Rustica

Yield: 1 12- by 8-inch rectangular pie, *or* a 10- to 12-inch springform pan.
Serves 8 as a main course or 10 to 12 as an appetizer.
Crust Suggestions: Basic Pizza, Sicilian-style, Pepper-Lard, Semolina dough.

PIZZA RUSTICA IS A general title for any deep-dish egg- and cheese-based pie. These densely rich country (rustica means *from the country*) pizzas are the ancestors of the French Quiche Lorraine, which was also at one time made with a bread dough. Most modern recipes for *pizza rustica* call for a pastry crust (*pasta frolla*) but I prefer to use the traditional bread dough, because it is much easier to handle than ordinary pie pastry, and I think it tastes better. Yeast-raised crusts are stronger and have less tendency to leak.

These pizzas are so rich that a little goes a long way. Serve small pieces of this pastry as a first course or with a fresh tomato salad as a main course. Be sure to let the pie sit for 20 to 30 minutes before slicing into it, or the filling will ooze out.

1 recipe pizza dough, ready to use
½ pound sweet Italian sausage meat, removed from the casings and crumbled and cooked in 1 tablespoon of olive oil until just browned
2 pounds ricotta
½ pound smoked mozzarella, shredded
3 extra large eggs, beaten Freshly ground black pepper to taste

1. Preheat the oven to 400 degrees. Lightly coat a 12- by 8-inch baking pan or a 10- to 12-inch springform pan with oil.

2. Combine the sausage meat, ricotta, smoked mozzarella, eggs, and black pepper in a large bowl. Set aside until needed.

3. Divide the dough into two portions, making one two-thirds the size of the other.

4. Roll out the larger ball into a 12- by 15-inch rectangle and fit it into the baking pan leaving an overhang of ½ inch.

5. Spread the filling evenly over the dough shell.

6. Roll out a second rectangle of dough to 10- by 13-inches and fit it onto the top of the pie.

7. Fold the dough edges together around the dish and crimp to seal the pie. Use any remaining extra pieces of dough for decoration of top of the pizza. Cut out leaves and flowers and attach them to the top of the crust with a damp pastry brush. Make a steam hole in the dough at the center of the pie.

8. Brush the dough with a little olive oil or with an egg white glaze (1 egg white beaten with 1 tablespoon of water) before baking.

9. Bake for 50 to 60 minutes, or until golden brown. Let the pie sit for 20 to 30 minutes before slicing.

Variation

Add only 1 pound of ricotta and 2 pounds fresh spinach or 2 10-ounce packages frozen spinach, cooked, chopped, and squeezed dry, to the custard base.

Substitute ½ pound salami cut into ½-inch cubes for the sausage meat.

Fig. 25

Torta Rustica

Yield: 1 *torta* serves 8 to 10 as a main course or 14 to 18 as an appetizer or as part of a cold buffet.

ONE CAN SEE HOW pâtés en croûte might have developed from *tortas rusticas*. The beautiful mosaic-like filling and golden shiny outer crust make *torta rustica* a truly elegant buffet or brunch centerpiece (*Fig. 25*). And it's easy to prepare as well. Keep in mind that the entire dish must be prepared ahead of time.

1. Preheat the oven to 400 degrees. Lightly coat a 9½- to 10-inch springform pan with oil.

2. In a bowl, beat the 6 eggs with a fork and then season them with Parmesan cheese, marjoram, and black pepper.

3. Make 2 *frittatas* in a 10-inch frying pan: Heat 1 tablespoon of olive oil in the frying pan. Pour in half the eggs, cover the pan, and cook over low heat until the eggs are just set on top. Loosen the *frittata* with a spatula and slide it from the pan onto a plate. Repeat the procedure for the second *frittata*. Set the *frittatas* aside until needed.

4. In another bowl, combine the spinach, ricotta, black pepper, and parsley. Set aside until needed.

5. Cut one quarter of the dough off and return it to the bowl. Roll out the other larger portion into a 16-inch circle and fit it into the prepared pan, leaving an overhang of 1 inch.

6. Lay the filling down in the following order: One *frittata*, half of the spinach-ricotta mixture, half of the ham, half of the Fontina and all of the sun-dried tomatoes. Repeat the layers again finishing with a layer of Fontina.

7. Divide the remaining dough in half and roll half into a 10-inch circle. Fit that circle over the top of the *torta*, pinch the edges together and fold them under. Crimp the outer edge of the *torta* with a fork.

8. Roll out the remaining dough and cut out leaf shapes with a cookie cutter. Decorate the top of the *torta* by arranging the leaves over the crust and brushing them with a damp pastry brush to attach them.

9. Beat the egg yolk with the 2 tablespoons of water and brush the top of the *torta* lightly with the glaze. Don't attempt to use all of the glaze; most of it will be leftover.

10. Bake for 35 to 40 minutes, or until the *torta* is deep brown. Remove from the oven and let cool on a wire rack for 15 minutes before loosening the sides of the springform.

11. Let the *torta* cool for at least 30 to 45 minutes before serving. It is not supposed to be served hot, or all of the filling just slides out. (If thin, 2-inch slices are desired, the *torta* must be completely cold before it is cut.)

1 recipe **Rich Egg Dough (see recipe page 69), ready to use**

6 **extra large eggs**

¼ **cup freshly grated Parmesan cheese**

½ **teaspoon dried marjoram or dried oregano**
  Freshly ground black pepper to taste

2 **tablespoons olive oil**

2 **pounds fresh spinach, or 2 10-ounce packages frozen spinach, cooked, squeezed dry, and chopped**

½ **cup ricotta**

1 **tablespoon chopped fresh parsley leaves**

1 **pound boiled ham in one piece, cut into ½-inch cubes**

1 **pound Italian Fontina cheese, cut into slices**

10 **whole oil-packed sun-dried tomatoes, drained and cut into bite-sized pieces**

1 **egg yolk**

2 **tablespoons water**

Pizza Pasqualina (Italian Easter Pie)

Yield: 1 12- by 8-inch rectangular pie, *or* a 10- to 12-inch round springform pan.

Serves 8 as a main course or 10 to 12 as an appetizer.

Crust Suggestions: Basic Pizza, Sicilian-style, Pepper-Lard, or Semolina dough.

EASTER IS THE BIGGEST holiday of the year in many parts of Europe, particularly in Italy. The Italians look to the holiday as an occasion for serious feasting on special delicacies, both sweet and savory. One of the most celebrated of all those pastries is the egg-rich *pizza Pasqualina*.

Each family has its own version of this Eastertime classic, which is almost identical to *pizza rustica*. In this version, I have kept the number of eggs down to a minimum and still come up with an indecently rich, cheesy filling.

1 **recipe pizza dough, ready to use**

1½ **pounds ricotta**

½ **pound mozzarella, shredded**

½ **cup imported Provolone, shredded**

½ **cup freshly grated Parmesan cheese**

½ **pound salami, *prosciutto*, or ham, or sausage, or a combination of any 2 or 3, cut into ½-inch cubes**

3 **extra large eggs, beaten Freshly ground black pepper to taste**

1 **tablespoon finely minced fresh parsley leaves**

1. Mix together the cheese, meat, eggs, and pepper in a large bowl until well blended. Fold in the parsley with a few swift strokes. Don't overmix or the filling will turn green. Set aside until needed.

2. Follow all the directions given for *pizza rustica*, page 199, substituting this filling instead.

Bonata—rolled pizza—are traditionally filled with meat sauces, greens, cheeses, and sausage, but the filling possibilities don't stop there. There are other, more innovative fillings that are equally enticing. Rolled pizza may have been around for ages, but it is only now beginning to catch on.

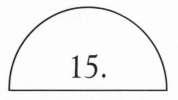

Master Rolled Pizza Recipe

Yield:

1 large 5- by 16-inch flavored bread
8 to 10 2-inch pizza rolls
1 full-size 6- by 16-inch rolled pie. Serves 4 to 6 as a main course or 8 to 10 as an appetizer.
2 half-size 4- by 16-inch rolled pies for smaller party slices (about 32)

Method

1. 1 recipe for pizza dough, ready to use.
2. 1 large 12- by 17-inch jelly roll pan or baking sheet, lightly oiled.
3. Roll the dough out into an even 14- by 16-inch rectangle, lifting it from time to time and dusting it with flour, if necessary, to prevent sticking. Position the longer edge of the finished dough sheet parallel to you, with the shorter edges at either side.
4. Spread the filling evenly over the dough, leaving a 1-inch border all around (*Fig. 26*) and continue layering the ingredients as called for in each recipe in the same manner.
5. Roll the dough up in a jelly roll fashion, starting from the top and rolling toward you, ending with the seam side down (*Fig. 27*).

Fig. 26

Fig. 27

Fig. 28

6. Tuck in the ends and pinch them into points. Lift the roll onto a prepared baking pan with 2 spatulas at either end (*Fig. 28*) and let it rise in the pan for 30 minutes before baking. (For a thinner outer crust and a less bread-like interior, bake immediately.)

Fig. 29

7. Preheat the oven to 400 degrees for 30 minutes.

8. Brush the pie with a little olive oil and bake for 35 to 45 minutes, or until it is golden.

9. Let the roll sit for at least 15 minutes before slicing for neater portions (*Fig. 29*). The colder the roll, the easier it will slice. Most rolled pies are great at room temperature.

For Two Smaller Rolled Pies

1. Proceed with steps 1 to 3 of the Master Recipe.

2. Cut across the center of the dough sheet and make 2 7- by 16-inch rectangles.

3. Divide the filling between the two (you will need slightly less filling, therefore, don't try to cram it all in) and continue with the Master Recipe from step 4 on.

Note: Smaller rolled pies take about 5 or 10 minutes less time to cook.

Freezing

Half-cook pizza breads, rolls, or pies until they just begin to color and let them cool off totally before wrapping in foil and freezing.

Reheating

1. Reheat breads, rolls, and smaller sized rolled pies in a preheated 350-degree oven for 10 to 15 minutes; full-size rolled pies need an additional 5 minutes baking time.

2. To reheat frozen breads and rolls, let them defrost in the foil at room temperature for 3 to 4 hours and bake, uncovered, in a preheated 400-degree oven for 15 to 20 minutes. Remove the foil and finish baking for an additional 10 to 15 minutes.

3. Follow the same directions for full-size rolled pies but allow more time to reheat.

1. All fillings for rolled pizza should be finely minced to facilitate rolling and to prevent holes from being poked through the dough.

2. Avoid over-moist fillings or too much sauce as they tend to leak out and cause the pie to become soggy.

3. If you should wish to improvise other fillings for rolled pizza, try not to go beyond 2 cups of ingredients in all, or they may leak out.

Panino Saporito

Yield: 32 small-size spiral buns.
Crust Suggestions: Basic Pizza, Sicilian-style, Herb, Pepper-Lard, or
Semolina dough.

THESE LITTLE SAVORY BUNS were created in the spirit of the Italian *fare uno spuntino*—to have a snack. They are excellent hot from the oven, cold, as party offerings, or as side dishes with soup or salad. Because the rolls are cut from the pie before baking, the filling has a chance to nudge its way up from the dough spiral and expose its chewy morsels while each bun puffs up and browns.

1. Follow the directions given in the Master Rolled Pizza Recipe for steps 1 through 3 and prepare two smaller sized rectangles of dough.

2. Brush the garlic oil over each piece of dough. Then season the dough with black pepper. Sprinkle the remaining ingredients evenly over all.

3. Continue with the Master Recipe from step 5, but do not tuck and pinch the ends shut. Cut 1-inch-thick slices from each roll and place them on a prepared baking sheet. Do not brush with oil before baking; they already have enough.

4. Bake for 10 to 15 minutes, or until golden brown and crusty.

Note: To make garlic oil, peel and crush 1 garlic clove through a garlic press into ¼ cup olive oil. Let sit for 1 hour before using.

Anchovy-Sausage Rolls

- ¼ **cup garlic oil (see Note)**
  Freshly ground black pepper to taste
- 1 **2-ounce can anchovies, drained and roughly chopped**
- ¼ **pound sweet or hot Italian sausage meat, removed from the casings and crumbled**
- ¼ **cup freshly grated Parmesan cheese**

Pancetta Rolls

1 recipe garlic oil (see Note page 205)
Freshly ground black pepper to taste
1 cup *pancetta*, bacon, or *prosciutto* cut into ¼-inch cubes
½ cup freshly grated Romano cheese

Prosciutto-Mozzarella Rolls

¼ cup garlic oil (see Note page 205)
Freshly ground black pepper to taste
1 cup *prosciutto* cut into ¼-inch cube
½ cup mozzarella, shredded

Onion-Cheese Rolls

¼ cup garlic oil (see Note page 205)
Freshly ground black pepper to taste
1 cup minced onions, sautéed in 1 tablespoon olive oil until just wilted
¼ cup grated Romano, imported Provolone, or caciocavallo cheese

Pagnotta Piccante   (Spicy Hot Pepper Loaf)

Yield: 14 to 16 1-inch slices. Serve as a side dish.

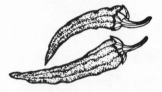

¼ cup garlic oil (see Note page 205)
15 to 20 pickled hot peppers, drained and finely chopped
¼ cup freshly grated Romano cheese
Freshly ground black pepper to taste

IF YOU LIKE HOT FOODS, this is the recipe for you. Timid palates, beware: This is a lusty, aggressive bread. It is especially good served cold with barbecued meats such as lamb, or sausages, or even ribs. Serve plenty of cold beer to put out the fire.

1. Follow the directions given in the Master Rolled Pizza Recipe for steps 1 through 3.
2. Spread the garlic oil evenly over the dough. Then sprinkle on the hot peppers, cheese, and black pepper.
3. Continue with the Master Recipe from step 5 to completion.

Pagnotta con Sugo (Gravy or Sauce Bread)

Yield: 14 to 16 1-inch slices. Serve as a side dish.

HERE ARE THREE variations for rolled pizza based on leftover tomato sauce, or "gravy," as it is customarily called.

1. Follow the directions given in the Master Rolled Pizza Recipe for steps 1 through 3.

2. Spread the sauce over the dough first; then sprinkle the remaining ingredients evenly over all.

3. Continue with the Master Recipe from step 5 to completion.

Tomato-Caper Filling

1 **cup leftover homemade tomato sauce or Basic Pizza Sauce (see recipe page 72)**
¼ **cup drained capers**
¼ **cup freshly grated Romano cheese**

Tomato-Black Olive Filling

Substitute 10 pitted and finely chopped oil-cured black olives for the capers

Meat Sauce and Cheese Filling

1 **cup leftover homemade meat sauce or Pizza Meat Sauce (see recipe page 72)**
½ **pound mozzarella, shredded**

Pagnotta con Pesto (Pesto Bread)

Yield: Approximately 14 to 16 1-inch slices.
Crust Suggestions: Basic Pizza, Sicilian-style, Herb, Cheese, Pepper-Lard, or Semolina dough.

THESE VARIATIONS ON the rolled pizza theme are really flavored breads and are more like *focaccia*. Some home cooks call them "sauce breads," because a thin layer of sauce and a few other ingredients are rolled up into the bread, where they soak into the layers like a sponge. The bread is then allowed to rise an additional 30 minutes in the pan, which results in a thick, chewy interior. To attain maximum flavor and serving ease, *pagnotta* should be cooled down to room temperature before they are sliced. Serve them as an accompaniment to soups and salads or on a buffet, sliced and set out with assorted cheeses.

Pesto loaf is especially good as a side dish with a hearty minestrone soup.

¾ **cup *Pesto* made with 1 finely minced garlic clove (see recipe page 82)**

½ **pound mozzarella, shredded**

1. Follow the directions given in the Master Rolled Pizza Recipe for steps 1 through 3.

2. Spread the *Pesto* over the dough first and sprinkle the cheese evenly over all.

3. Continue with the Master Recipe from step 5 to completion.

Variation

Substitute 1½ cups Sun-Dried Tomato *Pesto* (page 78) for the *Pesto*.

Bonata con Tonno (Broccoli and Tuna Rolled Pie)

Yield: Serves 4 to 6 as a main course or 8 to 10 as an appetizer.

Crust Suggestions: Basic Pizza, Sicilian-style, Pepper-Lard, or Semolina dough.

THIS RECIPE MUST be served cold to get the full flavor of the broccoli and tuna. It's a thoroughly Italian mixture.

1. Heat the oil in a large frying pan. Add the broccoli to the pan and sauté for 2 minutes over high heat. Add the garlic and pepper and sauté for 2 minutes longer. Set aside until needed.

2. Follow the directions given in the Master Rolled Pizza Recipe for steps 1 through 3.

3. Spread the broccoli evenly over the dough and top it with a layer of tuna.

4. Continue with the Master Recipe from step 5 to completion.

4 tablespoons olive oil
1 small head broccoli (about 1 pound), washed and finely chopped
4 garlic cloves, peeled and crushed
  Freshly ground black pepper to taste
1 recipe pizza dough, ready to use
1 7-ounce can Italian-style tuna packed in olive oil, drained and flaked

Bonata alla Verdura

(Rolled Pizza with Greens and Cheese)

Yield: 32 half-size slices. Serves 8 to 10 as an appetizer.
Crust Suggestions: Basic Pizza, Sicilian-style, Pepper-Lard, or Semolina dough.

SAUTÉED GREENS ARE excellent in rolled pizza. Use any one of the greens called for in the Master Greens Recipe on page 79. Use Fontina cheese or combine the greens as part of a more elaborate filling mixed with ricotta and *prosciutto*.

1 recipe sautéed Italian Greens (see recipe page 79), well-drained
½ pound Fontina cheese, shredded

1. Follow the directions given in the Master Rolled Pizza Recipe for steps 1 through 3.
2. Spread the sautéed greens over the dough and cover them with a layer of cheese.
3. Continue with the Master Recipe from step 5 to completion.

Variation
For *Bonata alla Vendura con Salsiccia*, substitute ¼ pound shredded mozzarella for the Fontina cheese, and add ½ pound sweet Italian sausage meat, removed from the casings, crumbled, and cooked in 1 tablespoon of olive oil until no longer pink.

Bonata alla Verdura con Prosciutto

Yield: Serves 4 to 6 as a main course or 8 to 10 as an appetizer.

1 recipe sautéed Italian Greens (see recipe page 79), well-drained
½ cup *prosciutto*, cut into ¼-inch dice
1 cup ricotta
½ cup freshly grated Parmesan cheese
Freshly ground black pepper to taste

1. Mix all of the ingredients together in a bowl and set aside until needed.
2. Follow the directions given in the Master Rolled Pizza Recipe for steps 1 through 3.
3. Spread the mixture evenly over the dough and continue with the Master Recipe from step 5 to completion.

Tomato-Based Bonata

SPECIAL CARE MUST BE taken when using tomatoes in rolled pizza. Use only canned or sun-dried tomatoes, because they have a much lower moisture content than fresh ones. Raw tomatoes give off liquid as they cook and tend to make a pizza soggy. Spicy tomato sauces or marinated sun-dried tomatoes permeate the pizza dough with their hearty flavors.

Tomato-based bonata are best served warm. They can be prepared in advance and reheated for 10 minutes or so before serving. I actually prefer them prepared early and warmed up because that gives the sauce more time to "perfume" the dough.

Sun-Dried Tomato and Ricotta Bonata

Yield: Serves 4 to 6 as a main course or 8 to 10 as an appetizer.

Crust Suggestions: Basic Pizza, Sicilian-style, Pepper-Lard, Herb, *Prosciutto*, Sausage, or Semolina dough.

1. Combine all of the ingredients in a medium-sized bowl and set aside until needed.

2. Follow the directions given in the Master Rolled Pizza Recipe for steps 1 through 3.

3. Spread the tomato-cheese mixture evenly over the dough. Then continue with the Master Recipe from step 5 to completion.

8 whole oil-packed sun-dried tomatoes, drained and chopped

2 cups ricotta

4 tablespoons freshly grated Parmesan or Romano cheese

2 tablespoons finely chopped fresh parsley leaves

2 garlic cloves, peeled and minced
Freshly ground black pepper to taste

Tomato, Mushroom, and Cheese Bonata

Yield: 32 half-size slices. Serves 8 to 10 as an appetizer.
Crust Suggestions: Basic Pizza, Sicilian-style, Pepper-Lard, Herb, *Prosciutto*, Sausage, or Semolina dough.

1 tablespoon olive oil
1 pound mushrooms, cleaned and thinly sliced
Salt and freshly ground black pepper to taste
1 garlic clove, peeled and minced
1 tablespoon finely minced fresh parsley leaves or basil
½ cup homemade tomato sauce or Basic Pizza Sauce (see recipe page 72)
½ pound mozzarella, shredded

1. Heat the olive oil in a medium-sized frying pan and sauté the mushrooms over high heat until all their excess liquid evaporates. Season with salt and pepper and toss in the garlic. Cook for 1 minute longer. Remove from the heat and stir in the parsley. Set aside until needed.

2. Combine the mushrooms and tomato sauce together in a small bowl.

3. Follow the directions given in the Master Rolled Pizza Recipe for steps 1 through 3.

4. Spread the tomato-mushroom mixture evenly over the dough. Top with a layer of mozzarella over all.

5. Continue with the Master Recipe from step 5 to completion.

Tomato-Anchovy Bonata

Yield: 32 half-size slices. Serves 8 to 10 as an appetizer.
Crust Suggestions: Basic Pizza, Sicilian-style, Pepper-Lard, Herb, *Prosciutto*, Sausage, or Semolina dough.

1 cup homemade tomato sauce
1 2-ounce can anchovies, drained and chopped
½ pound mozzarella or scamorza, shredded

1. Combine the tomato sauce and anchovies together in a small bowl.

2. Follow the directions given in the Master Rolled Pizza Recipe for steps 1 through 3.

3. Spread the tomato-anchovy mixture evenly over the dough. Top with a layer of mozzarella over all.

4. Continue with the Master Recipe from step 5 to completion.

Rose Bucci's Rolled Broccoli Pizza

Yield: Serves 4 to 6 as a main course or 8 to 10 as a light appetizer.

Crust Suggestions: Basic Pizza, Sicilian-style, Pepper-Lard, Sausage, *Prosciutto*, or Semolina dough.

AMY BUCCI INTRODUCED ME to the pleasures of rolled pizza many years ago with a version of her mother's broccoli roll.

1. Heat 4 tablespoons of olive oil in a large frying pan. Add the chopped broccoli and sauté for 2 minutes over high heat. Add the garlic and salt and pepper to the pan. Continue to sauté for 2 minutes more. The mixture should be bright green and crunchy. Set aside until needed.

2. Follow the directions given in the Master Rolled Pizza Recipe for steps 1 through 3.

3. Spread the broccoli evenly over the dough. Top the broccoli with a layer of cheese.

4. Continue with the Master Recipe from step 5 to completion.

Note: For an attractive presentation, form the roll into a half-moon shape once it is in the baking pan.

This pie is best served at room temperature for the fullest flavor.

4 tablespoons olive oil
1 small head broccoli (about 1 pound), washed and finely chopped
4 garlic cloves, peeled and crushed
Salt and freshly ground black pepper to taste
1 recipe pizza dough, ready to use
½ pound smoked mozzarella, shredded
Additional olive oil to brush on the dough before baking

Bonata with Broccoli, Meat, and Cheese

Yield: Serves 4 to 6 as a main course or 8 to 10 as an appetizer.

Crust Suggestions: Basic Pizza, Sicilian-style, Pepper-Lard, or Semolina dough.

MEAT, VEGETABLES, CHEESE, and bread are all rolled up in one convenient pie. Cut this pizza into generous inch slices and serve it warm with a hearty salad.

3 tablespoons olive oil
½ pound broccoli, washed
and finely chopped
2 garlic cloves, peeled
and crushed
Freshly ground black
pepper to taste
½ pound sweet or hot
Italian sausage meat,
removed from the cas-
ings and crumbled
½ pound mozzarella,
shredded

1. Heat 2 tablespoons of the olive oil in a frying pan. Add the chopped broccoli and sauté for 2 minutes over high heat. Add the garlic and black pepper and continue cooking for 2 minutes more. Transfer the contents of the skillet to a small bowl.

2. In the same frying pan, heat the remaining tablespoon of olive oil and sauté the sausage meat until it is no longer pink. Set it aside.

3. Follow the directions given in the Master Rolled Pizza Recipe for steps 1 through 3.

4. Spread the broccoli evenly over the dough first. Top with the sausage and end with a layer of cheese over all.

5. Continue with the Master Recipe from step 5 to completion.

Zucchini and Sun-Dried Tomato Bonata

Yield: 2 half-size rolled pies (4 by 6 inches) or 32 party size slices.
Serves 8 to 10 as an appetizer.
Crust Suggestions: Basic Pizza, Sicilian-style, Pepper-Lard, Sausage, *Prosciutto*, or Semolina dough

WHAT COULD BE BETTER than zucchini, Sun-Dried Tomato *Pesto* and cheese? Only zucchini, basil *pesto*, and smoked mozzarella. Serve at room temperature to develop the full *pesto* flavor.

2 tablespoons olive oil
2 cups zucchini, washed,
trimmed, and finely
chopped
1½ cups Sun-dried Tomato
Pesto (see recipe page
78)
½ pound mozzarella,
shredded

1. Heat the oil in a large frying pan and sauté the zucchini over medium heat for 4 minutes. Set aside until needed.

2. Follow the directions given in the Master Rolled Pizza Recipe for steps 1 through 3.

3. Spread the *Pesto* over the dough and then lay the zucchini over that. Top with a layer of mozzarella.

4. Continue with the master recipe from step 5 to completion.

Variation

Substitute basil *pesto* (page 82) for the Sun-dried Tomato *Pesto* and use smoked mozzarella instead of plain mozzarella.

Bonata con Fegato

(*Battuto* and Chicken Liver Rolled Pizza)

> Yield: Serves 4 to 6 as a main course or 8 to 10 as an appetizer.
>
> Crust Suggestions: Basic Pizza, Sicilian-style, Pepper-Lard, Cheese, or Semolina dough.

THE INSPIRATION FOR THIS unusual filling came by way of a spectacular dish presented by Giuliano Bugialli in *The Fine Art of Italian Cooking*. His recipe, *Pollo in pane*, calls for a whole stuffed chicken to be baked in a loaf of Tuscan bread. The result is a deliciously moist and tender chicken whose stuffing and juices leak out into the crusty bread shell. My favorite part of this dish is the underside of the loaf, where most of the chicken juices and stuffing collect in the chewy outer crust. The flavors of the stuffing marry so well with bread that I just had to create a rolled pizza based on those same tastes.

Battuto, a mixture of onions, carrots, and celery sautéed together in butter or olive oil, is a common basis for many Northern Italian stews, soups, and pasta sauces. Its slightly sweet flavor and crunchy texture are a perfect foil to the soft richness of the chicken livers and the saltiness of the *prosciutto*, and its bright orange, green, and gold tones lend a colorful touch to this rolled pie. Serve *battuto* bread warm or cold. It is especially good cold, cut into thin slices as an appetizer.

1. Heat 2 tablespoons of the olive oil in a medium-sized frying pan and sauté the onion, carrots, and celery over medium heat until the onion is soft, about 3 to 5 minutes. Transfer the contents of the pan to a medium bowl and set aside until needed.

2. In the same frying pan, heat the remaining 2 tablespoons of olive oil and sauté the chicken livers over medium heat for about 3 minutes. (They should still be pink inside.) Chop the chicken livers finely and add them to the *battuto*.

3. Stir in the *prosciutto* and the remaining seasonings. Taste to check the seasonings and adjust if necessary.

4. Follow the directions given in the Master Rolled Pizza Recipe for steps 1 through 3.

4 **tablespoons olive oil**
1 **small sweet onion, peeled and finely chopped (about ⅔ cup)**
1 **large carrot, peeled and finely chopped (about ⅔ cup)**
2 **celery stalks, finely chopped (about ⅔ cup)**
1 **pound chicken livers**
2 **ounces *prosciutto*, finely chopped**

5. Spread the filling evenly over the dough and continue with the Master Recipe from step 5 through completion.

1 garlic clove, minced
2 tablespoons finely minced fresh parsley leaves
¼ teaspoon freshly grated nutmeg
Freshly ground black pepper to taste

basil

Goat Cheese Rolled Pizza Variations

Crust Suggestions: Basic Pizza, Sicilian-style, Pepper-Lard, or Semolina dough.

GOAT CHEESE MAKES a first-rate base for a number of rolled filling possibilities because of its distinctive taste and low moisture content. Other creamy cheese, such as ricotta or Italian buffalo milk mozzarella, which contain a good deal of water, should be used sparingly. They tend to make the inner layer of rolled pizza soggy.

Sun-Dried Tomato Pesto and Goat Cheese Rolled Pizza

Yield: 32 half-size slices. Serves 8 to 10 as an appetizer.

SUN-DRIED TOMATO PESTO, goat cheese, and fresh herbs team up here in an absolutely delicious filling. Serve this pizza at room temperature.

11 to 12 ounces goat cheese
1 tablespoon finely chopped assorted fresh herbs, such as parsley, chives, mint, basil, etc.
Freshly ground black pepper to taste
1½ cups Sun-dried Tomato Pesto (see recipe page 78)

1. Mash the goat cheese, herbs, and black pepper together in a bowl with a fork. Set aside until needed.
2. Follow the directions given in the Master Rolled Pizza Recipe for steps 1 through 3.
3. Spread the cheese over the dough and then spread the *Pesto* over the cheese.
4. Continue with the master recipe from step 5 through completion.

Goat Cheese Rolled Pizza #1

Yield: 32 half-size slices. Serves 8 to 10 as an appetizer.

11 to 12 ounces goat
    cheese
2 teaspoons assorted dry
    or fresh herbs or *herbes*
    de Provence
1 garlic clove, peeled and
    minced
    Freshly ground black
    pepper to taste
2 ounces *prosciutto*,
    finely chopped

Goat Cheese Rolled Pizza #2

Yield: 32 half-size slices. Serves 8 to 10 as an appetizer.

11 to 12 ounces goat
    cheese
1 large sweet onion,
    peeled, thinly sliced,
    and sautéed in 1 table-
    spoon olive oil until
    translucent
2 teaspoons assorted dry
    or fresh herbs or *herbes*
    de Provence
    Freshly ground black
    pepper to taste

Goat Cheese Rolled Pizza #3

Yield: 4 to 6 as a main course or 8 to 10 as an appetizer.

1. For fillings 1 through 3, combine all of the ingredients in a medium-sized bowl with a fork. Set aside until needed.

2. Follow the directions given in the Master Rolled Pizza Recipe for
steps 1 through 3.

3. Spread the cheese mixture over the dough and continue with the
Master Recipe from step 5 through completion.

11 to 12 ounces herbed
    goat cheese
1 pound fresh spinach,
    washed, cooked,
    squeezed dry, and
    chopped, or 1 10-ounce
    package frozen spinach,
    cooked, squeezed dry,
    and chopped
½ cup finely chopped
    boiled ham

Provençale Shrimp Rolled Pizza

Yield: Serves 4 to 6 as a main course or 8 to 10 as an appetizer.
Crust Suggestions: Basic Pizza, Sicilian-style, or Semolina dough.

4 tablespoons sweet butter at room temperature
2 garlic cloves, peeled and minced
2 tablespoons finely minced fresh parsley leaves
2 tablespoons Pernod or other anise-based apéritif
Salt and freshly ground black pepper to taste
1 pound fresh shrimp, peeled, deveined, dried, and finely chopped

1. Combine the butter, garlic, parsley, Pernod, and salt and pepper. Blend into a smooth green paste.
2. Follow the directions given in the Master Rolled Pizza Recipe for steps 1 through 3.
3. Spread the butter mixture over the dough and lay the shrimp over that. Continue with the Master Recipe from step 5 through completion.

Tapenade Rolled Pizza

Yield: 32 half-size slices. Serves 8 to 10 as an appetizer.
Crust Suggestions: Basic Pizza, Sicilian-style, Pepper-Lard, or Semolina dough.

⅔ cup *Tapenade* (see recipe page 81)
½ pound mozzarella, thinly sliced

1. Follow the directions given in the Master Rolled Pizza Recipe for steps 1 through 3.
2. Spread the *Tapenade* over the dough first, and top it with a layer of cheese. Continue with the Master Recipe from step 5 to completion.
Variation
Add 1 cup thinly sliced sautéed Bermuda onion to the *Tapenade* mixture.

Rolled Pissaladière Variations

Yield: Serves 4 to 6 as a main course or 8 to 10 as an appetizer.

Crust Suggestions: Basic Pizza, Sicilian-style, Pepper-Lard, or Semolina dough.

VARIATIONS ON THE PISSALADIÈRE make exceptional rolled pizza fillings. They are the greatest "onion breads" this side of heaven!

1. Follow the directions given in the Master Rolled Pizza Recipe for steps 1 through 3.

2. Spread the onion filling over the dough first. Then continue making layers with the ingredients in each variation.

3. Continue with the Master Recipe from step 5 through completion.

Pissaladière Variation #1

- 1 recipe **Pissaladière** Onion Base with bay leaf removed (see recipe page 79)
- ½ pound smoked mozzarella, shredded

Pissaladière Variation #2

- 1 recipe **Pissaladière** Onion Base with bay leaf removed (see recipe page 79)
- 8 whole oil-packed sundried tomatoes, drained and torn into bite-sized pieces
- ½ pound mozzarella, shredded

Pissaladière Variation #3

- 1 recipe **Pissaladière** Onion Base with bay leaf removed (see recipe page 79)
- 1 2-ounce can anchovies, drained and chopped
- 20 oil-cured black or Niçoise olives, pitted and roughly chopped

The Stromboli Roll

Yield: Serves 4 to 6 as a main course or 8 to 10 as an appetizer.

Crust Suggestions: Basic Pizza, Sicilian-style, or Pepper-Lard dough, ready to use.

STROMBOLI ROLLS, as they are more commonly called in America, are slightly different from the jelly roll style of the rolled pies we've just encountered. Their fillings are solid and thick, and the dough which surrounds it is also thicker and breadier.

Stromboli rolls are customarily served warm, cut into wide slices, and accompanied with a zesty tomato sauce. The notion of the *bonata*—the *generous loaf* is fully realized in these hearty, rustic dishes. These can be served hot or cold.

Filling #1

1 recipe Italian Greens made with broccoli or broccoli rabe (see recipe page 80)

½ pound sweet or hot Italian sausage meat, removed from the casings and crumbled

½ pound mozzarella, coarsely shredded

Method

1. Lightly coat a 12- by 17-inch jelly roll pan with vegetable oil.

2. Mix all of the filling ingredients together in a large bowl and set aside until needed.

3. Roll a 12- by 18-inch rectangle out of the dough, dusting with flour if necessary.

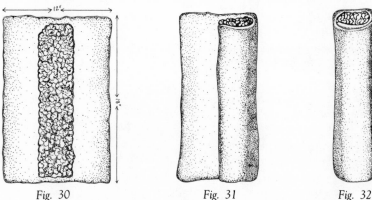

Fig. 30   Fig. 31   Fig. 32

4. Arrange the dough so that the shorter side is at the top and bottom.

5. Lay the filling evenly down the center of the dough (*Fig. 30*), leaving a 4-inch border on either side and a 1-inch border on the top and bottom.

6. Fold one side over the filling, repeat with the other side, and tuck in the dough at either end (*Figs. 31–32*).

7. Lift the roll onto a prepared baking sheet with 2 spatulas. Arrange the roll seam side down diagonally on the baking sheet and reshape it into an even log by pressing down on the dough and smoothing the filling beneath. (Don't press too hard, though, or you'll poke a hole into it.)

8. Cover with a towel and let rise 30 minutes before baking.

9. Preheat the oven to 400 degrees for 30 minutes.

10. Brush the roll lightly with olive oil and prick it with a fork in several places on top.

11. Bake for 45 minutes, or until golden and crusty.

Filling #2

½ **pound sweet or hot Italian sausage meat, removed from the casings, crumbled, and browned in 1 tablespoon olive oil**

½ **pound cooked potatoes, mashed**

1 **pound fresh spinach cooked, squeezed dry, and chopped, or 1 10-ounce package frozen spinach, cooked, chopped, and squeezed dry**

1 **small sweet onion, peeled, finely minced, and sautéed in 1 tablespoon olive oil until golden**

½ **2-ounce can anchovies, drained and roughly chopped**

½ **cup caciocavallo, shredded**

1 **garlic clove, peeled and minced**

1 **extra large egg, beaten Liberal amounts of black pepper**

Filling #3

1 **recipe Italian Greens made with broccoli or broccoli rabe (see recipe page 80)**

1 **cup ricotta**

½ **cup caciocavallo, shredded**

½ **cup scamorza or smoked mozzarella, coarsely shredded Freshly ground black pepper to taste**

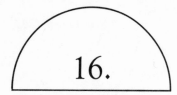

16.
NEW YORK-STYLE PIZZA

The first pizzeria in the United States, Lombardi's is now a full-fledged Italian restaurant, and although pizza is no longer on the menu, it can be had as an appetizer on special request. Jerry Lombardi, now the third generation of the family running the restaurant, is thinking of reopening a new pizzeria.

Signore Gennaro Lombardi was a *pizzaiolo* in Naples before he immigrated to the United States, in 1895. At first he worked as a baker, but a few years later, in 1905, he was able to purchase his own business—a pizzeria that also sold imported Italian goods. He then trained many of the *piazzaiolos* who later opened pizzerias of their own throughout New York City and the surrounding areas. The original owners of two of the best pizzerias in New York, John's and Totonno's, trained with Lombardi.

Lombardi's reputation grew and grew, and the place became very famous among lovers of good Italian food. One of his most famous patrons in the 1920s was Enrico Caruso, a noted pizza aficionado. The story goes that when Lombardi learned of Caruso's intention to come to his pizzeria the first time, he set a tablecloth on his best table. Caruso, a dyed-in-the-wool Neapolitan, pulled the tablecloth off and roared, "When I come here, I don't come to eat tablecloths! I come to eat pizza!"

The original Lombardi formula was the standard from which all New York-style pizza has evolved. It calls for dough made with a little bit of flour, water, salt, and a pinch of yeast. Each ball of dough is then stretched delicately over the fists into a circle that is no thicker than ¼ inch in the center. The cheese, freshly made mozzarella, is cut into thick chunks (never shredded!) and laid down on the dough before the tomatoes. The tomatoes, either fresh or canned, are then coarsely crushed right on top of the pie. Then comes the sprinkling of fresh chopped garlic, Sicilian oregano, grated Parmesan cheese, and imported Italian olive oil. The pie is then slipped into a searingly hot coal oven and baked to perfection: Its edges are puffed, crisped, and browned, its bottom has a charred bake and its topping is fused into a sizzling, heavenly scented whole.

Today less than a handful out of the thousands of pizzerias in New York City still make authentic New York-style pizza. Even though the genuine article is very rare, it is well worth seeking out, for it is one of the glories of American pizza. Here are some of the most noteworthy practitioners of the true style.

John's

The most renowned of all New York pizzerias is John's, on Bleeker Street in Greenwich Village, Mecca for the many fervent followers of authentic New York-style pizza. Frank Sinatra songs blast from the jukebox while waiters fly around taking orders from hungry patrons. Woody Allen, Johnny Cash, Warren Beatty, and the Rolling Stones are all devoted fans who are apt to pick up a pie or two. (John's doesn't deliver.)

The original owner, John Sasso, was one of many who started out with Gennaro Lombardi on Spring Street. The first John's pizzeria opened in the early 1920s on Sullivan Street. Later, in 1934, the pizzeria moved to its current location on Bleeker Street. At the age of fifteen, Pete Castellotti, the current owner, started making pizza at John's back in 1955. Now he oversees the entire operation and only makes pizza occasionally.

What makes John's pizza so delicious? Two things: the flavorful, crispy, chewy crust and the pizza sauce, cooked down from tomatoes and herbs. The sauce flavors the pie in a unique way, giving it more depth of flavor than is normally achieved with crushed tomatoes. Besides using whole milk mozzarella, fresh mushrooms, peppers, onions, excellent fresh handmade sausage and fresh garlic (better known as "essence" at John's), the pizza is always made with lots of tender loving care.

Tips for Successful Pizzeria Pizza at Home

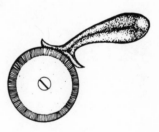

The Oven and Equipment. New York-style pizza must be baked directly on the oven deck so that it will puff up properly. Quarry tiles are the most effective oven liners and the cheapest, be sure to preheat the oven for at least 1 hour so that it has reached its maximum heat.

You'll need a pizza peel and a screen (if you're not yet adept at sliding a whole pie off the peel and onto the oven floor without breaking it). A pizza screen will give very satisfactory results but it will not have that browned, crusty bottom characteristic of New York pizza.

The Dough. Bread flour is the preferred choice of pizzerias, but excellent results can be had with unbleached all-purpose flour as well.

Notice the small amount of yeast in the recipe, this is the barest minimum needed to raise the flour without imparting a strong yeasty flavor to the dough. If the dough refuses to stretch, return it to the bowl and let it rise for another 30 minutes in a warm place. This should make it more manageable.

Shaping. New York-style pizza dough should never be rolled out with a rolling pin. This crushes the edges and affects the final texture of the dough. The Neapolitan stretching method is the only suitable way to achieve that light, thin crisp, airy crust.

Always use plenty of flour while stretching out the dough to keep it from sticking.

Assembling. Keep the ingredients 2 inches from the edge of the pie so that they won't leak off or prevent the rim from rising.

Don't crowd the filling into the center of the pie. Leave the center underfilled as the toppings tend to melt down naturally into the center during cooking. Don't pile too much on top of the pie or it will never leave the peel.

Move the pie around in the oven to make sure it cooks evenly.

The Ultimate New York-Style Pizza

Yield: 1 15- to 18-inch pie to serve 4, *or* 4 8-inch *pizzettes* to serve 4.

THIS RECIPE INCORPORATES the secrets I have learned from the best of New York's pizzerias into one incredible pie. The only thing missing will be that slight smoky charcoal taste from the coal oven, but the results will be so good that you'll hardly notice. I know that this recipe produces the real thing, for it was tested at John's by the first lady *pizzaiola* to make a pizza in his oven—me.

For the Dough

1 cup warm water (110 to 115 degrees)
1 level teaspoon active dry yeast
3 to 3½ cups bread flour or all-purpose unbleached flour
½ teaspoon salt

1. Follow the directions given in the Master Dough Recipe on page 224, using these quantities. Let the dough double in bulk.

2. Arrange quarry tiles on the floor of the oven according to the directions given in the Equipment chapter (page 39) and proceed, using the method for direct stone baking, preheating the oven to 500 degrees for 60 minutes.

3. While the dough is rising, prepare the sauce and the rest of the toppings.

4. When the dough has doubled in bulk (45 to 60 minutes), punch it down, knead it for 2 to 3 minutes. Then return it to the bowl and refrigerate for 15 minutes before shaping.

5. Shape and stretch the dough according to the classic Neapolitan method given on page 48.

6. Dust the pizza peel with flour and carefully lay the stretched dough on it. Quickly assemble the pie in the following order:

Lay the cheese over the dough shell, followed by any of the more burnable toppings, such as garlic, *pepperoni*, or meatballs.

Add the tomatoes next by the spoonful. Sprinkle with oregano and Parmesan cheese. Add any of the topping variations (No more than 2 kinds at once or decrease the quantities!). Drizzle the pie with olive oil and bake.

8. Give the peel a few jerks first to loosen the pie and facilitate its removal.

9. Bake the pizza for 5 to 10 minutes (15 if using a pizza screen), or until it is golden brown, puffed, and crusty. Serve immediately.

For the Topping

½ pound mozzarella, cut into ¼-inch-thick slices
2 large garlic cloves, peeled and minced
1 cup Basic Pizza Sauce (see recipe page 72) or 1 cup drained canned tomatoes, roughly chopped
1 teaspoon dried oregano
¼ cup freshly grated Parmesan cheese
Olive oil for drizzling over the pie before baking

Traditional Options

¼ pound additional sliced mozzarella for "extra" cheese
½ pound sweet Italian sausage meat removed from the casings and crumbled
1 2-ounce can anchovies, drained
½ pound mushrooms, cleaned, sliced, and sautéed in 1 tablespoon olive oil until all excess liquid has evaporated

Additional Options for American Tastes

32 to 36 slices *pepperoni*
½ pound meatballs, broken up or sliced
1 small sweet onion, peeled and thinly sliced
1 small sweet green pepper, seeded and thinly sliced

Patsy's

Another venerable New York pizza institution is a sleepy old pizzeria called Patsy's, on First Avenue near East 116 Street. By day the place is just about empty, but at night the clientele could include Frank Sinatra or even Jerry Lombardi.

Although the original owner, Patsy Lancieri, died a few years ago, his wife, Carmella, continues to run the show. She's the one who trains the new pizza-makers and who makes her fresh pasta dishes from scratch every day. Patsy's pizza is made in a coal oven, has a characteristically thin, light crust, and is one of the spiciest creations in town. The secret is in the hot, *hot* fresh Italian sausage that is piled on the pie along with plenty of garlic, tomatoes, and cheese. No one else in New York makes a pie like it.

Patsy's Hot Sausage Pizza

Yield: 1 15- to 18-inch round pie.
Serves 4 as a main course or 8 to 10 as an appetizer.

1 recipe New York-style Dough, ready to use
½ pound mozzarella, thinly sliced
1 cup Basic Pizza Sauce (see recipe page 72)
2 garlic cloves, peeled and finely minced
½ pound hot Italian sausage meat, removed from the casings and crumbled
Olive oil to drizzle on top of the pie

Follow the directions given for the Ultimate New York-style Pizza on page 221, using the ingredients given here.

Goldberg's Pizzeria

There's New York-style pizza and then there's Goldberg's, on East 53 Street. The story of Goldberg's pizza is a classic example of how new kinds of pizza evolve. But how did a nice Jewish boy from Kansas City become a magnate of the pizzeria trade?

Having migrated from Chicago to New York, Larry craved some of that thick, rich, Chicago-style deep-dish pizza. But all he could find in this thin-crusted town was pizza that tasted like "wallpaper with red paint!" Larry decided that New York was in need of some "real" pizza. After months of testing in his tiny home kitchen, Goldberg's pizza was born on Valentine's Day 1968.

Goldberg's pizza does not have the typical Chicago-style, corn-meal-rich, pastry-like crust. He uses a more traditional New York-style pizza dough, which contains olive oil to make it tender. The dough is pressed into a deep-dish pan and allowed to rise for 15 to 20 minutes before the toppings are added. This accounts for its fluffiness. The toppings are layered in the typical Chicago style: cheese down first; sausage, *pepperoni*, and onions next; more cheese; and then sauce (Larry uses a sauce instead of plain tomatoes) and seasonings. The ingredients are piled all the way out to the edge of the pie, which causes the crust to stay soft and moist on the inside and delicately crisp on the outside.

I met Larry on the first New York Pizza Taste-Off (forty-four people on a school bus ride around to four different pizzerias to consume thirty-two pizzas without leaving the bus), and we quickly became pizza confidants. I've since had the fun of working first-hand with Larry and his authentic pizza ingredients in my own kitchen, so I know that Goldberg's pizza can be a big hit when it's made at home.

The SMOG© Pizza

Yield: 1 15-inch deep-dish pie.
      Serves 4 to 6 as a main course.

THE MOST FAMOUS OF the Goldberg variations is the SMOG (Sausage, Mushroom, Onion, Green pepper).

1 **recipe Sicilian-style Dough, ready to use**
1 **pound mozzarella, shredded**
½ **pound sweet Italian sausage meat, removed from the casings, crumbled, and cooked until it is no longer pink**
½ **pound mushrooms, cleaned, cut into quarters, and sautéed in 1 tablespoon olive oil until all the excess liquid has evaporated**
2 **tablespoons olive oil**
1 **medium-sized sweet onion, peeled and roughly chopped**
1 **sweet green pepper, seeded and roughly chopped**
4 **cups Basic Pizza Sauce, see recipe page 72 (Goldberg doesn't use garlic in his—you decide for yourself.)**
1 **teaspoon dried oregano**

1. While the dough is rising, preheat the oven to 500 degrees and prepare the toppings.

2. Heat the olive oil in a medium-sized frying pan. Sauté the onion and green pepper for 3 to 5 minutes, or until they are tender.

3. Mix the sausage, mushrooms, onion, and pepper together in a bowl and set aside until needed.

4. Lightly coat a 15-inch deep-dish black pizza pan with vegetable oil.

5. When the dough has doubled in bulk, punch it down, knead it briefly, and press it evenly into the prepared pizza pan with your fingertips. Let the dough rise in the pan for 15 minutes.

6. Spread half of the cheese right to the edge of the dough. Distribute the sausage, mushroom, onion, and pepper mixture over the cheese. Sprinkle the remaining cheese over that. Cover all with the tomato sauce and finish by sprinkling on the oregano.

7. Press down lightly on all of the ingredients with a spatula before baking. (This helps compact the pie and mingle all of the topping together.)

8. Bake for 20 to 25 minutes, or until the bottom crust is golden. You can check on its progress by lifting a section with a spatula to see what color the bottom of the crust is. Serve immediately.

Totonno's

The only pizzeria that still makes pizza exactly as it was made eighty years ago is a tiny place with no name, out in the wilds of Coney Island, on Neptune Avenue. It is owned and operated by Jerry Totonno. His father was one of the very first to work with Signore Lombardi, and for over thirty years, Totonno has made pizza exactly the way his father did.

Totonno's is the only pizzeria that I know of that still uses hand-made fresh mozzarella on its pizza. (Jerry insists that it must be sliced by hand with a knife because this retains all of the cheese's natural moisture.)

In a small coal oven, Jerry Totonno bakes up a pie so light and delicious, it's absolutely ethereal. This very serious pizzeria offers nothing but plain tomato, mozzarella, sausage, mushroom, or anchovy pizza and a house specialty called pizza bianca—white pie.

Jerry Totonno's White Pie

Yield: 1 15- to 18-inch round pie.
　　　Serves 4 as a main course or 6 to 8 as an appetizer.

Follow the directions given for the Ultimate New York-style Pizza on page 224, using the ingredients given here. Remember: Use a knife to slice the mozzarella.

Variation
One 2-ounce can anchovies, drained, can be distributed over the pie after the garlic has been spread.

1　recipe New York-style **Dough, ready to use**
1　**pound fresh mozzarella or scamorza, thinly sliced**
2　**to 3 garlic cloves, peeled and minced**
1　**teaspoon dried oregano, or 5 to 6 fresh basil leaves, shredded Freshly ground black pepper to taste Additional olive oil for the top of the pie**

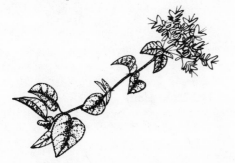

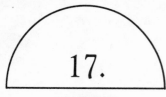

17.

NEW ENGLAND-STYLE PIZZA

During the 1930s, pizzerias started cropping up in some of the larger New England cities—Bridgeport, New Haven, Providence, and Boston. Like the earlier New York City pizzerias, many evolved from a family grocery store or bakery. The kind of pizza they made was Neapolitan but slightly different from the New York kind. In this region of rugged individualists, interpretations varied more from pizzeria to pizzeria.

New England pizza is not as easily classified as New York-style because there isn't a single recipe or method from which it all started. Crust thickness ranges from ultra-thin to ultra-thick. Toppings will also vary markedly. The tomato and cheese pie still reigns supreme, but the cheese is often white Cheddar instead of mozzarella, and other typical New England ingredients such as clams, tuna, chicken, and bacon are also common on pizza there.

This region boasts more first-rate pizzerias than just about anywhere else in the country. No fewer than four of the all-time greatest pizzerias in America are located in this region: Santarpio's in Boston and Pepe's, The Spot, and Sally's in New Haven.

Whether it is picked up for a take-out tailgate party or the Sunday evening supper, "apizza" (pronounced *ah-beetz* in Italian-New Englandese) has become as popular with New Englanders as their boiled dinners. New England pizza at its best combines old world traditions with Yankee ingenuity. The results, as this chapter shows, are some of the most delicious variations of typically American regional pizza ever.

New England Cheddar Pie

Yield: 1 15-inch round pie.
Serves 4 as a main course or 6 to 8 as an appetizer.

No one seems to know who first thought up this popular New England combination. My guess is that it came from some practical pizzeria owner who happened to have more white Cheddar cheese around one day than mozzarella. Or maybe it was an attempt to jazz up the taste of mozzarella. However it came about, the addition of white Cheddar to the cheese base lends a delicious sharpness to pizza and goes extremely well with tomatoes.

1. Preheat the oven to 500 degrees for 30 minutes.

2. Lightly coat a large pizza pan with vegetable oil and sprinkle it lightly with coarsely ground yellow cornmeal.

3. Press the dough evenly into the pan with your fingertips, forming a border 1-inch high up the sides of the pan.

4. Mix the cheeses together and spread them over the dough shell. Spoon the tomato sauce over the cheese. Make layers of the bacon and peppers next and then sprinkle the oregano and olive oil over all.

5. Bake for 15 to 20 minutes, or until the crust is golden.

Variation

Use all white Cheddar cheese, instead of the mixture of cheeses suggested.

1 recipe Basic Pizza or Sicilian-style Dough, ready to use
½ pound mozzarella, coarsely shredded
½ pound white Vermont (or similar) Cheddar cheese, crumbled
1 cup Basic Pizza Sauce (see recipe page 72)
1 cup cubed Canadian bacon
1 sweet green pepper, seeded and thinly sliced
1 teaspoon dried oregano
2 tablespoons olive oil

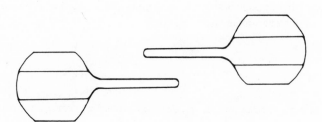

Santarpio's

One usually thinks of Boston as a center for eating seafood and baked beans, but it's also a great town for all kinds of good pizza. The great variety of pizza available in Boston is a result of its extremely large college student population, who come from many areas of the country, creating a lively market for all kinds of pizzas. But Boston, like New York, also has an old Italian community with its own pizza tradition. I can think of no other pizzeria that better embodies that tradition than Santarpio's in East Boston.

Santarpio's started out as a bakery in 1921, selling bread and baker's pizza. In 1933, Frank Santarpio opened the pizzeria that has served what many consider to be the best pizza in Boston for the last fifty years. Still housed in the building that was once the bakery, Santarpio's looks the part of the typical pizzeria—nothing fancy.

Frank Santarpio, the present owner and third generation of Santarpios to serve pizza in Boston, attributes his success to the best quality ingredients—and to his *pizzaiolo,* Joe Timpone. A master of the pizza-making art, Joe prefers to remain behind the scenes in Santarpio's kitchen. Wearing his trademark, a baker's cap fashioned from a brown paper bag, he works in front of a huge gas-fired revolving oven that can accommodate up to twenty-five pies at once. Even when the place is packed and the orders are jumping, Joe effortlessly spins out pie after pie.

His fans all appreciate his pizza, and whenever I go to Santarpio's, I go back into the kitchen to shake his hand. I've always asked questions about his dough and watched his technique. Over the years Joe has parted with enough information so that I've been able to make a pizza that might even meet his standard.

The Joe Timpone Special

Yield: 1 16- to 18-inch round pie.
Serves 4 as a main course or 6 to 8 as an appetizer.

THIS RECIPE SEEMS just like a New York-style pie, but there's a critical difference in the way they are cooked. A New York-style pizza is baked in a coal oven, and Joe's pizza is baked in a gas oven. Doughs cooked in coal ovens have a thin outer crust with a softer, chewier interior; doughs cooked in gas or electric ovens also tend to have a thin outer crust, but the interior is drier and the overall texture is much crisper.

The secret of Joe's pizza lies in the light crispiness of its crust and the way the separate ingredients combine on top of the pie as they cook. This pizza comes alive in the oven. The trick is to use whole milk mozzarella, a very lightly seasoned tomato sauce, fresh garlic, excellent quality Italian sweet (preferably fennel-flavored) sausage meat, and a liberal sprinkling of Romano cheese, oregano, and olive oil. The toppings mingle in such a way that they never lose their freshness. The effect is as close as you can get to the perfect pie.

1. Preheat a tiled-lined oven to 500 degrees for 60 minutes. Dust a pizza peel liberally with cornmeal.

2. Form a 16- to 18-inch dough shell, following the directions for New York-style Pizza on page 234. Or coat a 16- to 18-inch pizza screen lightly with vegetable oil and bake the pie on that.

3. Lay the mozzarella over the dough shell and sprinkle the cheese with the garlic. Spoon the Pizza Sauce over the cheese and distribute the sausage meat evenly over the pizza. Sprinkle on the Romano, oregano, and olive oil.

4. Give the pie a jerk on the peel to loosen it before baking and slide it onto the preheated tiles in the oven.

5. Bake for 10 to 15 minutes.

1 **recipe New York-style Dough, ready to use**
A small handful of coarsely ground yellow cornmeal
¾ **pound mozzarella, cut into ¼-inch-thick slices**
4 **garlic cloves, peeled and thinly sliced**
1 **cup Joe Timpone's Pizza Sauce (see recipe page 73)**
½ **pound sweet Italian sausage (preferably fennel-flavored), removed from the casings and crumbled**
1 **tablespoon freshly grated Romano cheese**
1 **teaspoon dried oregano Olive oil for the top of the pie**

New Haven-Style Pizza

New Haven, home of Yale University, is also the home of Pepe's, The Spot, and Sally's. Located on the same quiet side street, this trio is reputed by many pizza connoisseurs to serve the best pizzas in America.

New Haven's pizza tradition, like that of New York City, owes its beginnings to the inspiration of one great *pizzaiolo:* in this case, Frank Pepe. In 1925, Pepe, a native Italian and a baker by profession, rented a small bakery on Wooster Street. There he made the most delicious tomato pies, consisting simply of crushed tomatoes and grated cheese. The demand for these pies grew to the extent that Pepe made his living by selling them around town from a horsedrawn cart. By 1934, Pepe was able to purchase the building right next door to the bakery he had been leasing and to open his own Pizzeria Napoletana. Equipped with a coal oven large enough to bake 25 full-sized pizzas at once and a suitable capacity for tables and chairs, Pepe's was the first pizzeria to put New Haven on the pizza map.

Soon after Pepe's opened, the bakery next door was turned into a pizzeria named The Spot, owned by the Boccamiello family. And then a few years later, in 1938, Pepe's nephew, Salvatore Consiglio, opened his own place, Sally's, just down the street. For nearly 50 years now, this triad of pizzerias has made New Haven notorious among pizza fans.

Pepe's

Frank Pepe established the standards for all New Haven-style pizza and, even though each of the other pizzerias has its own idea about how to make a great pie, each still adheres to his basic principles.

Each day at Pepe's the dough is made fresh in the morning and the huge coal oven is stoked up (it uses over a ton of coal a week). Imported canned tomatoes are crushed, whole milk mozzarella is sliced, and other fresh toppings are prepared: fennel sausage, chicken, mushrooms, onions, peppers, garlic, bacon, and clams. Making pizza there is a three-man operation. One presses out the dough, another constructs the pizza, and the third mans the oven with a 10-foot pizza peel. A quick 5-minute blast from the furnace-like oven renders each disk into a sizzling, molten, crusty slab, which is then slid onto a large metal tray lined with white butcher paper. The drama of the event is always heightened when the pie (often as large as the table) arrives and eager patrons, equipped with knives and forks (which they rarely use) and a large stack of paper napkins (which they do use!) risk burning their mouths as they bite down onto each slice. Eating pizza and pizza only is the main event here—no side dishes, salads, or even plates detract from its glory!

Besides his fantastic tomato pies, Pepe was the originator of that most famous of New Haven specialties, the white clam pie. For this creation, he used only freshly shucked Rhode Island clams, chopped garlic, olive oil, a sprinkling of grated Romano cheese and oregano and that special New England twist—pieces of crispy bacon.

After Frank Pepe's death, in 1969, the task of upholding a noble tradition was left to his son-in-law, Ralph Rosselli.

Today, Ralph Rosselli still swears by the same techniques and even the same ingredient sources that his father-in-law before him used. If the clams aren't available from the one source in Rhode Island, the white clam pie doesn't make the menu that day.

Pepe's White Clam Pie

Yield: 1 16- to 18-inch round pie.
  Serves 4 as a main course or 6 to 8 as an appetizer.

THE LIGHT, CHEWY QUALITY of Pepe's crust is achieved by pressing out the dough rather than stretching it. Pressing the dough out allows more air to remain in the crust so a more developed crumb structure is formed inside.

1. Preheat a tile-lined oven to 500 degrees for 60 minutes.
2. Lightly flour your hands, the work surface, and the dough before working.
3. Form the dough into a 6-inch-wide flat circle and press it out with your fingers into a 16- to 18-inch circle. Avoid pressing the edges down and keep lifting the dough over and over again so that both sides are pressed out.
4. Dust the pizza peel liberally with cornmeal. Then lay the dough down and assemble the pizza. Or use a prepared 16- to 18-inch pizza screen.
5. Distribute the clams over the dough. Follow them with the garlic, bacon, Romano cheese, oregano, and a drizzle of olive oil.
6. Give the pie a jerk on the peel to loosen it before baking and slide it onto the preheated tiles.
7. Bake for 10 to 15 minutes, or until the crust is golden.

1 recipe New York-style **Dough, ready to use**
  A small handful of coarsely ground cornmeal
2 **cups chopped, freshly shucked clams or 2 10-ounce cans clams, drained**
4 **garlic cloves, peeled and minced**
4 **strips bacon, cut into bite-sized pieces**
2 **tablespoons freshly grated Romano cheese**
1 **teaspoon dried oregano Olive oil for the top of the pie**

The Spot

When it opened, The Spot was the smallest and the least glamorous of the New Haven pizza triad, but it did have its own loyal following. Eventually, though, the Boccamiello family closed the place down, and it lay abandoned for some time until Francis Rosselli (Ralph Rosselli's son and Frank Pepe's grandson) decided to breathe some life into the old pizzeria.

In 1980 Francis Rosselli, a classically trained musician, renovated the old pizzeria. The grand old bakery oven (the largest of all three pizzerias) was reconditioned, the bricks were sandblasted, and the original enamel-top tables and ice cream parlor-style chairs were stripped and refinished. The old style pizzeria with its clean, modern overtones—spare white walls, large glass windows and a skylight—creates a very pleasant atmosphere.

Francis is a staunch upholder of the Frank Pepe tradition—he uses the same family recipes and techniques—but he has his own unique style of presentation. The Spot turns out pizza every bit as scrumptious as Pepe's next door, but they look a bit more refined, more arranged.

The Spot's White Chicken Pie

Yield: 1 15- to 18-inch round pie.
Serves 4 as a main course.

THIS UNUSUAL PIZZA is another New Haven specialty. Drained canned tuna is often substituted for the chicken. Sometimes bits of bacon are added and even a cup of tomato sauce, which turns it into a red chicken or tuna pie.

1 recipe New York-style Dough, ready to use
A small handful of coarsely ground cornmeal
½ pound mozzarella, thinly sliced

1. Preheat a tile-lined oven to 500 degrees for 60 minutes.

2. Lightly flour your hands, the work surface, and the dough before working.

3. Form the dough into a 6-inch-wide flat circle and press it out with your fingers into a 16- to 18-inch circle. Avoid pressing the edges down and keep lifting the dough over and over again so that both sides are pressed out.

4. Dust the pizza peel liberally with cornmeal. Then lay the dough down and assemble the pizza. Or use a prepared 16- to 18-inch pizza screen.

5. Lay the mozzarella over the dough shell. Then distribute the chicken, mushrooms, garlic, onion, Romano cheese, oregano, and salt and pepper over the cheese. Finish with a drizzle of olive oil.

6. Give the pie a jerk on the peel to loosen it before baking and slide it onto the preheated tiles.

7. Bake for 10 to 15 minutes, or until golden and bubbly.

Variation

Add 1 cup Basic Pizza Sauce (page 72) over the mozzarella and continue topping the pie as indicated in step 5.

1 cup chopped cooked chicken or drained canned tuna
½ pound thinly sliced, sautéed mushrooms
3 garlic cloves, peeled and minced
½ a small sweet onion, sliced paper thin
1 tablespoon freshly grated Romano cheese
1 teaspoon dried oregano
Salt and freshly ground black pepper to taste
Olive oil for the top of the pie

Sally's

For over 42 years, Sally's has been the place where Yalies and neighborhood regulars have feasted on some of the best pizza on this side of heaven. Everyone wants to return again and again to Sally's because Salvatore (Sally) and Flo Consiglio treat you like family. Returning to Sally's is like going home.

But the friendly atmosphere of Sally's is not the only reason for its popularity; pizza here comes loaded right to the very edges with copious amounts of topping. Sally's version of the white clam pie classic, luxuriant with clams, garlic, and mozzarella, is my favorite New Haven pizza. This pizzeria also features more unusual variations than the other two members of the trio. Most of them, such as fresh tomato pizza bianca and a broccoli di rape-sausage pie, are seasonal specialties.

Sally, a slight, wiry man, looks almost too fragile to attend his huge coal oven, but he knows that oven like the back of his hand and the delicious pies he produces attest to his mastery.

Sally's White Clam Pizza

Yield: 1 16- to 18-inch round pie.
Serves 4 as a main course or 6 to 8 as an appetizer.

ALL OF SALLY'S PIZZAS have a crust that is so light it's almost like cake. Sally presses out his dough in the Pepe tradition, but he finishes the job with a few quick stretches, which makes his crust just a bit more delicate.

1 recipe New York-style Dough, ready to use

2 heaping cups chopped clams, or 2 10-ounce cans whole clams, drained

8 garlic cloves, peeled and minced

4 tablespoons finely minced fresh parsley leaves, or 1 teaspoon dried oregano

4 tablespoons olive oil Salt and freshly ground black pepper to taste (if using canned clams, omit the salt) Small handful of coarsely ground yellow cornmeal

½ pound mozzarella, cut into ¼-inch-thick slices

¼ cup freshly grated Parmesan cheese Oil for the top of the pie

1. Preheat a tile-lined oven to 500 degrees for 60 minutes.

2. Combine the clams, garlic, parsley, 4 tablespoons of olive oil, and the seasonings in a bowl. Set aside until needed.

3. Lightly flour your hands, the work surface, and the dough before working.

4. Form the dough into a 6-inch-wide flat circle and press it with your fingers into a 12-inch circle. Avoid pressing the edges down and keep lifting the dough over and over again so that both sides get pressed out. To develop the rim, press the dough down 1 inch in from the edge and continue pressing in toward the center until you have formed a 14- or 15-inch circle. Stretch the dough out over your fists for the final 2 to 3 inches, until the circle is about 16 to 18 inches wide.

5. Dust the pizza peel liberally with cornmeal. Then lay the dough down and assemble the pizza. Or use a prepared 16- to 18-inch pizza screen.

6. Lay the mozzarella over the dough shell. Then spread on the clam mixture, the Parmesan cheese, and a sprinkling of olive oil.

7. Give the pie a jerk on the peel to loosen it before baking and slide it onto the preheated tiles.

8. Bake for 10 to 15 minutes, or until the pie is golden and bubbly.

Some Interesting Variations

Omit the mozzarella.

Substitute equal quantities of raw bay scallops, peeled shrimp, or mussels, or any combination of the three for the clams.

Red Clam Pie: Omit the olive oil and parsley and add ½ cup coarsely crushed drained whole tomatoes. Season with 1 teaspoon dried oregano and 5 fresh basil leaves, shredded.

Sally's Spring Greens Pizza

Yield: 1 16- to 18-inch round pie.

Serves 4 as a main course or 6 to 8 as an appetizer.

A HEARTY COMBINATION OF broccoli rabe, sausage, and cheese makes this springtime specialty a favorite at Sally's. Sally and Flo put this on the menu only when locally grown rabe is available, but rabe from California is on the market from late fall into the summer, so you can make this pie all year 'round.

1. Preheat a tile-lined oven to 500 degrees for 60 minutes.

2. Heat 4 tablespoons of the olive oil in a large frying pan. Add the broccoli rabe, cover, and cook, tossing for 3 to 5 minutes, or until the broccoli is wilted. Add the garlic and season with salt and pepper. Cook for 2 to 3 minutes longer. Drain the cooked broccoli in a colander and set aside. (Save the broth for soups or pasta sauces.)

3. Prepare the crust following the directions given in Sally's White Clam Pizza (page 238), steps 3 to 5.

4. Lay the mozzarella over the dough shell. Then make layers of the broccoli and the sausage meat. Sprinkle the Parmesan cheese and olive oil over all.

5. Give the pie a jerk on the peel to loosen it before baking and slide it onto the preheated oven tiles.

6. Bake for 10 to 15 minutes, or until the crust is golden.

4 tablespoons olive oil, plus 2 tablespoons for the top of the pie
1 pound broccoli rabe, washed and cut into 1-inch pieces
4 garlic cloves, peeled and minced
Salt and freshly ground black pepper to taste
1 recipe New York-style Dough, ready to use
Small handful of coarsely ground yellow cornmeal
½ pound mozzarella, cut into ¼-inch-thick slices
½ pound sweet Italian sausage meat, removed from the casings and crumbled
¼ cup freshly grated Parmesan cheese

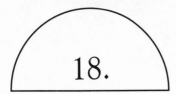

18.

CHICAGO-STYLE PIZZA

There is no other city in America whose name is more associated with pizza than Chicago. Chicago-style pies are the first and the most famous of the distinctly American Regional genres of pizza.

The development of pizza in Chicago is distinct. It has no real connection with pizza in the East except that the end product, a tomato and cheese pie with a yeast crust, is also called pizza. Back in the East, the pizzas they made were of the classic Neapolitan tradition. Pizzerias were family-run businesses, started by first- or second-generation Italians, who passed the craft down from father to son. All of the earliest pizzerias in the East were located in Italian neighborhoods, and they began by catering to the tastes of an Italian clientele. (Remember, pizza didn't become nationally popular until after the Second World War. To most Americans, pizza was a foreign food.)

The tale of how Chicago-style pizza was born starts out most improbably with the formation of a partnership between Ike Sewell, a free-wheeling Texas businessman, and Ric Riccardo, an Italian restaurateur and bon vivant, to open a Mexican restaurant. At the time, Mexican food was very popular in Texas, and Sewell thought it would catch on in Chicago. Riccardo, who had never even tasted Mexican food, agreed to set up the restaurant if Sewell would finance it. The partners had gone as far as to rent a place before Riccardo actually had his first taste of Mexican food. Sewell recalls that the meal made Riccardo so sick, he fled to Italy to recover. While in Italy, Riccardo discovered Neapolitan pizza, and when he finally returned to Chicago, he was convinced they should forget about Mexican food and open up a pizzeria instead.

Sewell was not opposed to the idea of a pizzeria, but he had reservations about pizza itself. He thought pizza was too foreign for American tastes and that the thin pizza Riccardo had in mind lacked the substance necessary to sustain a sit-down restaurant clientele. Sewell maintained that pizza must be considered a gourmet meal before it would make it in a town like Chicago. After several months of experimentation, the two men finally developed the now famous Chicago Deep-Dish Pizza, and in 1941 they opened Pizzeria Uno.

Some three refinancings and 20 million pizzas later, Pizzeria Uno and the newer one, Pizzeria Due, caught on like wildfire. (Ric Riccardo died in 1954, before the success of his venture had been realized.) The tremendous popularity of the deep-dish pizza fostered a proliferation of pizzerias in Chicago, all of which served a similar pie. Several enterprising Chicagoans have since developed other variations on the deep-dish theme—such as the Stuffed Pizza and the Pizza Pot Pie (upside down pizza), which have caused even more ripples in the Chicago pizza scene.

Pizzeria Uno's

Pizzeria Uno's of Rush Street still makes the best pie in town. The combination of a rich biscuit-like crust, gobs of mozzarella, thick Italian sausage, sweet tomatoes, and seasonings has become Chicago's culinary claim to fame.

Ike Sewell is now a 79-year-old, extremely engaging and dapper gentleman who doesn't look a day over 60. He attributes his success to his use of only the finest ingredients, but there are two other secrets to his wonderful pie—the women who've been making it for him all these years, Elnora Russell and Aldean Stoudamire.

Elnora has been with Sewell since 1950 and Aldean since 1957, and both know their craft so well that they are able to produce the same results over and over again by touch and taste alone. Perhaps this is why competitors have always had a tough time uncovering Sewell's secret; it's such a simple recipe that it's deceptive. There are so many variables within the ingredients and technique that commercial operations find it hard to duplicate, but the home cook can easily buy top-quality ingredients and master the technique and make a very respectable Chicago-style pizza at home.

Sewell's secret formula has been the victim of espionage in his kitchens, theft of his garbage, and even bribery of his employees. With a wry smile, Sewell says that he has no secrets, and that anyone can reproduce his pizza by experimenting as he and Riccardo did. And, he was right.

Chicago-Style Deep-Dish Pizza

Yield: 1 15-inch deep-dish pie.

Serves 4 to 6 as a main course.

THE RICH BISCUIT-LIKE crust of Chicago-style pizza is a result of a basic yeast dough enriched with crunchy cornmeal and oil. The dough is pressed into the pan with oiled fingertips—never rolled or stretched—and allowed to rise a bit before finishing the pie. The addition of cornmeal and oil to the dough makes it light, crispy, and wonderfully chewy. Pressing the dough into the pan allows it to develop a more delicate crumb structure.

The basic assembly of Chicago-style pizza is somewhat different from that of classic Neapolitan pizza. The cheese goes down first, lining the crust so that it won't get soggy. Raw sausage or whatever other flavoring goes on next. (If the sausage appears particularly fatty, precook it and drain off the excess fat.) Well-drained whole tomatoes, coarsely crushed, go over the topping. And the pie is finished with a sprinkling of fresh garlic, oregano, and Parmesan cheese.

Deep-dish pizza bakes at two temperatures: a higher one for the first 15 minutes and a lower one to finish cooking the pie without burning it. The pies take about 40 minutes to cook and they can be reheated.

For the Crust

1 **cup warm tap water (110 to 115 degrees)**
1 **package active dry yeast**
3½ **cups flour**
½ **cup coarsely ground yellow cornmeal**
1 **teaspoon salt**
¼ **cup vegetable oil**

1. Pour the warm water into a large mixing bowl and dissolve the yeast with a fork.

2. Add 1 cup of the flour and all of the cornmeal, salt, and vegetable oil. Mix well with a wooden spoon.

3. Continue stirring in the flour ½ cup at a time, until the dough comes away from the sides of the bowl.

4. Flour the work surface and your hands and continue to knead the ball of dough until it is no longer sticky.

5. Preheat the oven to 500 degrees.

6. Let the dough rise in an oiled bowl, sealed with plastic wrap, for 45 to 60 minutes in a warm place.

7. When the dough has doubled in bulk, punch it down and knead it briefly. Press the dough into an oiled 15-inch round deep-dish pizza pan until it comes 2 inches up the sides and is even on the bottom of the pan. Let the dough rise in the pan for 15 to 20 minutes before filling.

8. While the dough is rising, prepare the filling.

9. Lay the cheese over the dough shell. Then distribute the sausage and garlic over the cheese. Top with the tomatoes. Sprinkle on the seasonings and Parmesan cheese.

10. Bake for 15 minutes at 500 degrees. Then lower the oven temperature to 400 degrees and bake for 25 to 35 minutes longer. Lift up a section of the crust from time to time with a spatula to check on its color. The crust will be golden brown when done. Remove the pizza from the pan and serve immediately.

Variations

Substitute 4 ounces of sliced *pepperoni* for the sausage meat and/or add 1 sliced sweet green pepper and 1 sliced onion (sautéed together in 2 tablespoons of oil until just tender) instead of or with the sausage or *pepperoni*.

For the Filling

1 pound mozzarella, sliced

1 pound sausage, removed from casings and crumbled (Cook the sausage until it is no longer pink and drain it of its excess fat.)

1 28-ounce can whole tomatoes, well drained and coarsely crushed

2 garlic cloves, peeled and minced

3 teaspoons dried oregano, or 5 fresh basil leaves, shredded

4 tablespoons freshly grated Parmesan cheese

Chicago-Style Stuffed Pizza

The stuffed pizza is a double-crust sibling of pizza in a pan. It can have a similar biscuit crust or a thinly rolled Sicilian one. The filling and lots of cheese are mixed together and encased between two layers of dough. The sauce goes over the top crust, but just at the last moment, so that the crust doesn't get soggy. The effect is similar to a *torta pasqualina* or *pizza rustica*, which are often served with a tomato sauce over them, except that none of these have any ricotta in them. (It would make a fine addition, though!) The following recipes are adaptations of the pies I tried in Chicago.

Nancy's Stuffed Pizza with Sausage

Yield: 1 15-inch round pie.

Serves 4 to 6 as a main course.

ROCCO PALESE OF NANCY'S (named after his wife Annunziata) takes his recipe for stuffed pizza from a similar Eastertime family pizza called *scarceidda*. The pizza that I sampled at his place in the Rush Street area had a Chicago-style biscuit crust that was especially light and crispy. The pie was filled with excellent Italian sausage and mozzarella and topped with another layer of crust and finished with a well-balanced tomato sauce on top.

After Rocco and I had a serious pizza conversation, he gave me a lesson on how to make his own brand of stuffed pizza. He showed me all of the ingredients that go into his dough, and I learned that the secret to its lightness comes from the addition of a bit of beer to the batter. Then we put an actual pie together. He explained that the fillings—spinach and other greens—must be cooked with some olive oil, garlic and seasonings to give them flavor before adding them to the pie. The dough is pressed into a prepared pizza pan and left to rise for a while before the pie is assembled. After the dough has risen for 15 to 20 minutes, the desired filling mixed together with coarsely shredded mozzarella cheese is added to the dough shell. The pie is then covered with a thin, even disk of additional dough and topped with a finishing touch of sauce before baking.

Thanks for the lesson, Rocco. Here's my version . . .

For the Dough

¾ **cup hot tap water (115 to 130 degrees)**

1 **package active dry yeast**

½ **cup beer at room temperature**

¼ **cup vegetable oil or melted butter**

1. Preheat the oven to 500 degrees.

2. Follow the directions given for Uno's Chicago-style deep-dish crust (page 242) from steps 1 through 5, substituting the above quantities. (Add the beer and oil together in step 2.)

3. When the dough has doubled in bulk, punch it down and knead it briefly. Remove one quarter of the dough from the ball and return the smaller part to the bowl. Press the other larger ball into an oiled 15-inch deep-dish pizza pan until it comes 2 inches up the sides and is even on the bottom. Let the dough rise for 15 to 20 minutes.

4. In a bowl, mix together the mozzarella, sausage meat, and garlic. Set aside until needed.

5. Spread the filling evenly inside the dough shell.

6. Roll out the remaining ball of dough into a 14-inch circle and fit it over topping. Crimp the edges and prick the dough in several places to let the steam escape.

7. Bake for 15 minutes at 500 degrees. Lower the oven temperature to 400 degrees and bake for 10 minutes longer.

8. After 25 minutes' total baking time, add the sauce and sprinkle with cheese. Bake for 5 to 10 minutes longer. Lift up a section of the crust from time to time with a spatula to check on its color. The crust will be golden brown when done. Remove the pizza from the pan to serve.

Note: To prepare in advance, cook three-quarters of the way through and omit the sauce. Reheat in a preheated 400-degree oven for 15 to 20 minutes, adding the sauce and cheese during the final 5 minutes of baking time.

½ **cup coarsely ground yellow cornmeal**

4 **to 4¼ cups flour**

1 **teaspoon salt**

For the Filling

1 **pound mozzarella, coarsely shredded**

1 **pound sweet or hot Italian sausage meat, removed from the casings and crumbled**

2 **garlic cloves, peeled and minced**

2½ **cups Basic Pizza Sauce (see recipe page 72), warmed up**

¼ **cup freshly grated Parmesan cheese**

Edwardo's Stuffed Chicago-style Pizza with Spinach

Yield: 1 15-inch round pie. Serves 4 to 6 as a main course.

A RELATIVE NEWCOMER to the Chicago pizza scene, Edwardo's, on North Dearborn Street, has quickly gained a reputation with a specialty called "Spinach Soufflé Pizza." The pizza contains not a single egg, and it doesn't bear even the slightest resemblance to a soufflé. But it *is* one of the best stuffed Chicago-style pies in the city.

Ed Jacobson, owner of Edwardo's, is justly proud of his pizza, and he's not in the least bit secretive about what goes into it. In fact, the ingredients are displayed in a refrigerated case for all the world to see. Baskets of garden fresh spinach, bunches of broccoli, green peppers, onions, and fresh white mushrooms frame a 50-pound bag of unbleached

white flour, blocks of fresh yeast, and whole milk mozzarella in an edible still life. Cans of imported Italian tomatoes and olive oil line the wall, and an entire front window is devoted to the hydroponic garden in which he grows all of his basil.

The spinach-stuffed pizza and its fresh broccoli variation are much lighter than most Chicago-style stuffed pies, because they are made with a thin Sicilian-style crust that contains no cornmeal. The filling is composed of shredded raw spinach or blanched, chopped broccoli mixed together with shredded mozzarella. And the final layer of dough is blanketed with roughly crushed whole tomatoes, fresh basil, Parmesan cheese, and slivers of elephant garlic. When the pie comes out of the oven, it slices into pretty white, green, and red wedges. This is truly the most elegant of all the Chicago-style pies.

In this adaptation, I have opted for cooking the spinach or broccoli in olive oil, garlic, and seasonings rather than using them raw or blanching them, as Edwardo's does. Cooking stabilizes the excess moisture of the greens and infuses the filling in general with much more flavor. I prefer the headier flavor of the filling to contrast with the refreshingly delicate combination of the tomatoes, cheese, and fresh basil on top of the pie.

1 recipe large-size Sicilian-style Dough, ready to use
1 tablespoon olive oil
2 pounds fresh spinach, washed, dried, and chopped
4 garlic cloves, peeled and minced
½ dried hot red pepper, lightly crushed
Salt and freshly ground black pepper to taste
1 pound mozzarella, coarsely shredded

1. While the dough is rising, preheat the oven to 500 degrees.
2. Heat the olive oil in a large frying pan. Add the chopped spinach and the garlic. Season with the hot red pepper and salt and black pepper. Stir over high heat until the spinach wilts and most of the excess liquid has evaporated. Discard the red pepper and drain the spinach through a sieve. Set aside until needed.
3. When the dough has doubled in bulk, punch it down and knead it briefly. Remove one third of the dough, return that to the bowl and cover it with plastic wrap. Roll the other portion of the dough out into a 16-inch circle and fit that into a prepared 15-inch round deep-dish pizza pan. The dough should come 2 inches up on each side.
4. Mix the spinach together with the shredded mozzarella and fill the dough shell with it.
5. Roll out the remaining dough into a 14-inch circle and fit that on top of the filling. Crimp the edges and prick the top dough with a fork to allow the steam to escape.

6. Let the pie rise in the pan 15 minutes before baking.

7. Bake at 500 degrees for 15 minutes. Then lower the oven temperature to 400 degrees and bake for 20 to 25 minutes. Add the tomatoes, basil, and Parmesan cheese during the last 10 minutes of baking time. Lift up a section of the crust from time to time to check on its color. The crust will be golden brown when done. Remove the pizza from the pan to serve.

Variation

Substitute 1 pound finely chopped broccoli for the spinach. Cook the broccoli in 2 tablespoons olive oil and the same seasonings for 2 to 3 minutes, until bright green and crunchy.

1 28-ounce can whole tomatoes, well drained and roughly crushed
5 fresh basil leaves, shredded, or 1 teaspoon dried oregano
¼ cup freshly grated Parmesan cheese

Chicago Pizza and Oven Grinder Co. Pizza Pot Pie

Located just across the way from the site of the Saint Valentine's Day Massacre, on North Clark Street, the Chicago Pizza and Oven Grinder Co. makes one of the most unusual variations of pizza that the city has to offer—Pizza Pot Pie, or Upside-Down Pizza.

The owners, Charles Smital and Albert Beaver, had been serving pizza in a pan until one night when Beaver got the idea for pizza pot pie. After much experimentation, the partners developed a new perspective on pizza. They began to make it upside-down. They even had ovenproof bowls specially made to their specifications.

When the pizza goes into the oven, it resembles a crust-covered deep-dish pot pie, but when it is done, the waiter detaches the crust from the bowl and deftly flips it over at your table. Voila! Upside-down pizza pot pie!

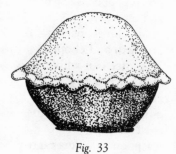

Fig. 33

Chicago Pizza Pot Pie

Yield: Serves 4 as a main course

PIZZA POT PIES are fun to prepare, but they can be tricky to handle. I would propose making 4 individual sized ones. (Those ovenproof onion soup bowls tucked away in nearly everyone's cupboard make perfect containers.)

All of the pie's filling components except the cheese are cooked together in a thick sauce. That sauce is spooned in first, followed by a layer of mozzarella cheese and a cap of dough over all. The pies are baked until the crust is crisp, and then they are flipped over to reveal a pizza (*Fig. 33*). Do practice before you serve pizza pot pie to guests. Flipping hot pies may be fun, but it can also be messy.

1 recipe Basic Pizza Dough, ready to use
4 teaspoons olive oil
1 pound uncooked ground beef or sweet or hot Italian sausage meat, removed from the casings and crumbled
1 medium-sized sweet onion, peeled and chopped
1 medium-sized sweet green pepper, seeded and chopped
2 garlic cloves, peeled, crushed, and chopped
1 28-ounce can whole tomatoes, roughly crushed
3 ounces canned tomato paste
1 teaspoon dried oregano or dried basil
2 tablespoons minced fresh Italian parsley leaves
   Salt and freshly ground black pepper to taste
½ pound mozzarella, thinly sliced
   Vegetable oil for the bowls

1. Prepare a recipe for pizza dough and let it rise in the refrigerator for 1½ hours.

2. Preheat the oven to 500 degrees for 60 minutes.

3. Prepare the sauce while the dough is rising.

4. Heat 2 teaspoons of the olive oil in a medium-sized nonaluminum saucepan. Add the meat and cook it until it is no longer pink. Remove the meat and drain off the fat.

5. Heat the 2 remaining teaspoons of olive oil in the same saucepan and sauté the onion and green pepper until the onion is just translucent. Stir in the garlic and cook for 1 minute.

6. Add the sautéed meat, tomatoes, tomato paste, oregano, parsley, and salt and pepper. Stir and simmer, uncovered, for 45 to 60 minutes. Stir from time to time to prevent burning.

7. Oil 4 1- to 1½-cup ovenproof bowls, inside and out. Oil a baking sheet.

8. Spoon the cooked sauce into each bowl, leaving at least ½ inch of space at the top of each bowl. Lay the mozzarella over the sauce in each bowl.

9. Remove the dough from the refrigerator, punch it down, and divide it into 4 pieces. Roll each piece out with a rolling pin until it is just large enough to overhang the bowl's edge by 2 inches.

10. Set the bowls on the oiled baking sheet and bake for 15 to 20 minutes. The dough is done when the crust is golden and sounds hollow when tapped.

11. To serve, put a dinner plate on top of the dough, and with oven mitts protecting your hands, quickly invert the pie. Loosen the dough all around the edge with a knife before removing the bowl. The pies can also be served in their bowls without inverting them. Let each person break through the crust to get to the filling—just as they would with another type of pot pie.

Note: The dough is refrigerator risen so that it will be stiff when it is rolled out. When the dough is too soft, it can slip and expand too much on the bowl.

One of the most formidable of all American regional cuisines is that of the southern border states of Texas, New Mexico, and Arizona known as Tex-Mex. Tex-Mex cookery is a mixture of Mexican influences and contributions of the varied ethnic cultures who settled those states during the late nineteenth century. Such specialties as tacos, chili, and burritos, making lavish use of corn flour, chili peppers, beef, and beans are among its best-known preparations. In recent years, another ethnic dish has made its way south of the border and has turned into some pretty original variations: pizza. Perhaps there are not yet any Tex-Mex pizzerias, but there are enterprising cooks who have adapted pizza to their own down-home style.

Tex-Mex pizza is not really so strange as it sounds. After all, tacos and burritos are the New World relatives of those ancient styles of pizza cooked on hot stones and wrapped around a savory filling. Of all American regional pizza, Tex-Mex has the least resemblance to a Neapolitan pizza. The fillings for Tex-Mex pizza can include an assortment of fiery hot chili peppers, salsa, chili (with or without beans), avocados, and Monterey Jack cheese. Typical south of the border seasonings are onion, garlic, oregano, fresh cilantro (also known as Chinese parsley), cumin, and chili powder (2 or 3 alarm!). It's not very Italian, but it's very American and it's great on pizza!

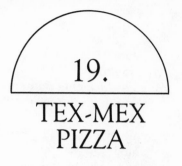

19.
TEX-MEX PIZZA

Lone Star Chili Pizza

Yield: 1 15-inch pie.

Serves 4 to 6 as a main course.

Method: Use a prepared deep-dish pan for this sumptuous pizza.

Crust Suggestions: Basic Pizza, Sicilian-style, Pepper-Lard, or Chicago-style dough.

AUTHENTIC TEXAS CHILI contains only meat—no beans. And although it is true that Texans are especially fond of hotter than hot chili con carne on their pizza, any spicy chili recipe (even with beans) will make a fine topping. So the next time you prepare a potful of your favorite chili, save some for pizza Texas-style.

1 **recipe pizza dough,
ready to use**
3 **cups thick chili with or
without beans (see rec-
ipe page 77)**
½ **cup minced sweet
onion**
¾ **pound Monterey Jack
cheese or a mild white
Cheddar cheese,
shredded**

1. Preheat the oven to 450 degrees.

2. Lightly coat a 15-inch round deep-dish pizza pan with vegetable oil. Sprinkle it lightly with coarsely ground yellow cornmeal.

3. Press the dough into the pan with your fingertips until it comes up the sides of the pan about 2 inches and the bottom is even.

4. Let the dough rise in the pan for 20 minutes before filling.

5. Spread the chili over the dough shell and sprinkle the onions over the chili.

6. Bake for 30 to 35 minutes. Add the cheese during the final 10 minutes of baking. The pie should bake for 40 to 45 minutes in all.

Taco Pizza

Yield: 1 15-inch pie.
Serves 4 to 6 as a main course.
Crust Suggestions: Basic Pizza, Sicilian-style, Pepper-Lard, or Chicago-style dough.
Method: A prepared deep-dish pizza pan is in order for this generously filled pie.

YOU MAY WANT to serve this spicy pizza with some sour cream on the side.

1 **recipe pizza dough,
ready to use**
1 **tablespoon vegetable oil**
1½ **pounds very lean
ground beef**
2 **garlic cloves, peeled,
crushed, and minced**
½ **teaspoon ground cumin**
1 **teaspoon dried oregano**
2 **to 3 tablespoons chili
powder
Salt to taste**

1. Preheat the oven to 500 degrees.

2. Lightly coat a 15-inch round deep-dish pizza pan with vegetable oil. Sprinkle it lightly with coarsely ground yellow cornmeal.

3. Press the dough into the pan with your fingertips until it comes up the sides of the pan about 2 inches and the bottom is even.

4. Let the dough rise in the pan while you prepare the taco filling.

5. Heat the oil in a medium-sized frying pan. Add the meat and season it with the garlic, cumin, oregano, chili powder, and salt. Cook, breaking up the meat with a fork, until it has browned. Set the meat mixture aside until needed.

6. Spread half of the shredded cheese over the dough shell. Use a slotted spoon to drain off any accumulated fat from the beef and spoon the beef over the cheese. Spoon the *Salsa* over the meat and finish with a layer of onions.

7. Bake at 500 degrees for 20 minutes. Then lower the oven temperature to 400 degrees and bake for 25 to 30 minutes longer. Add the remaining cheese during the last 5 to 10 minutes of baking so that it melts without burning.

1 **pound Monterey Jack or white Cheddar cheese, shredded**
2 **cups drained *Salsa* (see recipe page 73)**
1 **small sweet onion, peeled and chopped**

Jalapeño Pizza

Yield: 1 16- to 18-inch round pie. Serves 6 to 8 as a side dish.

Crust Suggestions: Basic Pizza, Sicilian-style, or Pepper-Lard dough.

Method: Jalapeño Pizza is best with a thin crust. Use a prepared pizza pan or the direct stone method to bake it.

1. Preheat the oven (if using the direct stone method) to 500 degrees for 30 minutes for a pizza pan or 60 minutes for pizza tiles or stones.

2. Lightly coat a large pizza pan with vegetable oil and sprinkle it lightly with coarsely ground yellow cornmeal. Or lightly coat a large pizza screen with oil or dust a pizza peel with flour.

3. Roll out or stretch the dough into a thin circle and fit it onto the prepared pan, screen, or peel.

4. Spread the shredded cheese over the dough shell. Then distribute the chiles, onion, tomato, and garlic over the cheese. Season the pie with the cumin and cilantro.

5. Bake for 15 to 20 minutes, or until the crust is golden brown and the topping is puffed.

1 **recipe pizza dough, ready to use**
1 **pound Monterey Jack cheese or other white Cheddar cheese, shredded**
2 **4-ounce cans green chiles, drained, seeded, and roughly chopped, or 4 fresh jalapeño peppers, roughly chopped**
1 **small sweet onion, peeled and chopped**
1 **large tomato, seeded and roughly chopped**
2 **garlic cloves, minced**
1 **teaspoon ground cumin**
1 **tablespoon minced fresh cilantro, optional**

South-of-the-Border Pizza

Yield: 1 15- to 18-inch round pie.

Serves 4 as a main course or 6 to 8 as an appetizer.

Crust Suggestions: Basic Pizza, Sicilian-style, or Pepper-Lard dough.

Method: This pizza is best on a light, thin crust. Use a prepared pizza pan or the direct stone method to bake it.

SMOOTH AVOCADOS AND Monterey Jack cheese contrast with the spiciness of Salsa on this version of tomato and cheese pizza. The delicate blending of flavors is reminiscent of some of the new California interpretations of Mexican-style pizza.

1 recipe pizza dough, ready to use

½ pound Monterey Jack cheese or similar white Cheddar cheese, shredded

1 cup drained Salsa (see recipe page 73)

2 garlic cloves, peeled and minced

1 small avocado (preferably the small rough skinned ones from California), peeled and cut into ½-inch cubes

12 water-packed, pitted black California olives, halved

1 teaspoon ground cumin

1 tablespoon chopped fresh cilantro (Chinese parsley)

1. Preheat the oven (if using the direct stone method) to 500 degrees for 30 minutes for a pizza pan or 60 minutes for tiles or stones.

2. Lightly coat a large pizza pan with vegetable oil and sprinkle it lightly with coarsely ground yellow cornmeal. Or lightly coat a large pizza screen with oil or dust a pizza peel with flour.

3. Roll out or stretch the dough into a thin circle and fit it onto the prepared pan, screen, or peel.

4. Spread the shredded cheese over the dough shell. Then spoon the Salsa over the cheese. Distribute the garlic, avocado, and black olives over the sauce. Season the pie with the cumin and cilantro.

5. Bake for 15 to 20 minutes, or until the crust is golden.

Variation

Substitute 1 cup sliced chorizo sausage for the olives.

The latest page of pizza history is being written in California, where superstardom has struck the dish and made it a big hit. Californians, employing indigenous produce and imported products along with a liberal sprinkling of imagination, are creating all kinds of new variations. California pizza can be composed of just about anything that strikes the cook's fancy. A list of some of the most popular toppings might include combinations as varied as sun-dried tomatoes, buffalo mozzarella, and lamb sausage, or chorizo, hot chili peppers, Monterey Jack cheese, and cilantro, or smoked salmon, caviar, and sour cream. Some of the toppings may seem somewhat outlandish because they depart from the standard concept of American pizza, but once we get over the tomato-and-cheese pie block, different combinations atop pizza shouldn't seem odd at all.

The vanguard of the pizza innovators in California are Alice Waters of Chez Panisse in North Berkeley, and Wolfgang Puck of Spago in the Hollywood section of Los Angeles. They have done more to change the face of pizza in this country than any other commercial establishment.

20.
CALIFORNIA PIZZA

Chez Panisse

Alice Waters, owner and driving force behind one of America's most renowned eating establishments, Chez Panisse, is famous for her novel approach to cuisine. In 1980, when she opened the café above the restaurant, another new concept in American dining was launched. Offering simple, robust fare, such as pasta, pizza, sautées, and light salads, the café's menu was composed of what used to be thought of as appetizer courses in more formal restaurants. The café was also the first restaurant in America to present pizza in a traditional Italian—and a non-Neapolitan—style.

The café quickly gained notoriety as a new kind of pizzeria, one that served up a concoction called *California nouvelle pizza*. But Chez Panisse is not a pizzeria, and the folks at Chez Panisse say there is nothing *nouvelle* about their pizza at all—or even new for that matter. Their outlook on the dish departs from a traditional Italianate point of view. Their inspiration comes from classic pizza and pasta combinations. Still other variations were developed from French Provençale, Mexican, and Mediterranean flavors, or whatever ingredients are fresh at the moment.

Pizza Chez Panisse Style

CHEZ PANISSE USES A wood-burning brick oven to bake their pizza. The wood fire (which is not as intensely hot as coal) creates a softer, chewier crust. Their delicious crust is developed through an initial sponge rising of the dough and the addition of a small amount of rye flour, which lightens its texture and adds a subtle taste. At Chez Panisse, pizza is always stretched over the fists in the classic manner and given a final flip (just for show) before it is assembled, but their *calzone* is rolled out with a rolling pin. Both pizzas and *calzoni* are baked directly on the oven floor until they are golden and well puffed. Then as soon as they are removed from the oven, they are brushed lightly with extra-virgin olive oil, sprinkled with fresh herbs, and dusted with Parmesan cheese.

1 **package active dry yeast**

½ **cup hot tap water (120 to 130 degrees)**

2½ **cups unbleached white flour**

½ **cup rye flour (available at most supermarkets or health food stores)**

¼ **cup warm tap water (110 to 115 degrees)**

¼ **cup extra-virgin olive oil plus 4 tablespoons**

½ **teaspoon salt**

1. Mix the yeast and ½ cup of the white flour together. Stir in the hot tap water with a fork until all of the raw flour combined. Cover the bowl tightly with plastic wrap and let it rise in a warm place for 30 to 45 minutes. When the sponge bubbles up and almost doubles, it is ready.

2. Deflate the risen sponge by stirring it with a wooden spoon.

3. Add the rye flour, warm water, oil, and the salt and stir well.

4. Add 1 cup of the white flour and mix well until the dough forms a soft sticky ball and comes away from the sides of the bowl.

5. Turn the dough out onto a floured surface and knead in the remaining cup of flour. Knead in only as much flour as it takes for the dough to no longer stick to your hands. The whole kneading process should take about 5 minutes or so.

6. Lightly oil a bowl with vegetable oil and roll the dough ball around in it so it is coated with a thin film. Seal the bowl with plastic wrap and let the dough rise in a warm place for 30 to 45 minutes, or until it has doubled in bulk.

7. Punch the dough down and knead it briefly. Refrigerate the dough for at least 30 minutes before stretching it out.

8. Roll out or stretch the dough into a 15-inch round large pie or 4 6-inch individual sized ones. (See Note.)

9. Brush the dough shell with some extra-virgin olive oil and fill with the toppings of your choice.

Note: This dough is rather soft and has a tendency to stick to the pizza peel. Don't stretch the dough any thinner than ¼ inch at the center and leave a 1-inch rim of dough around to attain the very puffed edges characteristic of a Chez Panisse pizza. If the dough should stick to the peel, try loosening it with a large spatula. (Avoid letting the raw pizza sit too long on the peel before baking as this makes it stick.)

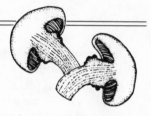

Pizza with Mushrooms, Prosciutto, Mozzarella, Parmesan, and Gremolata

Yield: 1 16-inch round pie, *or* 4 6- to 8-inch *pizzettes*.
   Serves 4 as a main course or 6 to 8 as an appetizer.

1. Preheat the oven to 450 degrees.

2. Heat the olive oil in a medium-sized frying pan and sauté the mushrooms over high heat until they give off their liquid and are nicely browned. Season lightly with salt and pepper and set aside.

3. Measure out 1 rounded tablespoon of *gremolata* and set aside. Toss the rest with the mushrooms.

4. Prepare the pie (or pies) shell, following the directions given in the Master Recipe, steps 8 and 9.

5. Lay the mozzarella, mushrooms, and *prosciutto* over the dough shell.

6. Bake for 15 to 20 minutes, or until the pie is golden and well puffed.

7. To serve, brush the crust edges with some more extra-virgin olive oil, dust with Parmesan cheese, and sprinkle with the remaining tablespoon of *gremolata*.

Note: To make *gremolata*, combine the finely grated zest of 1 lemon with 3 to 4 minced garlic cloves, and 2 tablespoons finely minced fresh parsley leaves.

4 tablespoons olive oil
1½ pounds fresh mushrooms, thickly sliced
   Salt and freshly ground black pepper to taste
1 recipe *gremolata* (see Note)
1 recipe Chez Panisse Pizza Dough, ready to use
½ pound mozzarella or Fontina cheese, thinly sliced or cut into 1-inch cubes
4 ounces julienned, *prosciutto, pancetta,* or boiled ham
   Extra-virgin olive oil for brushing on the baked crust
2 tablespoons freshly grated Parmesan cheese

Pizza with Pancetta, Leeks, and Fresh Mozzarella

Yield: Serves 4 as a main course or 6 to 8 as an appetizer.

THIS BEAUTIFUL COMBINATION is very much like a *pizza bianca*. Normally it would be made with onions, but the mellow flavor and pretty green color of the leeks is an inspired adaptation.

2 tablespoons sweet butter or olive oil
3 cups chopped leeks (white and green parts)
   Salt and freshly ground black pepper to taste
1 recipe Chez Panisse Pizza Dough, ready to use
½ pound mozzarella, cut into ¼-inch-thick slices or 1-inch cubes
4 ounces julienned *pancetta, prosciutto,* or boiled ham
   Extra-virgin olive oil for brushing on the baked crust
2 tablespoons freshly grated Parmesan cheese
1 tablespoon finely chopped fresh herbs, such as parsley, chives, oregano, marjoram, or thyme (any one or combination of herbs)

1. Preheat the oven to 450 degrees.

2. Melt the butter in a medium-sized frying pan and quickly sauté the leeks over high heat, tossing until they turn bright green, about 1 minute. Off the heat, season lightly with salt and pepper and set aside.

3. Prepare the pie (or pies) shell, following the directions given in the master recipe, steps 8 and 9.

4. Lay the mozzarella, leeks, and *pancetta* over the dough shell.

5. Bake the pie for 15 to 20 minutes, or until the crust is golden and the topping is well puffed.

6. To serve, brush the crust edges with some extra-virgin olive oil, dust with the Parmesan cheese, and finish with a sprinkling of fresh herbs. Delicious hot or cold.

Pizza with Onion Confit, Prosciutto, and Mushrooms

Yield: 1 16-inch round pie, *or* 4 6- to 8-inch *pizzettes.*
Serves 4 as a main course or 6 to 8 as an appetizer.

THE FLAVORS OF PROVENCE come to life in this interpretation of the classic Pissaladière. Chez Panisse is fond of using red onions for this dish, since they are particularly sweet and mild, but any similar onion will do.

1. Preheat the oven to 450 degrees.
2. Heat the olive oil in a large frying pan and sauté the onions over medium heat, stirring frequently, until they are quite soft and reduced, about 30 to 45 minutes. Season with salt and pepper and set aside.
3. Sauté the mushrooms and garlic in the butter over medium heat, until they release all of their liquid and turn golden.
4. Prepare the pie (or pies), following the directions given in the Master Recipe, steps 8 and 9.
5. Spread the onion mixture over the dough shell. Then distribute the *prosciutto* over the onions and finish with a layer of mushrooms.
6. Bake for 15 to 20 minutes, or until the pie is golden and well puffed.
7. To serve, brush the crust edges with some more extra-virgin olive oil, dot with olives, and sprinkle with the fresh herbs.

4 tablespoons olive oil
3 pounds red onions, peeled and thinly sliced
Salt and freshly ground black pepper to taste
½ pound thinly sliced mushrooms (or wild mushrooms, such as *cepes, chanterelles,* or golden oak, well washed and dried)
1 garlic clove, minced
3 tablespoons sweet butter
1 recipe Chez Panisse Pizza Dough, ready to use
4 ounces *prosciutto* or boiled ham, julienned, or 1 2-ounce can anchovies, drained
12 to 15 Niçoise olives for garnish, optional
1 tablespoon assorted fresh herbs, such as parsley, thyme, or marjoram, finely minced

Goat Cheese Calzone à la Chez Panisse

Yield: Serves 4 as a main course.

THE GOAT CHEESE CALZONE is by far the most popular item on the menu at the Chez Panisse Café. This *calzone*'s soft, oozing, cheesy interior, heady with garlic and herbs, makes my mouth water at the mere recollection of its taste!

½ pound Boucheron goat cheese, crumbled (Chez Panisse uses Boucheron, but any other tangy goat cheese will do), with the rind removed

½ pound mozzarella, coarsely shredded

2 garlic cloves, peeled and minced

2 tablespoons finely minced fresh chives

2 tablespoons finely minced fresh parsley
Freshly ground black pepper to taste

1 recipe Chez Panisse Pizza Dough, ready to use

4 thin slices *prosciutto*, folded in half

½ cup extra-virgin olive oil

2 tablespoons freshly grated Parmesan cheese

1. Preheat the oven to 450 degrees.

2. Mash together the goat cheese, mozzarella, garlic, chives, parsley, and black pepper with a fork.

3. Lightly coat a large pizza pan or pizza screen with vegetable oil or a pizza peel with flour.

4. Divide the dough into 4 equal portions and roll each one out into an even 8-inch circle on a floured surface.

5. Place a folded strip of *prosciutto* on the bottom half of each circle. Divide the cheese mixture in 4 portions and spread that over the *prosciutto*, leaving a ½-inch border all around.

6. Fold the top half of the circle over the bottom. Then fold the border over and crimp the edges with your fingers or the tines of a fork.

7. Carefully remove each *calzone* to a prepared baking pan, screen, or peel and brush lightly with olive oil. (Note: If using a pizza peel, put the *calzoni* on the peel and into the oven one at a time.)

8. Bake for 20 to 25 minutes, or until golden and puffed.

9. To serve, brush each *calzone* with more olive oil and sprinkle with some Parmesan cheese. They are best piping hot, but cold isn't bad either.

Spago

Spago's has been called the pizzeria of the stars—or for anyone else who can get a reservation. It's hardly your average neighborhood pizzeria. Even though pizza seems to receive the top billing, it surprisingly makes up only about 10 percent of the entire menu.

Wolfgang Puck, the originator of this very successful restaurant, saw pizza—along with pasta and *grillades*—as part of the solution toward the lighter, healthier cuisine that Californians were looking for. He had always loved pizza himself and wanted to serve a really great pie in his restaurant. Like Alice Waters, Wolfgang Puck relies upon both regional and imported produce and products of the utmost quality. For instance, he never uses anything canned on his pies—not even imported tomatoes.

Puck's approach to pizza is unique because he is not interested in traditions; his outlook on pizza is totally personal. Although he is a classically trained chef, a fact that is very apparent in many of his dishes, he firmly believes that pizza is not *haute cuisine*. For him pizza is first and foremost peasant food: hearty, direct, and savory. Using whatever strikes him at the moment, Puck is capable of creating a lusty pizza thick with cheeses, sausages, peppers, onions, and garlic, and whimsical enough to combine delicate herbs, smoked salmon, golden caviar, and sour cream on another pie.

What the home cook can learn from this rather freewheeling approach to pizza is that nearly anything goes—or can go—atop a pie. As long as the ingredients are of good quality and the combination is pleasing to the cook, the possibilities are limitless.

Pizza à la Spago

Yield: 1 15-inch round pie. Serves 4 as a main course or 6 to 8 as an appetizer.
4 8- to 9-inch round pies. Serves 4 as a main course.
6 6-inch round pies. Serves 6 as an appetizer or luncheon.

Method: Direct stone baking, a prepared pizza screen, or a prepared pizza pan.

SPAGO'S CRUST IS tender on the inside and lightly crisp on the outside. Its exceptionally light texture comes from a touch of honey and olive oil added to the dough, and its crispness comes from brushing the empty pie shell with olive oil before baking (which also promotes the browning and lovely flavoring of the crust). Like Chez Panisse, Spago uses a wood-burning brick oven to bake their pies. The pizzas are cooked directly on the oven floor and served hot and sizzling on special plates.

The Dough

1 package active dry yeast
¾ cup warm tap water (110 to 115 degrees)
1 tablespoon honey
3 cups (approximately) all-purpose white flour
1 teaspoon salt
5 tablespoons olive oil, plus 2 tablespoons additional to brush over the dough

1. Dissolve the yeast in the water along with the honey.

2. Stir in 1 cup of the flour, the salt, and 3 tablespoons of the olive oil with a wooden spoon. Mix well.

3. Add a second cup of flour and continue mixing until the dough forms a soft sticky mass and comes away from the sides of the bowl.

4. Flour the work surface and your hands and turn the dough out of the bowl. Continue kneading in the remaining flour until the dough is smooth and elastic.

5. Put the dough in an oiled bowl and seal the bowl tightly with plastic wrap. Let the dough rise in a warm place for 30 to 45 minutes, or until it has nearly doubled.

6. Punch down the dough, knead it briefly, and divide it into 4 equal parts. Roll each piece into a ball and refrigerate for 15 minutes before using. (If you wish to leave the dough in the refrigerator for an extended period of time, return it to the oiled bowl, seal it with plastic wrap, and let it rise slowly again. Let the dough sit out at room temperature for 30 minutes before using it after prolonged refrigeration.)

Note: Puck suggests baking the pies directly on pizza stones or tiles for the best results.

Prosciutto Pizza

Yield: 1 15-inch round pie, *or* 4 8-inch pizzettes.
    Serves 4 as a main course or 6 to 8 as an appetizer.

AT SPAGO'S, PIZZA with the *works* is infinitely more elegant than what we are generally accustomed to. These generously topped pies—along with a salad and some wine—can be an entire meal in themselves.

1. Preheat the oven to 500 degrees.
2. Mix the olive oil and hot red pepper together. Let stand until needed.
3. Roll out or stretch the dough into 4 equal 8- to 9-inch circles. Assemble each pizza one at a time on a prepared pizza peel, or on 4 prepared pizza screens, or in 2 large prepared 12- by 17-inch pizza pans.
4. Brush the pizzas with the hot pepper oil. Distribute the mozzarella and Fontina cheeses first, followed by the plum tomatoes, garlic, basil, *prosciutto*, onion, green pepper, and goat cheese.
5. Bake for 10 to 15 minutes, or until golden and bubbly. Serve immediately.

Note: 1 15-inch round pizza serves the same number of people and takes less time to prepare; cut into attractive wedges, it looks just as good as the individual pies.

1 recipe pizza dough, ready to use
5 tablespoons olive oil
1 tablespoon dried crushed hot pepper (Crush 1 dried red pepper in a mortar with a pestle until coarse flakes are obtained.)
½ pound fresh mozzarella, thinly sliced
½ pound Fontina cheese, thinly sliced
6 ripe plum tomatoes, seeded and thinly sliced
4 large garlic cloves, peeled and thinly sliced
10 fresh basil leaves, shredded
4 ounces *prosciutto*, julienned
1 medium-sized sweet red onion, thinly sliced
2 sweet green peppers, seeded and julienned
6 ounces fresh chèvre (goat cheese), crumbled

Pizza with Smoked Salmon and Golden Caviar

Yield: 4 8- to 9-inch luncheon or brunch size.
6 6-inch appetizer size.
Method: Direct stone baking, a prepared pizza screen, or a prepared pizza pan.

THIS IS DEFINITELY one of Puck's more exotic creations. It is reminiscent of that classic combination: lox and bagels. Consequently, I would rather serve this elegant pizza at a special brunch or in smaller portions as a light appetizer than as a main course.

1 recipe pizza dough,
   ready to use
6 tablespoons minced
   fresh chives
4 tablespoons olive oil
1 cup sour cream
4 ounces smoked salmon,
   julienned
4 heaping tablespoons
   American golden caviar

1. Preheat the oven to 500 degrees.
2. Knead in 2 tablespoons of minced chives into the dough after it has risen. (If the dough becomes sticky, knead in a few dustings of flour until it no longer sticks.)
3. Roll out or stretch the dough into 4 8- to 9-inch circles. Brush each one with olive oil and bake for 10 minutes, or until golden brown and puffed.
4. Remove from the oven. Spread with sour cream and top each pie with the salmon strips, chives, and a spoonful of golden caviar.

Pizza with Sweet Pepper, Garlic, Confit, and Herbed Feta Cheese

Yield: Serves 4 as a main course or 6 to 8 as an appetizer.
Crust Suggestions: Basic Pizza, Semolina, Chez Panisse-style, or Spago's-style dough.
Method: Direct stone baking, prepared pizza screen, or a prepared pizza pan.

SMOKY PEPPERS, MILD sautéed whole garlic, and zesty herbed feta cheese make an irresistible combination atop this pizza. Blanching the garlic cloves unpeeled for 1 minute in boiling water facilitates peeling and removes the pungent flavor. Furthermore, by gently sautéing the cloves in extra-virgin olive oil until they are golden and meltingly sweet, you add a completely new dimension to garlic on pizza.

Try to use sweet red peppers for the best color contrast but green ones will also work well. This pie is excellent hot or cold cut into thin wedges as an hors d'oeuvre.

1. Preheat the oven following the directions for your choice of crust.

2. Gently sauté the red peppers in 3 tablespoons of the extra-virgin olive oil, over low heat, covered, for 25 minutes, or until they are just tender.

3. While the peppers are cooking, drop the garlic cloves into 1 quart of boiling water and cook them for 30 seconds. Drain and peel each clove.

4. Put the garlic in a small saucepan. Add enough olive oil to just cover the garlic cloves. Cover and cook over very low heat, stirring frequently to prevent burning, until just tender and golden, about 20 minutes. Drain and reserve the oil. Set the cooked garlic aside until needed.

5. Mash the cheese, herbs, and black pepper together with a fork.

6. Roll out or stretch the dough and fit it onto the prepared 15-inch pizza pan, pizza screen, or on a floured peel.

7. Brush the dough shell with some of the oil in which the garlic was cooked.

8. Spread the dough shell with the cooked peppers and their oil. Then make a layer of the herbed cheese on top of the peppers. Sprinkle the cooked garlic cloves over the top of the pie and drizzle 2 tablespoons of the garlic cooking oil over all.

9. Bake for 15 to 20 minutes, or until the crust is golden.

10. Brush the outer crust of the pie with a little of the garlic cooking oil just before serving.

Note: Any remaining oil can be brushed on toasted bread, tossed with cooked pasta, or used in a salad dressing.

Extra-virgin olive oil

½ **pound sweet red peppers, seeded and julienned**

½ **pound sweet yellow or green peppers, seeded and julienned**

20 **garlic cloves, separated but unpeeled**

½ **pound feta cheese, drained**

2 **tablespoons finely chopped herbs, such as parsley, chives, thyme, marjoram, mint, or basil in combination**
Freshly ground black pepper to taste

1 **recipe pizza dough, ready to use**

Pizza with Shrimp, Leeks, Tomatoes, and Goat Cheese

Yield: Serves 4 as a main course or 6 to 8 as an appetizer.
Crust Suggestions: Basic Pizza, Semolina, Herb, Chez Panisse-style, or Spago's-style dough.
Method: Direct stone baking, prepared pizza screen, or a prepared pizza pan.

THE QUINTESSENTIAL CALIFORNIA PIZZA is elegant and light yet robustly flavored, and nothing fits that description better than this lovely shrimp and leek pizza. Serve it as an elegant first course or as a light entrée with chilled, dry, California Sauvignon or Fumé Blanc wine.

2 tablespoons sweet butter
3 cups chopped leeks (white and green parts)
  Salt and freshly ground black pepper
8 ounces goat cheese
2 garlic cloves, minced
3 tablespoons assorted fresh chopped herbs, such as parsley, thyme, chives, oregano, marjoram, or basil
1 recipe pizza dough, ready to use
4 tablespoons extra-virgin olive oil
4 ripe plum tomatoes, seeded and thinly sliced
½ pound fresh (33 to 35) medium-sized shrimp, peeled, with tails left on, and deveined

1. Preheat the oven, following the directions for your choice of crust.
2. Melt the butter in a medium-sized frying pan and sauté the leeks over high heat for just 1 minute. Season them lightly with salt and pepper and set them aside.
3. Mash together the goat cheese, garlic and 2 tablespoons of the herbs with a fork until they are just blended.
4. Roll out or stretch the dough and fit it onto the prepared 15-inch pizza pan, pizza screen, or a floured pizza peel.
5. Brush the dough shell with 2 tablespoons of the extra-virgin olive oil.
6. Spread the leeks over the dough shell. Then crumble on the seasoned goat cheese and finish with a layer of tomato slices.
7. Bake for 10 to 20 minutes—depending upon the crust type and method chosen—and add the shrimp during the final 10 minutes of baking time.
8. To serve, drizzle with the remaining extra-virgin olive oil and sprinkle with the remaining tablespoon of fresh herbs.

Pizza alla Mexicanna (Pizza with Onions, Peppers, Tomatoes, Monterey Jack Cheese, and Chorizo)

Yield: 1 16- to 18-inch round pie.
Serves 4 as a main course or 6 to 8 as an appetizer.
Crust Suggestions: Basic Pizza, Semolina, Chez Panisse-style, or Spago's-style.
Method: Direct stone baking, a prepared pizza screen, or a prepared pizza pan.

FOODS ON A MEXICAN THEME pervade California cuisine.

1. Preheat the oven following the directions for your choice of crust.

2. Heat the olive oil in a large frying pan and sauté the onion and peppers over medium heat, for 3 to 5 minutes, or until they are just tender.

3. Roll out or stretch the dough and fit it onto the prepared 15-inch pizza pan, screen, or on a floured pizza peel.

4. Lay the cheese over the dough shell. Then make layers of the onions and peppers, garlic, tomatoes, and chili peppers. Top with the chorizo. Sprinkle the pie with cumin, oregano, and cilantro.

5. Bake for 15 to 20 minutes, or until the crust is golden brown. Serve hot or cold.

- 4 tablespoons olive oil
- 1 medium-sized sweet onion, thinly sliced
- 2 sweet green bell peppers, julienned
- 1 recipe pizza dough, ready to use
- ½ pound Monterey Jack cheese or other similar, mild white Cheddar cheese, shredded
- 4 garlic cloves, minced
- 6 ripe plum tomatoes, seeded and thinly sliced
- 2 fresh hot chili peppers, seeded and chopped, optional
- ½ pound chorizo or other hot sausage, removed from the casings and crumbled
- ½ teaspoon ground cumin
- 1 teaspoon dried oregano
- 2 tablespoons finely minced fresh cilantro

Appendix:
SOURCES OF SUPPLIES AND EQUIPMENT

NEW YORK CITY

Balducci's
424 Sixth Avenue
New York, NY 10009
Fine imported and domestic
groceries and mail order.

Broadway Panhandler
520 Broadway
New York, NY 10012
Kitchen equipment.

Dean and Deluca
121 Prince Street
New York, NY 10012
Specialty imported and
domestic foods, cooking
equipment and mail order.

Dipalo Dairy Store
206 Grand Street
New York, NY 10013
Homemade mozzarella and
other domestic and imported
cheeses.

Faicco's Pork Store
260 Bleecker Street
New York, NY 10014
Pork products, Italian groceries,
and cheeses.

Ottomanelli & Sons, Butchers
281 Bleecker Street
New York, NY 10014
Meat, sausages.

H. Roth & Son
1577 First Avenue
New York, NY 10028
Herbs, spices, and flours.

Saint Remy
818 Lexington Avenue
New York, NY 10021
Provençale herbs, olives, olive
oil, and mail order.

Todaro Brothers
557 Second Avenue
New York, NY 10016
Italian specialty foods and mail
order.

CHICAGO

Il Conte Di Savoia
555 Roosevelt Road West
Chicago, IL 60607
Italian groceries and cookware.

Speko Products, Inc.
1014 N. Kolmar Ave
Chicago, IL 60651
Brick Oven Black Steel
Bakeware

Old Stone Oven Corporation
6007 Sheridan Road
Chicago, IL 60660
Baking stones.

SAN FRANCISCO

Williams-Sonoma
576 Sutter Street
San Francisco, CA 94102
Olive oil, pizza-making
equipment, and mail order.

BEVERLY HILLS

Williams-Sonoma
438 North Rodeo Drive
Beverly Hills, CA 90210
Olive oil, pizza-making
equipment, and mail order.

Bibliography

Bevona, Don. *The Love Apple Cookbook.* New York: Funk and Wagnalls, 1966.

Boni, Ada. *Italian Regional Cooking.* New York: Bonanza Books, 1979. (Translated from the Italian by Maria Langdale and Ursula Whyte.)

————. *The Talisman Italian Cookbook.* New York: Crown Publishers, 1950. (Translated from the Italian by Matilde La Rosa.)

Bugialli, Giuliano. *The Fine Art of Italian Cooking.* New York: Times Books, 1977.

Clayton, Bernard, Jr. *The Complete Book of Breads.* New York: Simon and Schuster, 1973.

David, Elizabeth. *Italian Food.* Harmondsworth, Middlesex, England: Penguin Books, Ltd., 1972 (reprint).

Dupree, Natalie. "Beyond All Purpose," *The Cook's Magazine.* Westport, Connecticut: Vol. 2, No. 1, Jan/Feb 1981 (pp. 54–57).

Hazan, Marcella. *The Classic Italian Cookbook.* New York: Knopf, 1973.

————. *More Classic Italian Cooking.* New York: Knopf, 1980.

Minervini, Roberto. *History of the Pizza.* Napoli, Italy: Ente Provinciale Per Il Turismo, 1956.

Muffoletto, Anna. *The Art of Sicilian Cooking.* Garden City, New York: Doubleday and Doubleday, Inc., 1971.

Root, Waverley. *The Food of Italy.* New York: Vintage, 1977 (reprint).

The Pizza Maker, published monthly by Paisano Publishing Co., Raleigh, North Carolina.

Thorne, John. *Pizza: The Art of the Pizzaiolo.* Boston: The Jackdaw Press, 1981.

Index